EVERYTHING
I NEED TO KNOW ABOUT
TEACHING

... THEY FORGOT TO TELL ME!

STACEY JARVIS
BOB ALGOZZINE

CORWIN PRESS
A SAGE Publications Company
Thousand Oaks, California

For information:

Corwin Press
A Sage Publications Company
2455 Teller Road
Thousand Oaks, California 91320
www.corwinpress.com

Sage Publications Ltd.
1 Oliver's Yard
55 City Road
London EC1Y 1SP
United Kingdom

Sage Publications India Pvt. Ltd.
B-42, Panchsheel Enclave
Post Box 4109
New Delhi 110 017 India

Printed in the United States of America.

Library of Congress Cataloging-in-Publication Data

Jarvis, Stacey.
Everything I need to know about teaching . . . they forgot to tell me! / Stacey Jarvis, Bob Algozzine.
    p. cm.
Includes index.
ISBN 1-4129-1691-7 (cloth : alk. paper) — ISBN 1-4129-1692-5 (pbk. : alk. paper)
    1. First year teachers. 2. Teacher effectiveness. 3. Effective teaching.
I. Algozzine, Robert. II. Title.
LB2844.1.N4J37 2006
371.1—dc22   2005025997

This book is printed on acid-free paper.

05   06   07   08   09   10   9   8   7   6   5   4   3   2   1

Acquisitions Editor:	Kathleen McLane
Editorial Assistant:	Jordan Barbakow
Production Editor:	Diane S. Foster
Copy Editor:	Jacqueline Tasch
Typesetter:	C&M Digitals (P) Ltd.
Proofreader:	Dennis W. Webb
Indexer:	Molly Hall
Cover Designer:	Scott Van Atta

Contents

Preface

Teachers are leaving education in droves. Many leave after teaching only a few years. Continuing concern in the education field, as well as in the United States and society at large, is focused on the high rate at which beginning teachers leave the profession. Most teachers who leave have fewer than 10 years of teaching experience. Many reports indicate that 25% to 50% of beginning teachers leave during their first three years of teaching, and nearly 10% leave in their first year.

Why do new teachers leave? Everyone knows that teaching is difficult, especially after leaving the relatively protected world of undergraduate or graduate studies in education. Research tells us that five major concerns make it even more difficult for novice teachers:

- Workload, time management, fatigue
  - ✓ How can I get it all done?
  - ✓ Do I have a life anymore?

- Content and curriculum knowledge
  - ✓ What is *really* important to teach?
  - ✓ How should I spend my teaching time?

- Relationships with students, parents, colleagues, and supervisors
  - ✓ Will students like me?
  - ✓ Will parents see me as a legitimate teacher?
  - ✓ Will my colleagues believe that I know what I am doing?
  - ✓ Will I satisfy the expectations of district evaluators?

- Evaluation and grading
  - ✓ What am I measuring?
  - ✓ What do I do when the numbers are "not too good?"
  - ✓ What about the pressures of accountability and keeping my job?

- Autonomy and control
  - ✓ Can I teach the way I believe is best for my students?
  - ✓ Who tells me what and how to teach?

The loss of new teachers is catastrophic in human and professional terms.

Everything I Need to Know . . . is a compendium of tools compiled during one teacher's first year of teaching. It is a book of real-life experiences and problems turned into helpful guidelines and solutions for beginning teachers. Our approach is practical applications of "effective practices" for managing the workload of new teachers, engaging the curriculum, building productive relationships, using assessments and evaluation effectively, and establishing control that nourishes rather than deprives the beginning teacher.

We hope you enjoy the book.

ACKNOWLEDGMENTS

Jointly we want to thank Kathleen McLane and the professional staff at Corwin Press. Kathleen's continuing support for the book and her insightful comments helped to make the project a joy to complete and the assistance we received in editing, production, and all aspects of producing the book was outstanding.

From Stacey Jarvis . . .

I want to thank so many people who gave me guidance and support in my first year of teaching. First and foremost, I want to thank my parents, Ron and Kathy. They offered constant encouragement and reassurance that this is what God has intended for me to do with my life. They were also there to listen to me vent and whine after a bad day, and not once did they complain. They themselves as parents are wonderful teachers; I am who I am because of them.

Next, I want to thank my partnership teacher, Richelle Dombroski. I could not have asked for a better mentor. Not only did she have great lessons to teach me about being a teacher, but she saw the potential that I had and helped me to develop into the teacher that I am now. If I ever become the caliber of teacher that she is today, I will have reached my ultimate goal.

The North Carolina Teaching Fellows Program provided me with invaluable experiences throughout my four years in college, helping me not only to survive as a teacher, but to thrive. From my campus director, Kathleen Benzaquin, to the program's director, Gladys Graves, everyone involved with making this program work has my gratitude.

And last, but definitely not least, I want to thank all the supportive teachers who helped me endure every day during that first year. Heather, Molly, Abby, and Shilpa: I know you took time out of your day to listen to and help me when I needed you. Because you remembered what that first year was like, you helped me through mine, and for that I am forever grateful.

From Bob Algozzine . . .

I have never written a book without the constant and continuous support of my family. Although they may not see it and often do it in very clever ways, they inspire me, and I am grateful for that. I am also thankful for the children, teachers, administrators, parents, and other professionals who remind me on a daily basis that teaching is important, that teaching requires attention, and that teaching is a great way to spend your life.

A Personal Promise

T his is an unusual book, a collection of the experiences of a first-year teacher—that's me—as seen through my eyes and those of a college professor, Bob Algozzine, whom I met after I had been a successful teacher for a few years. I kept a journal throughout my first year of teaching at the advice of my mentor teacher. Every day, I noted the lessons I had learned, the mistakes I had made, and the joys I constantly found in becoming and being a teacher.

If I can help just one first-year teacher by sharing some of the things I learned in my first year, I know in turn that I will have helped a student, and that is the reason I am a teacher. I want to continue teaching for many years, and I want to be surrounded by good teachers. Good teachers don't just show up; they work hard and get better every day. If I can make the work a little easier by sharing some first-year teacher advice, I am hoping new teachers will become better every day and that they'll stay around for a while.

Just like a great team and its players, a strong school is made up of strong teachers. You will only become stronger if you keep practicing, and your practice takes place in a classroom, in front of students. Schools often set new teachers up for failure by giving them difficult students, a troublesome schedule, added paperwork, excessive meetings, and sometimes, not even their own room. First-year teachers need to know that we've all been there and that there is light at the end of those long, tough first 180 days.

Most of the book "speaks" from and to the heart of teaching. We wrote the book this way to keep the voice and message personal, practical, and real. We hope you enjoy it.

—Stacey Jarvis

About the Authors

Stacey Jarvis received a North Carolina Teaching Fellows Scholarship while in high school and graduated from the University of North Carolina at Wilmington in 2000. She is currently teaching social studies in an urban high school in North Carolina. She is now a National Board certified teacher and is working on obtaining her master's degree in secondary education. She has spoken at numerous conferences and seminars across the state addressing the struggles of first-year teachers, and she has presented workshops and lectures to provide those individuals entering the teaching profession with advice and guidance.

Bob Algozzine earned his doctorate from The Pennsylvania State University in 1975, joining the faculty there that same year and moving to the University of Florida in 1977. During his 10-year tenure at the University of Florida, he served in various teaching, research, and service capacities, including a term as behavior disorders program coordinator. Since 1987, he has been a faculty member at the University of North Carolina at Charlotte, serving as coordinator of the research program in the Department of Educational Leadership and as research mentor for the faculty in the College of Education. Dr. Algozzine is widely known for his research on effective teaching practices in the area of behavior disorders and on critical issues in the field of special education. He has been a featured speaker at local, state, national, and international professional conferences and has conducted professional development workshops for general and special education teachers across the country.

CHAPTER ONE

The College Years

Avoiding a Long Walk off a Short Pier (Blindfolded)

I was never an "undecided" college student. I had received a scholarship in high school that would pay for my college education in return for my years of service in the public school systems of North Carolina. I knew my college major and my life's work before I even met my adviser for the first time. I was ready to plan for four years whereas other college students seemed to be planning for the next day.

I had lots of great real-world experiences in college. I had hours upon hours of coursework, observations, and other educational experiences (e.g., tutoring, attending professional development seminars, meeting with friends to "talk teaching"). I had the most wonderful partnership teacher an intern could ask for. I heard numerous guest speakers who were the cream of the crop in public education. I even heard one of the greatest educators ever, Dr. Harry Wong, speak for six hours. I was a substitute teacher for two years. I read every piece of education literature I could find. I started the fall of my freshman year with an education course, and by the spring of my senior year, I thought I knew everything I needed to know about teaching. I was very successful in college, and I heard on numerous occasions that I would make a great teacher (where were those people on the first day of school?).

Confident and eager to interview, I set out to find the perfect system, the more perfect school, and the most perfect teaching job ever. It took only two interviews for reality to hit. Of course, "perfect" is a tough thing to find, and I soon found myself looking for a job that would be "a good place to start." As a certified Grades 9 to 12 social studies teacher, I struggled to find a high school that "fit." Finally, I received an offer from a struggling middle school in a big urban system. I began my teaching career in an eighth-grade classroom in a new city and I was all alone.

If you had to go back and do college all over again, you would probably do it a little differently (experience is a great teacher, isn't it?).

Here are a few things that I believe can help you succeed—and I doubt anyone in your teacher preparation program will tell you about them.

BUILD YOUR OWN ROLODEX

Create a contact book with names, addresses, phone numbers, e-mail addresses, and other information for people who contribute in positive ways to your career. Whenever you hear a guest speaker or have a professor whom you want to use as a resource in the future, add his or her name to your book. Anytime you complete an observation, add that teacher to your book. Start your file at the beginning of your freshman year, or as soon as possible, and by the time you graduate, you will have a database of wonderful people who will help you thrive in your teaching career. A sample of a form for your contact book is included in the Survival Guide at the end of this book. Keeping track of the date you added the contact helps; it is a useful reminder of the time in your career when you met the person. Brief information about the circumstances of the meeting or what the person said or the resource he or she might offer will also help you remember why you included him or her in your book.

BUILD A PROFESSIONAL LIBRARY

Save *everything*! A bag of tricks can never be too full. When you receive handout after handout, lesson after lesson, article after article in your education courses, *save them!* And those textbooks that you thought you didn't really need could turn out to be some of the most valuable resources you have in the first year of teaching. Bloom's taxonomy is crucial knowledge when you have, sitting side by side, a student who can barely read and a student who could make a perfect score on the SAT. Understanding multiple intelligences will be your saving grace when an administrator pops his or her head in your door to talk about alternative assessment. Make sure you collect textbooks that are not in your planned or current area of teaching. For example, you might take several courses in special education even if you don't plan to get a special education certificate. During your first year of teaching, those textbooks will be invaluable to you, as you will probably teach students with disabilities in an inclusion classroom.

KEEP AN OPEN MIND

You have to know and understand where your students are coming from to prepare them best for where they are going. Take every opportunity to learn from a new experience, even if, at the time, you think that it may not be helpful. Your teaching career may take you places you never thought it would, so if you are prepared, you will be successful.

LEARN FROM EVERY OPPORTUNITY

Talk to the students and the teachers when you are in their class observing, and take notes on what they tell you. Teachers seldom ask their students what they thought "worked" and "didn't work" in a classroom or what really makes a good teacher. Those same students, however, can teach you a great deal about what they find most helpful. When you are assigned to observe a particular teacher, there is a reason. Schools don't want you to see their weakest link, so ask the teachers you observe what makes them the best of the best. They will probably know what it is that they do that other teachers don't. Keep a notebook of what you learn whenever you learn it (see the Survival Guide for a professional development log that you can use). Encourage other teachers within your school to do the same, and plan informal meetings to share what you have learned.

TREAT YOUR FIRST TEACHING JOB LIKE YOUR FIRST CAR OR HOUSE

Most people would not buy a car without looking around and deciding on a few top choices. Nobody buys a house, sight unseen. You should not take a teaching job without knowing where you are going because you are making a huge investment and you want to be successful. Here are a few things to think about as you move from student to teacher:

- When you begin to apply for jobs, first decide what type of students you want to teach. There is a big difference between urban schools and rural schools, impoverished schools and well-to-do schools, and small schools and overcrowded schools. If you are not sure who, what, or where you want to teach, do some research. It is better to spend a few days visiting schools to see how they are different than to pay for the "lesson learned" during your first year of teaching.
- If you have decided on a location (city or county) where you would like to teach, look at schools individually. If at all possible, arrange an interview and tour of the school when it is still in session; this way you will have a sense of how things look on a daily basis.
- Even the best school systems can have low-performing schools or schools with a special focus, and it helps to know where they are, if that is where you want to teach.

- Many school systems hire teachers without assigning them to a specific school; they wait for transfer periods to end, retirements to be finalized, enrollment allotments to be made, and other human resources issues to be settled. This means you may not know where you will be teaching until very near your first day of teaching. If this doesn't suit you, see if the range of possibilities can be reduced, and try to visit some of the potential schools.
- Web sites maintained by state education agencies are a great resource for information to consider if you have a choice on where to teach. Test scores are usually easy to find; here are some other things to consider:
  - ✓ teacher turnover rates
  - ✓ percentage of students on free/reduced cost lunch
  - ✓ dropout/graduations rates
  - ✓ student-to-teacher ratios
  - ✓ percentage of English Language learners
  - ✓ magnet programs or special areas of study
  - ✓ Special programs under IDEA, No Child Left Behind, or other federal or state initiatives

SHOW WHAT YOU KNOW WHEN YOU LEAVE THE NEST

Moving from student to teacher is an exciting transition, but often, it is one that is not "covered" in preparation programs. When you move into your first year of teaching, you will need to have a few things ready as you enter the profession.

The first is a *personal educational philosophy* that reflects the beliefs, opinions, attitudes, and values that will direct the way you teach and continue to learn as a teacher. You may be asked to share this information during an interview, but more important, your philosophy will be the foundation for what you do in your classroom and what you become as a teacher. Most states have standards or expectations for teachers, and your philosophy should blend with them. An educational philosophy is a great item to include in your teaching portfolio. As you prepare it, be sure to include your views on the purpose of education and learning, the value of a curriculum, and the role of teachers. This is also a good place to describe your teaching style and your preferences for schools, classrooms, and professional interests (e.g., extracurricular activities, special skills and talents). The length and depth of your philosophy will depend on what you want to share. Try to be concise without leaving out important information. This can usually be done in two to three pages.

When you apply for teaching positions, you will need a cover letter, résumé, and list of references, as well as records of your teacher preparation experiences. Your *cover letter* should include accurate information for the school system and contact person, an introduction, a few statements of self-promotion, information about your professional development experiences, and a summary closing statement. This document should be prepared with careful attention to details. Double-check it for grammatical, spelling, or style errors; have a friend or two proofread it. This is the first impression you will make, and you know what they say about first impressions. Take this one very seriously: You are introducing yourself, creating interest in yourself as a teacher, and trying to convince the reader that you deserve an interview. Your *résumé* is a broader picture of your abilities and experiences, which will help others to see your potential for success (see Survival Guide for a sample). As you prepare it, take one or two pages to describe yourself, including personal information, career objectives, educational experiences, teaching and related experiences, special areas of interest and expertise, and other relevant information (such as leadership positions in school and community organizations, professional memberships, awards). You can also include a list of professional *references* as part of your résumé, or you can prepare a separate document with this information. When you list someone as a reference, be sure they know that you have done it. It is also helpful to let them know your plans for applying for teaching positions.

CHAPTER TWO

Finally Teaching? Not Yet!

There is no feeling quite like it; getting your first "real" job. So once you are hired, what do you do? Many teachers learn of their new jobs a month or so before the next school year is to begin, but be prepared for anything. You may have to struggle through the summer, interview after interview, road trip after road trip, before you finally get that wonderful call: Yes! You have a job, and you are going to be a teacher.

Once you are hired, your school will have a new-teacher orientation to acquaint you with practices, procedures, and professional expectations related to your new job. Before you go, here are a few words of wisdom that might be useful in moving from student to first-year teacher.

BUDGET YOUR MONEY WISELY, VERY WISELY

It is sad but true: You may have had more money as a college student than you will have as a first-year teacher. You can determine your salary based on the state scale plus any local supplements for "special" teaching assignments or duties, but don't forget Uncle Sam, college loans, bills, bills, and more bills. You cannot afford to add more stress to your world because you have to have the "ultimate" cable package. Anyway, during your first-year teaching (as with many other new jobs), watching TV will be a luxury you can rarely afford. Cut spending corners wherever you can, and plan your budget carefully so you leave some money for unexpected expenses.

Most teachers are paid once a month, so you should plan your expenditures accordingly. Many companies will take automatic payments from your checking account—you could schedule them for a day or two after you're paid, so you are sure there's money in it. This can be very helpful to a poor, hard-working teacher on a limited budget. When in doubt, talk with other teachers, new and experienced, and use what you learn to manage your budget. This will make your first year of teaching a little easier.

MAKE LIFE EASIER WITH AN EARLY MOVE

If you have to move to your new job, do it sooner rather than later. It is not a good idea to try to move into a new home during the last days before school starts. There will be plenty of work at school to keep you busy, and you probably will not want to unpack a kitchen or a bedroom while you are doing school work.

TAKE ADVANTAGE OF YOUR POSITION

There probably are businesses in your community that will offer discounts to teachers. These discounts range from waiving security deposits to reduced rates for services such as copying. Don't be afraid to ask.

LEARN FROM EVERY OPPORTUNITY

No matter how good your college preparation program was, the "real" world is different. You need to give your orientation to teaching as much attention as you would give to a college course. Pretend you are a sponge, and soak up every bit of information around you. Keep a folder with all your new-teacher "stuff" in it; health insurance, dental insurance, life insurance, contract, human resources contacts, professional development requirements (which will vary by system and state), and other papers that you will probably need from time to time. Use a monthly schedule to keep track of meetings (see Survival Guide for a sample to copy).

JOIN A PROFESSIONAL ORGANIZATION

As a professional, you should participate in a professional organization that supports teachers. If your state has a teachers' union, do some research (information should be accessible online) so that you fully understand what's required of you and the services you can receive. If teachers in your state are not unionized, other groups can provide support to supplement the school system in which you work. One of the most successful new teaching mentoring programs in the country was developed by a group of new teachers. Find an organization that fits your needs. If you joined a professional group in college, be sure your membership information is updated. Larger school systems may have their own teacher organizations. Most states have at least one teacher organization as well, and there are national organizations. These groups do charge membership dues, but usually, you can have these withdrawn monthly from your paycheck, so you won't even miss it. Think of it as medical insurance; you pay for it even when you don't need it, but when you do need it, it's a good thing to have.

Now the fun begins!

CHAPTER THREE

The Days Before the First Day of School

Y ou may have very helpful people around you and still not be able to find help when you need it. There is no checklist for the first day of school, and no syllabus outlining the agenda for the days, weeks, and months to come. Fortunately, you are not alone. Make a point of getting to know the other first-year teachers at your school.

No matter how many books you read about teaching methods, you will not find the chapter that tells you about all those little things that have to be done before the kids arrive. They cannot tell you who in your school has the copier codes or your class lists, not to mention how to deal with all the paperwork required just to get a key to your room. Once inside your first classroom, you may find a mess: bare walls, empty shelves, and desks everywhere. You may spend several workdays getting your classroom ready.

Don't Worry! Be Happy!

The first day of school is an important day—one that receives a considerable amount of emphasis, but not one that will always go as planned. Relax, and don't attempt to control the things that are out of your control—incorrect rosters, irregular bells, late buses, and so on. Try your hardest to get a good night's sleep and eat a good breakfast. Your body will be challenged the first time you meet 50 students or more in one day, and it needs fuel to keep going. And you have 179 more days to go: Come June, no one will remember what you wore on the first day of school, or if you stuttered . . . all in all, it's just another day!

Use Other People's Money as Often as You Can

Most schools have some sort of supply room in which you can get items of classroom décor. It's OK to spend a few dollars of your own here and there, but that first paycheck is often already committed to your own living expenses before you get it. Be smart and pace your spending at the teacher store. One sure-fire way to get good stuff for free is to find that veteran teacher down the hall who might be cleaning out his or her room: Ask for hand-me-downs. Teachers accumulate a bunch of "stuff," and it's hard to just throw it away. Most veteran teachers would love to give or let you borrow stuff, just ASK!

GET TO WORK EARLY, ESPECIALLY THE FIRST DAY

It is a fact that more mothers take their children to school on the first day than on any other day all year. These moms sometimes watch their child all the way through the doors, or they mistakenly park in the faculty lot, leaving you trying to scope out a spot just as you hear the bell echo through the lot. Traffic will be heavier than usual on this special day due to slow-moving buses, new bus drivers with new bus routes, and just the sheer madness that develops in the carpool lane. The earlier you arrive, the more time you'll have to do the things you need to do: Relax, check your box for any roster or schedule updates, and put finishing touches on your "first-day plan." You don't ever want your students to beat you to your class, especially on the first day of school.

CHAPTER FOUR

The First Day of School

Once Is Enough!

I arrived at school a good hour and a half early on my first day. I picked up more forms and schedules and made my way down the hall to my room. My sign—identifying me as Ms. Jarvis—was still there, cute as it was yesterday, and my classroom looked almost ready. All it was missing was the 23 kids who were on my roll. I rehearsed their names, hoping to figure out those tricky ones before I embarrassed myself or the student. I made sure I had a seating chart set up just like Harry Wong, author of *The First Days of School* had advised, and I waited until the bell rang.

All of the sudden, dozens of nervous teenagers poured into the hallway like horses when the gate goes up at the start of the Kentucky Derby. Looks of confusion and excitement crossed their faces as they scrambled to find the right room. Then, it hit me; I was the calm one. I already knew where I was supposed to be, and I found comfort in that, at least for a while. One by one, students approached me, "Are you Ms. Jarvis?" they innocently asked. I confirmed their suspicions, introduced myself, and invited them into "our" room. This process seemed to last forever, but I didn't mind. Finally, they were all in, and I began my first "First-Day Speech."

The first day is the longest but shortest day ever. Cherish the first day while it lasts, and then be thankful that you will never have to do it again and that the remaining days will be much easier. First days never go completely according to plan. You can learn a lot about your students on your first day at school, and they can learn about you. Take advantage of this time. Here are a few things for the first day that no one tells you in your teacher education courses.

TELL THEM UP FRONT WHO YOU ARE AND WHAT YOU STAND FOR

Teaching is more than standing in front of a group and telling them what you know (and what they are expected to know). A good deal of teaching, especially for new teachers, is discipline and classroom management. If you are "easy" on the first day, just think about how you will appear on the 24th day. Kids love honesty, so be honest with them about your expectations, rules, consequences; and most important, tell them why you became a teacher. Explain the importance of high expectations and how they contribute to success. Share some experiences that helped you to develop your philosophy of teaching. Also, share a few thoughts that will help them to see who you are:

- I refuse to let one student ruin the educational opportunities for many others, so don't be the one!
- I will accept you the way you are, but I will expect you to be a little (or a lot) different after I have taught you!
- The best thing I can spend on you is time, and I am ready to spend it!

The important thing to remember about classroom management is that it is much easier to loosen up as the year goes by than to fight for control two weeks down the road.

DON'T EVER TELL YOUR CLASS THAT YOU'VE NEVER DONE THIS BEFORE

They will "eat you for lunch" if they think they can get away with it. It is your classroom, and you are in charge. Look in control, even if you feel that you are losing it. If you don't know the answer to one of their random questions, tell them you will look it up and have an answer for them tomorrow. You can tell them, "There is no question that I cannot answer except the one you don't ask. It may take me longer than normal to find some answers, but I promise you if you ask, I'll find!"

WEAR LOOSE CLOTHES AND COMFORTABLE SHOES

Your physical activity—walking, bending, stretching, passing out papers—will be greater on the first day of school than on any other school day. Stress and anxiety will also be greater, and you may find yourself sweating a bit despite the new air conditioner. Not to mention, all eyes will be on you all the time on this day and this day only. If a button is missing or a waistband is too tight, the students will see it. If you are lucky, they won't let you know; nonetheless, they watch you and notice the details, so pay attention to what you say and how you look.

BE PREPARED TO BE UNPREPARED FOR SOMETHING

No one can be prepared for everything. You might have a student in your room who is not on your roster. Keep in mind that this sort of thing happens to every teacher, and every teacher is doing the same thing today (form after form, rule after rule). All these problems can and will be solved . . . they are just part of teaching. Relax! Your students are actually the "nervous ones."

HAVE YOUR CLASSROOM RULES CLEARLY POSTED

Classroom rules should be written positively, kept to a minimum number (three to five), and, above all, taught just like any other content. Do not assume that everyone will agree with your rules or know how to follow them. For example, your Rule 1 may seem simple: Be respectful of all persons and property at all times. But in a matter of days or weeks, you may find some students are behaving in ways that you find disrespectful—and they think it is perfectly fine. So take a few minutes of each class period to define and practice respectful behavior:

- No hitting, touching, teasing, or bothering others or their belongings.
- We all say *thank you, please,* and *you're welcome* when appropriate.
- We handle personal matters in the quietest of ways and outside the door, if possible.
- We leave the room cleaner than we found it.
- We help each other to be successful and do what is asked of us at all times.
- We choose our words and what we say wisely (*shut up* is not respectful).
- We use a reasonable volume when addressing someone.

Explain to your students that if someone breaks Rule 1, there will be an appropriate consequence, just as there is when a school rule is broken. Rules define expectations, so set them early, teach them to all of your students, and reteach them whenever you can. Whatever you do, don't assume that students will come to your classroom knowing "how to behave."

ESTABLISH YOUR CLASSROOM PROCEDURES

The first day is also a perfect time to establish classroom procedures (e.g., "This is how we do it here.") and, if possible, have them posted as well. For example, you might have a sign on your desk that says, "The bell doesn't dismiss you, I do." This lets your students know an important procedure (or way of doing things) in your room. Depending on the age of your students and what content you are teaching, your procedures may vary.

On the first day of school, have your students rehearse several times the way you want things done, such as passing papers in, lining up to leave the room, entering the room, moving the desks into groups, getting art supplies, and sharpening pencils. This practice can be a great way for students to interact with each other while learning newly expected procedures. It also allows for some personalities to be presented. Your leaders, followers, shy students, best friends, and "center of attention" students can become clear. To identify these students on the first day is time well spent. Again, don't assume that you won't have to teach behavior; in fact, teaching behavior may be more important than teaching anything else, especially the first days of school.

GET TO KNOW YOUR STUDENTS

Information is power. As you begin teaching, collect information using weekly surveys to help you learn about your students. Focus the first surveys on information that helps you to "get to know" your students (see Survival Guide) and provides a basis for compiling files on each of them. Throughout the year, use surveys to update the information that you have. You can also use the surveys to provide a great integrated lesson option by asking students to chart some of the data (e.g., number of classmates at various ages, favorite foods, reading habits) and compare it to other information they find in newspapers or magazines and on the Internet or by surveying other classes. You do not have to be a scientist to conduct research; even kids can do it, if you lead the way.

EMBRACE TEACHING'S BIGGEST DISILLUSIONMENT

Ask any teacher, and she will tell you that the biggest problem for new teachers is discipline. Ask any new teacher, and he will tell you that he was not prepared as well to manage behavior as he was to present content. Ask any new teacher, and she will tell you that many teachers (and the professors who taught them) don't think that teaching behavior is "her job." Nothing could be further from the truth.

Just because you're teaching high school, don't assume your students will know how to behave in your classroom. You have to teach this to them, just as you have to teach them about history, geography, physics, or mechanical engineering. Nobody assumes that students know all there is to know about an academic subject when they show up to be taught; if they did, why would we need to teach them? If a child can't read, we teach him. If I child can't compute, we teach her. If a child can't behave, we have to teach him that, too.

CHAPTER FIVE

One Lesson After Another

My partnership teacher gave me the idea of keeping a journal during my first year of teaching. I bought a special one-subject composition notebook, which I kept in my desk so that whenever anything happened that I thought was special or unique, I could write it down. Needless to say, I filled that notebook up, and then some, by the end of the year. Every once in a while, I would flip through the pages and read what I had written down. Sometimes, I was surprised by the simple things I was writing: "Talk slower." "Always keep change for a dollar in desk." "Smile, even when it is not your first choice." "Apologize first, last, and often." Simple phrases with profound meanings and a wealth of knowledge represent wisdom that grows with teaching. These are all the little things I learned in that first year that I think can help new teachers. I am in no way a "know-it-all"; most of these hints are things I learned because I did something wrong!

THINK BEFORE YOU SPEAK

Believe it or not, your students are listening. Don't say mean things you can't take back, dumb things you never intended to say, or condescending comments about other people (trust me, it will get back to them). Kids can be mean. They are guaranteed to let you know when they don't like your outfit, when they think you've gained weight, when you have a new haircut and they think it looks bad, when you have a blemish on your face, or when you have food in your teeth. Many of them live for these moments. Manners are stored in lockers, and public embarrassment is something some students look forward to with great relish. No matter how mean they get—and there is always one kid who will love to be mean to you—you have to remember that you are the teacher, and your job is to teach.

CHOOSE YOUR WORDS WISELY

Your words may be the only words a child hears from an adult all day. Words can last in a child's memory for years to come, so make sure they are words of kindness and compassion. If your students hear you say hateful and mean things, they will think it's OK for them to do the same. Your words will get back to their mother, so be sure you use words you'd want her to hear. It's OK to mess up and say things you wish you could take back, as long as you make the time as soon as possible to take them back. "I'm sorry" and "I made a mistake" are very powerful things to say.

ALWAYS HAVE EXTRA CASH AND LOOSE CHANGE

During your student-teaching experience, kids probably didn't ask you for money; however, when you are a teacher, expect to be asked for money fairly often. Your students won't need much, a quarter here, 50 cents there. The significance of this is that your students need something, and you are able to give it to them. The banking system is easy; they ask, you give, no questions asked and no payment schedules devised. You might think you will lose quite a bit of money by the end of the year. On the contrary, you earn much more than you give. When a student needs a dollar because she left her money at home, you give her a dollar. Two weeks later, when she has an extra quarter or so, she will repay you. The same thing will happen if someone needs a quarter to get a snack out of a machine. If you supply the quarter, often by the end of the lunch period, that student will offer you a chip or a cracker. The lesson to be learned in all of this is when you give something to a student unconditionally, whether it is money, food, or just a smile, they will return it . . . unconditionally, and often with interest. This will build relationships that cannot be broken.

PREVIEW VIDEOS AND USE THEM CORRECTLY

OK, now this is one of those "well duh?" things that can really get you. Although videos are approved by school systems and even recommended by a standard course of study, you need to watch them by yourself before you show them to students. When you watch the video, pretend you are watching through the eyes of a student the age you are teaching. Also, look for anything in the video that may catch your student's eye for the wrong reason.

Research your system's video library and viewing rules. Some systems require parent consent forms if you show a video with a particular rating. Be sure to be aware of this before you risk anything. I have seen every history movie produced since 1990, but I have seen only a few through the eyes of a middle school student. You can predict what questions your kids will ask, and you can go ahead and take time to prepare an answer. You can familiarize yourself with the plot and prepare a viewing guide, a quiz, or a study guide to go along with the video. You will appear very informed to your students, and that is important.

Be careful to use, not abuse, videos in your classroom. Avoid showing a video that has nothing to do with what you are teaching, and always offer some follow-up to a 90-minute visual lesson. Clips are great; don't waste an hour of time when showing 10 minutes of a video would have been just as effective. Use videos as a reward and for reinforcement, not as a time killer when there is a sub. Teachers around the school won't respect you if they hear that all you do is show videos . . . in fact, they may even resent you.

Test the Equipment to Avoid the Catastrophe

Arrive early on days you are using technology with which you are not familiar or that you don't use daily. Be sure you have the right cables, you know what channel the TV goes on, and you have the tape already forwarded to the exact place you want it (and, be careful, "free time" while fast forwarding is often a great time for a breakdown in classroom management). Whenever possible, have a backup plan to cover for any unexpected bumps in your hi-tech lessons.

Plan Ahead for Accidents

At all times, you should have tissues, Band-Aids, lotion, hand sanitizer, wet wipes, and paper towels on hand. You will be amazed at how many times students will want a pass to leave the classroom to get these items. If you have them on hand, you have saved a student a long trip to the office and a loss of instructional time. Of course, remember that you cannot give students any medicine, including cough drops or aspirin; this is a big teaching "no-no" that you don't want to learn about the hard way.

Be Flexible

Without fail, your lesson plans will be interrupted sometimes. It may be a last-minute assembly, a pep rally that runs long, some form of testing (and FYI, standardized testing *always* runs over), or another surprise event that you cannot control or that you might not be aware of until 10 minutes before it happens. You need to be able to flip-flop lessons, lengthen and shorten them according to plan, and reschedule tests.

There are several ways to do this. If you have a class of students for only 15 to 20 minutes, we suggest using a game of some sort like Trivial Pursuit or Twenty Questions. You can divide the class into teams or partners, and the game can go on for as little time or as much time as needed. Always keep score and reward the winners. This will help to ensure that you have 100% participation from everyone in the class. If a regular class period is extended due to a special event, such as testing that has run overtime or an assembly that is not quite ready to begin, find creative ways to fill the time. For example, if you teach social studies, you can come up with a topic for a reflective paper or drawing that covers a time period discussed in class. Then, assign a one-page paper answering the question, "If you could travel back in time, what era would you travel to and why?" or, "If you could interview any historical figure, who would it be, and what would you ask him or her?" Another activity would be a drawing or illustration of a key event or historical figure that has been covered in class. You have to adapt your extended lessons to your content, of course, but make sure you have a few ideas ahead of time. Being prepared and in control is crucial in deepening your students' learning and preventing discipline problems.

Keep a Calendar Handy

You will need more than one calendar in your classroom. Put extra calendars in important places. For example, you might use a calendar desk pad for recording your parent conferences and special events. Keep a school staff calendar on your Events bulletin board to highlight meetings, workdays, deadlines, and duties, and check it frequently. You want never to miss something that the principal has scheduled. Keep a huge wall calendar next to the white board for students to see and use. Keep quiz dates and test dates clearly marked, along with school sporting events and social functions. You might even let students mark their own birthdays on the calendar. This helps them to feel a part of the classroom. When dates are clearly marked on a calendar, you can answer the comment, "I didn't know we had a test today?" simply by pointing to the calendar. This will make your point very clearly without having to say too much. Having a calendar in a prominent place also stresses the importance of time management and organization, especially at the middle and high school levels. You will also find that reviewing the calendar periodically (e.g., Mondays) is time well spent. It is also helpful to have students keep track of assignments and progress on standardized sheets that you provide rather than on slips of paper or other bits likely to be lost. To eliminate chances of forgetting, keep a copy of the sheets in a notebook for each student.

DON'T REVEAL TOO MUCH ABOUT YOUR PERSONAL LIFE

Your students don't need to know your first name or your husband's, wife's, boyfriend's, or girlfriend's name. They don't need to know where you live, your home phone number, what kind of car you drive, how much money you make, or what you do on weekends. This information has nothing to do with you as a teacher. Students will find out who you are as a teacher by your actions in the classroom; finding out about your weekend activities may confuse them. Students, especially teenagers, look at you as a role model—although they may not always show it. The flaws that they can find—and trust me, they will find them—can and possibly will become a justification for *their* flaws. This hint is especially important to young teachers. Don't try to be cool in front of your kids by talking about your social life; they will respect you more if you keep your professional and personal lives separated. Students will invent plenty of stories about you on their own. If the stories have any truth, you will lose the respect of your peers and run the risk of losing effectiveness in the classroom.

ALWAYS LOOK LIKE A TEACHER

Your physical appearance in and out of school is very important to your relationship with your students. If you look like you just rolled out of bed each morning, your students will think that you don't think it's very important to get up in time to get ready for your job. And at the other extreme, if you look too made up for a school teacher, your students will start caring more about what you are wearing than what you are teaching. As a rule of thumb, when in doubt, don't wear it. Nothing should be too tight, too short, too low-cut, too see-through, or too baggy, and, of course, everything should be clean. Be sure you are appropriately dressed on your own time as well. Be aware, that you may meet students—or their parents—when and where you least expect it: at Wal-Mart, the movies, the post office, or McDonald's.

KEEP A CLEAN AND INVITING CLASSROOM

You will spend an amazing amount of time in your classroom, so be sure that it is clean and that you like its appearance. Also, make students accountable for the condition of the classroom. Have them pick up trash, straighten desks, and put away supplies at the end of every class. This gives them ownership of a place where they spend time. It is a good idea to display student work on the walls and to make the room colorful and appealing (see later section, "Display Students' Work," for more information). If your room is bright, colorful, inviting, warm, and student centered, your students will be more likely to enjoy the time they spend there. Also, by knowing in advance that you display selections of their work, some students may be more motivated to excel so they can get their work on the wall. Elementary school teachers tend to do a better job of this than middle school and high school teachers. When parents come to visit, they should be able to see exactly what goes on in your room. If the walls are bare and the floors are covered with balls of paper, they'll wonder what it is that you're teaching.

SARCASM CAN BACKFIRE

Many—even most—adults use sarcasm in their everyday conversation. However, teenagers have a hard time distinguishing truth from sarcasm, and truth is what they want and need to hear. Students may take your witty sarcasm as truth. Then, when a student acts inappropriately by taking something you said literally, you may be misunderstood and lose credibility with your peers. Don't answer the question "Do I have to do this?" with the statement, "No, you don't have to do your homework, you never have to do any work in school if you don't want to," because many students will take it literally; the important message will be lost. Watch your words carefully for the literal and out-of-context meaning. Your words will be repeated when you least expect it and in a manner you never intended.

PROOFREAD *ALL* HANDOUTS

It is extremely important to proofread everything twice. Your students should think that you are one of the smartest people they know, but they won't if you constantly misspell words, leave out the *fanboys* (for, and, nor, but, or yet, so), or use *you're* and *your* or *there* and *their* incorrectly. Another common error that students always notice is adding an extra letter somewhere that will really stand out (*us* becomes *ass*). They will wonder how you got through college. It is lots of fun and beneficial to create your own worksheets and overheads, but be sure to check them twice before you pass them on to your students.

TRUST YOUR STUDENTS

Teachers often make the mistake of not trusting the character of their students. Although they may have a tendency to not tell the whole truth, kids can be honest. If you are always second-guessing and disregarding students' word, they will begin to not trust your word. This is especially important if you are teaching at-risk students or students living in poverty. These kids have already been taught that nobody trusts them or believes what they have to say. By trusting them, you have validated them as people, and you may be the first person who has ever done this in their lives. When it comes time for them to behave and act appropriately in your presence, they are more likely to do so. You can begin by telling your classes that each and every student has 100% of your trust and what they decide to do with that is their choice. If they lose your trust by being dishonest, let them know it may take the rest of the year before they can earn it back.

FIND A "BUDDY" IN EACH CLASS

Although you should try to build a special relationship with each and every student you teach, you need to start small. Try to identify one student in each class who can be your eyes and ears. This is the student you can talk to one-on-one about what happened in another class, how hard an assignment really was, and the behavior of the class in your absence. The student can even help you get a clue into the social world students live in at school and away from it. You have to choose this student wisely, as he or she will be self-conscious, yet confident of his or her role. You want to make sure that you talk with this student in private and that you make it clear that the conversation is to stay between the two of you. By having an "inside source," you can get a glimpse of your students without their even knowing it. Your goal is not to find a "snitch," but more to get to know your class one student at a time.

ASK YOUR STUDENTS WHAT THEY THINK

Students need to know that they matter. They need to know that teachers care about them. Every once in a while, ask your class what they think about a current event or a new movie, how they would change an assignment, or how they can be more successful. You will be amazed at the amount of input they have and the quality of what they think. You are treating them like adults, and hey, they may even begin to act that way. Of course, there are no guarantees, but what do you have to lose?

LEARN TO IMPROVISE

Organization and control may be strengths in some ways, but as a teacher, they can be huge weaknesses as well. You have to improvise to be successful. Things don't always have to be just like you wrote them in your plan book. As long as you reach your final destination, it is OK if the path takes a different turn. Don't let your students see your disappointment when things don't go exactly your way; they need to know that you approve and believe in what is going on in the classroom. Sometimes your way isn't the best way for your students.

MAKE YOUR COPIES AHEAD OF TIME

A rule of thumb for teachers, especially new ones: When you need the copier most, it will be (1) broken, (2) in use by a teacher with hundreds of copies, who will not let you jump in front of her, or (3) out of something (paper, toner, power). Make sure that all copies are made a minimum of one day ahead (and be sure to make a few extras for accidents and lost papers). Those experienced teachers down the hall will make you understand this. They can copy weeks and maybe even months ahead. But you, the novice teacher, will be doing well to stay just a day ahead. A teacher who is unprepared and without materials is like a race car leaving the pit without any gas. Of course, there are those rare mornings when you realize that you forgot to make an overhead, or you forgot about the new student who came yesterday, and you will have to rush down and hope for the best.

WHEN IN DOUBT, *ASK*

One of the biggest misconceptions that first-year teachers have is that asking for help is a sign of weakness. Wrong! Find the best teachers in your school, and ask them about their first year of teaching; you can bet that, at some point in that first year, they had to ask for help. Asking for help shows that you care enough to try and be a better teacher. Ask experienced teachers about what they did in their own classes with classroom management and discipline. Ask the media specialist for assistance in ordering videos and books. Ask the guidance counselor for behavior contracts for students. Ask the academic facilitator for ideas and lesson plans for different units. Ask other teachers for advice on everything, ranging from hard-to-handle parents, to failing students, to state test scores. Ask, ask, ask! There are plenty of great people in your school who will be happy to help you, and they will respect you more for asking for help than for not asking and constantly falling short.

LEARN THE SYSTEM

Each school is its own little world. There are so many people with so many jobs that figuring out who does what can be a nightmare. Before the first day, try to get acquainted with the staff in the front office. Work on putting names with faces and learning where everyone's office is located. Take notes of what first-day forms go where and who can provide specific things when you need them. It is particularly important to know the financial secretary, the attendance secretary, the registrar secretary, anyone who deals with lunch numbers and lunch money (depending on grade), and the staff member who is in charge of substitutes. Depending on the size of your school and the district, one person may serve in all these roles, or two or three people may share the workload. It is important as a first-year teacher to learn where forms are to be submitted and who students need to see with certain problems. If you seem like the only one in the building who has no clue where to send locker money, don't panic. Ask the office staff or another teacher. By the way, it's OK if you have to double-check an answer with another teacher; it is also OK to ask your students for help.

DISPLAY YOUR STUDENTS' WORK

A visually appealing classroom is often filled with student work. Professional posters are great for motivation and decoration, but make sure you leave room for what matters most—the products of your students' efforts. Students of all ages and abilities need to know that their work matters and that it is good enough to be displayed. Be selective in what you display and how you display it. Choose major student projects that reveal a great deal of student effort. It is also important to leave the work up for awhile—say, for the duration of the next project (one to two weeks) or until another assignment worthy of display is completed.

Make sure that every student has the chance to show off his or her success. Although a few students will always do awesome artwork or have A+ papers, share the spotlight with all of your students. You will soon find all of them trying hard to do well on an assignment, just to get their work displayed. Displaying student work also gives you something for your bag of tricks; tell students that you are going to pick the best three assignments, and those will be the ones you hang around the room. You will be surprised with the effort some students will put forth to be recognized for what they have done.

IF A DISAGREEMENT ARISES WITH
A STUDENT, ADDRESS IT ONE ON ONE

A public argument with one of your students is probably the fastest way to lose respect and control of your classroom. When a student engages in a power struggle with you, try not to drop down to his or her level and argue back. You are the adult, and you are in control. Ask the student calmly and respectfully to speak with you in the hallway. Once outside of the public eye, treat the student as you would like to be treated if your superior was talking with you. Don't begin by insulting and accusing the student; start by stating that you didn't appreciate the language, tone, volume, or message that the student used with you in front of your class. You will feel much more successful when you exhibit this kind of control. In addition, by taking the time to speak to a student one on one, you are showing an interest in that individual, and that may help make his or her behavior a little bit better.

DON'T PUNISH THE WHOLE CLASS
WHEN ONLY ONE STUDENT DESERVES IT

This is one of those lessons you will learn the hard way if you're not careful! More often than not, you will have only a handful of students who are making it "tough to teach" your lesson or who are acting inappropriately. The best plan is to discipline only those students. Try not to make the other kids pay for something they did not do. If you do, they will soon realize that good behavior does not pay off in your class, and then they will be more inclined to misbehave.

One strategy is to use a system of probation for misbehavior. For example, you might use art supplies probation (the most popular with middle school students), hall pass probation, choice probation (this means you get to choose a student's seat, partner, group, line order, or other place), and so on. If you are having a fun activity such as a game in class, allow those students who completed their homework to play while the others finish, but be careful to avoid inadvertently punishing students with disabilities or anyone who has a good reason for not handing in work quickly. Be creative and consistent, and the behavior of your students will improve.

ISSUING IDLE THREATS MAKES YOU LOOK WEAKER

Disciplining by intimidation is not effective. Don't say, "I'll call your mother . . ." or "Let me just talk to the coach . . ." unless you are ready to follow through with the threat. Don't threaten or promise something that you cannot do. Sadly, some students are used to adults not keeping their word (e.g., If you don't eat your vegetables, I'll shoot the dog!). If you fall into that category, you will lose any respect you may have gained. Remember to choose your words carefully because once you say them, you can't take them back.

BE COMPASSIONATE AND UNDERSTANDING WITH ALL OF YOUR STUDENTS

This can be one of the hardest lessons to learn. Your students know where they stand with you. If they see you treat them differently, they may feel rejected or hurt. You can make a student's day simply by being kind. Simple questions and actions can mean a great deal to almost any student. Ask about the day, write a nice comment on a paper, or compliment a student. It may take only a second, but the benefits may last a long time. This kind of investment and return is well worth the effort. Find some time for it, and you will be very happy with the results you see sooner as well as later.

DON'T ENGAGE IN A POWER STRUGGLE WITH A STUDENT

Almost every first-year teacher makes this mistake at some point. You have to remember that you are the adult, you are in charge, and you are the one who gets the last word, even if you do not say it! Some students will thrive on getting you to come down to their level and argue with them. Don't do it. Don't let anybody get you into a situation where you are verbally defending your decision or explaining yourself. You do not owe any student that, and the audience (which is usually your class) will be watching and listening to your every word.

If you fall into the power struggle trap, you will feel angrier at yourself in the end than at the student. When you step into an argument with a child, you allow them to question your authority. So, how do you learn to avoid this? Watch an experienced teacher address a disrespectful and disorderly student. The student will begin the argument in the class, and the experienced teacher will ask the student to step into the hallway. Once the student is removed from the audience, the teacher turns the argument into a stern conversation. The student still may not agree with the teacher, but the teacher refuses to give in to the student. If necessary, an administrator can be called to remove the student from the hallway. The power struggle is over before it began. The teacher still has the last word, her point is understood by the student, and, most important, she demonstrates to the rest of the class that she is in charge.

PICK YOUR BATTLES

We all know that education has a few faults. Some of these will be out of your control. Let them go. The only thing you can control is what goes on in your classroom. If you can address discipline issues yourself, you should do it. Once you turn it over to another person, it is out of your control, and you may not agree with the way it was handled. Learning to manage the things that are in your control takes time. Remember the serenity prayer: Grant me the serenity to accept the things I cannot change, the courage to change the things I can, and the wisdom to know the difference. Pick battles wisely. Depending on the age and abilities of your students, you may not be able to enforce everything. You need to ask yourself what is worth fighting for. Ask yourself this before you go crazy over small things like chewing gum or not having a pencil. In no way does this mean that you should not set high expectations and hold your students to them, but be reasonable and remember why you are there. Students can learn with gum in their mouths, they honestly can forget a pencil, and sometimes, they really have to go to the bathroom. When you pick your battles wisely, your students will be able to see your compassion and purpose in their life.

Make mental notes of the battles you avoid and how you avoided them. Then in the future, if another battle arises with the same student or one acting the same way, you have leverage and experience to make a difference. One first-year teacher had an experience that illustrates this point.

I recently worked with a student who at 14 had a terrible temper and couldn't control it. During the middle of a lesson, he exploded in anger at the young lady sitting near him because she asked him to pick up her paper that she had knocked off her desk. The young lady was horrified, and I was shocked. I asked the young man to step outside and wait for me. I finished giving directions and went to speak with him.

I began our conversation with a soft, caring tone. I told him that last week I didn't say anything to him when he fell asleep in class (which is not acceptable behavior in my class) and I gave him the benefit of the doubt that it wouldn't happen again. But now the benefit of the doubt was gone and we needed to address his behavior and find a solution. As we talked calmly, he began to tell me that his newborn sister had colic (constant crying), and he had not been able to sleep in weeks (he shares a two-bedroom apartment with six other people). His lack of sleep, he claimed, was the reason for his irritability and outburst.

I explained that I understood, and that next time he becomes irritated with someone, he should take five deep breaths before he speaks. I then allowed him to pick his punishment. As he pondered for two minutes, I made the suggestion that he write a letter to the young lady, explaining his situation and then apologizing for what he had done. By doing this, his apology would be accepted, and only she and I would know what he did. As the young man began to get more control of his temper, he was able to make it the rest of the year without any more outbursts.

Sometimes by not punishing students for every little infraction, the discipline that you do administer may be more effective.

SHOW INTEREST IN THEIR PICTURES AND THEIR STORIES

The middle school world is sometimes a rude awakening to teenage life. By showing an interest in your students' art work (whether they are real photos or "doodles") and listening to their stores (and boy, do they have some stories), you will encourage a bond with them. The same is true for students of any age. Showing interest will go a long way. For high school teachers, this may be tough. Learn about the bands or groups that they like. Check out what they are watching on television or the movies that they are seeing. Simple things like being seen at their games, plays, concerts, or club events mean a lot to them, even if they never tell you.

SOMETIMES TEXTBOOKS CAN WAIT

Unless instructed to do so by a superior, do not pass out textbooks until you absolutely have to do it. You may be in a teaching situation in which some students change classes in their first weeks of school. If you have already given out textbooks, they may leave with the students. This also can mess up a numbering system that is already in place, or it can throw your textbook counts off at the beginning of the year, leaving you short until more books arrive.

Create lessons in which you are the deliverer of the information, whether it is in the form of notes, stories, centers, team projects, or independent activities. By doing this, you do not have to hand out textbooks early in the year, and your students can learn about your teaching style without being tied to material presented by others. When you do assign textbooks, be sure to keep copies of your distribution lists and have students sign them, acknowledging that they are responsible for what they have received. This is definitely a case of an ounce of prevention being worth a pound of cure.

CREATE FOLDERS AND SAVE EVERYTHING

You will soon discover that filing is a skill that all teachers need. Use manila folders and label them according to topics such as locker combination, lunch numbers, textbook numbers, seating charts, department information, staff meeting minutes, fire drill maps, classroom seating charts, PTSA newsletters, special education students' records (modifications, IEPs, 504 plans), disciplinary referrals, professional development, workshop "stuff," observations, and so on. Have a folder for everything. By organizing papers like this, you will be able to find what you need quickly, and you won't lose anything. It is also very helpful to have a summary (e.g., see Special Education Modification Chart in Survival Guide) of the information in some of your folders.

DEVELOP A GRADING SYSTEM AND STICK WITH IT

Education is very numbers oriented, especially in light of efforts to document student outcomes on high-stakes tests. This means you need to be consistent and accurate in grading. On the first day, explain your grading scale, and have it posted somewhere. You need to be able to justify the numbers at any time to anyone. Many teachers also find that rubrics can be very helpful for grading projects and papers. As a novice teacher, you may be questioned by people about your grades. A clear grading scale and rubrics are keys to your defense. Some examples of general rubrics are provided in the Survival Guide.

MEASURE SUCCESS IN MANY WAYS

Even students who struggle academically have successes throughout the year. It is important that you focus not just on grades but on other aspects and successes within your classroom so that every student can experience a sense of accomplishment. Specific praise for behavior is as important as recognition for academic performance. For example, you may have a student who keeps forgetting to raise his hand before calling out an answer or a little girl who is constantly late to class. If you see improvement in their behavior, acknowledge it with a note, a call home, or a simple "thank you." If you can make all of your students feel successful in some way, you will see a difference in the atmosphere of your classroom.

TEACH RESPONSIBILITY

Students often blame teachers when they are unsuccessful. When report cards come out, you will often hear, "Why'd you give me this?" or "How'd I get a D, I do everything?" You might be tempted to respond, "look at your grades" or "what do expect if you don't turn everything in." Instead, you can place the responsibility where it belongs: I don't *give* grades; you earn them, and I am merely a recorder of your success.

Repeated often enough, this can help students take responsibility for their own actions.

Be Involved, But It's OK to Say No

Being involved in your school is important. Find an activity that you like to do, and go for it. Whether you want to coach a sport, sponsor a club, or serve on a committee, being involved is critical to the success of the school. Be careful, however; in the first few years, you may be asked to do much more than you can handle. Don't feel pressured to always say yes. If you spread yourself too thin, the people who suffer first and foremost are your students, and they do not deserve that.

Pick one or two things to do in that first year, and see how it goes. Then next year, once you have some stability, add something new. Administrators and colleagues won't think poorly of you if you aren't "super teacher" in your first year; in fact, they will respect you more because you know your limits, and you are putting the success of your students first.

To Keep Your Sanity, Create a "To Do" List

In your first year of teaching, if you make a list of everything you have to do, you may find that there are not enough hours in the day to get them all done. Instead of one long list, make a three-part list: Things I Have to Do Today, Things I Need to Do This Week, and Things I Should Do When I Get the Chance. This will be a big relief. By ordering things based on a time frame, you can get more done. Rework the list everyday. Things you need to do this week can be moved up to tomorrow. Things that can be done when you get the chance— reorganizing a notebook, cleaning your desk, or laminating projects— can be set as a last priority so that they do not cause any stress. You need to do them, but when there are more important things to be done, priorities matter. Don't get overwhelmed by your list; break things down into manageable amounts, and you will be more successful.

Have Good Sub Plans and an Emergency Plan . . . Just in Case

As a first-year teacher, you will more than likely miss a day or so of school because of illness. You can wash your hands, disinfect your classroom, and take all the vitamins you can ingest, but you are still likely to get sick during your first year of teaching. When you know ahead of time that you will be absent, take time to create plans for your substitute teacher. Plan as if the substitutes have no idea about how a school works, and tell them everything: a seating chart, bell schedule, lunch procedures, and helpful nearby staff. Always leave more than enough work for your students to do.

You also need to have emergency lesson plans ready for those days when you wake up and know you can't come to school. Some schools may require you to submit an emergency plan, but if they do not, you should have one ready yourself. Ideally, emergency plans should be simple and OK to implement at any time in the curriculum. Have any required copies ready, and list the instructions very clearly. Then, show the teacher next door where this plan is located. Having good plans for substitute teachers is crucial. And, of course, your colleagues will not be happy with you if you aren't there one day and your kids are going crazy because they have nothing to do.

CHAPTER SIX

Student-Teacher Relationships

A s you learn how to relate to your students, keep in mind that you have to make it clear that you are not their friend. You have to show them—not just tell them—exactly where the line is between teacher and friend. You may see other first-year teachers blur the line, and you will see that the results of this are not good. If students think you are their friend, they may try to manipulate your judgment or make you lower your expectations, and they may lose respect for you. No matter what your students' age, children know that friends can come and go, and if you are a friend, you run the risk of falling into that category. Instead, be an adult, maybe the only adult in their lives whom they can always count on and trust.

From the outset, make it clear that you are the teacher, and within that role, you are a listener, an adviser, and a trusted adult, but not a friend. Do not say to your students, "you hurt my feelings" or, "please don't be mad at me," because they are expressions used more with friends or other peers.

You should care more about whether students are learning in your classroom than whether they like you. You do not want to be the teacher that the students run to with "hot" gossip. You want your students to respect you and to understand your purpose in their life as their teacher. Many times, children have watched adults in their life let them down; if you stick to your role as a teacher, you will not be one of them. First-year teachers may think that being "buddy buddy" with their students (especially if you teach high school) is the best way to manage their classroom. But before you know it, the students will start treating you like a teenager, and once that happens, there is no going back. Students should know just enough about you to respect you, but not enough to let them think that they know you. Do not reveal all of yourself to your students, or you will surely regret it.

Good relationships are also built on high expectations. Push your students to their limits, but do not make them feel like failures if they fail to achieve outstanding goals all the time. Be supportive and sympathetic to each individual student's needs, and watch out for blanket statements about the class that may come across as too harsh in the eyes of some of your students. Make sure you have an open-door policy if students need someone to talk to, but make it clear to them that, as an adult and an employee of the school system, you are under certain legal obligations if they reveal certain kinds of information.

Good student-teacher relationships also involve patience, flexibility, and understanding. In no way should you let the students in your class walk all over you. You must stand your ground and remain in control at all times. You can still create situations in which your students feel ownership and empowerment. Let them vote on two different ways of teaching the same assignment, or nominate students to fill different leadership positions at times (note taker, joke teller, name taker, VCR worker, line leader, table washer, calendar "up-dater," paper "passer-outer"—you get the point). No matter what the task, allowing students some choice and a feeling of control will gain you respect and cooperation, and this is a difficult thing to accomplish regardless of your years of experience in the classroom.

The way you respond to anger will also affect your relationships with students. If a student becomes disrespectful or rude toward you (and chances are good that at least one will), instead of reacting in anger, react with disappointment and try a different approach. Say, "Now, I don't speak to you like that (or use those words or speak that loud) so why do you think it's OK to speak to me like that?" Usually, the answer is "I don't know." Help your students learn how to express what they are feeling more effectively, choosing more appropriate words or tones or volume level. Whatever has caused them to lash out also needs to be addressed, but it is more important to teach them how to handle their anger now, so later in life, their reactions won't get them into bigger trouble. Remember, some of your students will never have been exposed to peaceful conflict resolution at home, so it is up to you to show them how it can be done.

One teacher summarizes the relationship between herself and her students like this:

> They [her students] know they can come to me with their problems and I'll give them tissues, but at the same time they know if they give me problems, they'll need tissues. Teddy Roosevelt said, "Speak softly and carry a big stick, you will go far." He wasn't referring to teaching, but his policy works. Yelling, screaming, and slamming doors does not work. It may get you a temporary fix to a problem, but it is harmful in the long run. When you scream, they see anger. Plus, you are supposed to be modeling good behavior; do you allow your students to scream at each other? By screaming, you lower the standards and the respect level your students have

for you. Think about it . . . have you ever heard a "Teacher of the Year" scream at the top of his or her lungs for a class to be quiet? He or she doesn't have to do it and knows that it is not good teaching behavior.

Some teachers use physical gestures to manage their students. Raising a hand, flicking the lights, or ringing a bell can all be quite effective. No matter how loudly you say "return to your seats please," the critical feature is that you have asked them to do something, and they know they should do it. If a student becomes upset when you ask them to do something, respond with a kind word (honey, kind lady, dear sir, sweetheart) and make a gentle physical contact (touch a shoulder, pat a back, rub a head) to get your point across to them with no anger at all and a change in behavior. If you start by loudly calling a student's name, the student will be less responsive and more defensive, and no change of behavior will result. Also, if you start by saying something positive, you are more likely to have their attention as you continue. For example, the words, "You are such a great student, I just wish you would work on listening to directions without talking," are much more soothing to a child than "Why can't you be quiet when I'm talking?"

Wait time (i.e., waiting before you discipline a student) can also be helpful. When a student's misbehavior is extreme, ask the student to step into the hall and wait for you. Take a few deep breaths and remind yourself that the student is only a child. Once you are calm, go outside the door and begin to talk. If you run out immediately, you are more likely to lash out and show anger. Showing disappointment and frustration are more effective than being angry. You have shown your student that it's OK to mess up: You still care about him or her and want the student to be successful.

Monitoring progress and keeping track of what your students are learning are essential parts of productive instructional relationships. If you have time, maybe on a workday or after school, review your students' career education records. Pick two or three students who you think need some attention. There is a wealth of information inside that will help you to better understand a student. Look at the student's birthday; is he or she old or young for this grade? Have students changed schools several times? Are their test scores consistent throughout their educational careers? Have they been retained? Look at their pictures: Have they changed much in appearance? Questions like these will help you get to know your students better, and the better you know them and understand them, the better chance you have of teaching them.

CHAPTER SEVEN

Parents

O f all the challenges you will encounter in your teaching career, dealing with parents can be a large one. You will learn that there are three general types of parents:

Type 1: The parents who love you. They bend over backward trying to help you, whether it is with supplies, tutoring, chaperoning, volunteering, or just giving you the little "teacher appreciation" gifts that will make you smile. We wish they were all like this!

Type 2: The parents whom you will never see. You see their children every day and their signatures every once in a while, and you might catch a glimpse of them at a school function, but as far as conversation and a relationship go, you won't have one. As long as their child is a perfect angel, this is OK, but how many perfect angels do you honestly think you'll have in your classroom? You will have to beg and plead with these parents for a conference, and when they do show up or you get them on the phone, speak fast, because you won't have much time.

Type 3: Last but not least, the parents of children who can do no wrong. These parents will defend their child to the end, even over the most trivial of things. These parents will undermine your authority based on your experience, your age, or the wonderful stories their child has invented about you. This group of parents loves to try to get the last word, and be ready, that last word may be unkind. But don't take it personally! They are lashing out at you the teacher, not the whole person. You have to learn to separate the two, or your life will be difficult.

So how do you deal with these parents, especially Type 3? Parents are as different as their children, and you must deal with them individually. Here are a few things that will help in working with all types of parents.

DON'T INSULT THEIR PARENTING

Although you may strongly believe that the parent with whom you are speaking has done very little positive parenting, don't say that. It is best to assume that parents are doing the best they can. Offer suggestions by using an example (whether real or not), such as, "I had another student who was having this same problem, and his mother found that by (insert your suggestion) he became much more successful." If you make parents feel as if they have already failed, why would they even attempt something different? Although it may be difficult, it never is too late to start being a parent.

ALWAYS BEGIN WITH A POSITIVE COMMENT

Opening the conversation on a positive note makes even the most difficult parents a little more inclined to listen to you. No matter how difficult the child, you should be able to find one good thing to say about him or her. Once you have made your positive comment, then lead into the real reason that you called. Make sure you sound optimistic by using lines such as "I know he can do the work," or "She has so much potential." Parents need to hear this. It is a mistake to think that parents won't want to help or become involved in their child's education. They have to see the light at the end of the tunnel, however, before they get on the train.

USE SEVERAL FORMS OF COMMUNICATION

There are many ways to keep in touch with parents. Telephone calls, e-mails, and letters sent home via the student or the postal service can all be effective. Find the one that works for you and stick with it. Another great strategy works like this: Give each student two envelopes, and have students address the envelopes (which can be a lesson in itself) to a parent or guardian that they want to receive good news. Then, ask the counselor for some awards or certificates or create some yourself. Periodically, mail as many letters home with "Most Improved," "Certificate of Achievement," "Citizenship," "Perfect Attendance," "Highest Grade on _____ " as you can. Students who receive them will be happy, their parents will be happy, and you will be happy.

DOCUMENT *ALL* PARENT CONTACTS

Even if you just write the date you contacted a parent, you need to keep a record. It is most helpful if you have a form or log that you use to record the name of the parent, date, time of day, method of contact, and reason for contact. This can become critical if problems continue and an administrator enters the picture, asking, "Have you contacted the parent?" Some schools even have policies that require you to contact the parent of each child who is failing your class. There is a sample log in the Survival Guide that you can use or adapt for yourself.

BALANCE

Although it may be difficult, try to make at least as many positive as negative contacts with parents. Having a positive conversation with a parent about a child's success is refreshing and rewarding. It also opens the door for communication if problems arise later in the year, or you need parent support for a field trip or financing a project.

CONFERENCES AND CONTRACTS

Parent conferences can be very challenging, for example, when a parent is angry or upset. At times like these, it is a good idea to bring in a mentor, counselor, administrator, or one of the student's other teachers. Take notes during the conference, and have each party sign it for verification. Depending on the grade and purpose of the meeting, it may also be a good idea to ask the student to participate in a parent conference—maybe not at the beginning, but at least near the end when recommendations and decisions are being made. This allows the student to have some ownership in the situation. This also may clear up any possible miscommunication. Writing behavior or academic contracts together during the conference is also effective. Everyone has equal input, the expectations are clear, and everyone agrees on what should happen next. This puts a motivational pressure on the student to uphold his or her end of the contract, which will probably result in a positive change.

CONSTANT CONTACT

It can also be effective to send a mass letter home with students every two weeks. The letters might address project announcements, class newsletters, athletic schedules, or requests for help. To encourage students to deliver the letters, ask them to have the letters signed and returned; you might also offer incentives such as extra credit, candy, homework passes, free lunch time, or whatever works for your students. You may find that almost all the letters are signed and returned when you do this.

Parents will appreciate your efforts to keep them updated and involved, even those Type 3 parents. Another approach is to compile an e-mail list of parents, and send a notice every Monday with a weekly agenda or other news. The bigger the team you can build focusing on improving a child's education, the greater the chance of continued success you will have.

BE A PROFESSIONAL WHEN TALKING WITH PARENTS

It is essential to keep your communications with parents on a professional level. This means, for example, not talking negatively about the school, administrators, or other teachers and not discussing other students, gossiping, or using profanity. Do not come late for a meeting, always shake hands, and do not argue with your supervisor in the parents' presence. Parents talk to each other, and you want them to have good things to tell the future parents of your future students. If parents already have a negative opinion about you based on the experiences you may have had with another parent, they are more likely to be Type 3 on the first day of school.

SUPPORT ALL FAMILIES AS THEY SUPPORT THEIR CHILDREN

Parents of children with special learning needs as well as children from diverse ethnic and language backgrounds often have to work harder to foster academic growth and development. Show your appreciation by helping families practice literacy skills at home. Encourage parents to engage their children in conversations about school—send children home with questions to ask their parents about things they are learning at school. Ask parents to set aside some time for talking about school with their children. Put together some homework that brings parents and children together to share a learning experience.

A teacher who we know used this approach very successfully. She developed a set of questions related to each unit of study during the year. Periodically, she would send a few questions home and ask parents to help their child answer them by using almanacs, encyclopedias, or other reference materials found in local libraries, community centers, or their homes. The teacher also allowed parents to answer the questions based on personal experience if technical resources were unavailable. For these activities, the answer was less important than the answering, and the goal was valuing the richness of personal experiences as well as academic resources.

CHAPTER EIGHT

Special Education

There was a time when most teachers did not have to know much about special education. Students in need of special education were taught in settings far removed from their mainstream neighbors and peers. Not anymore. Now students with special needs are taught with their peers without disabilities as much as possible. This trend is called inclusion. As a result, more than ever before, your classroom is likely to include students with special needs, and you must be able to teach them.

The thing that is distinctive about special education is that students have been identified as needing special services or specific modifications based on a disability. Students with disabilities are legally guaranteed a right to a *free, appropriate* public education. The Individuals with Disabilities Education Act (IDEA) is the current guiding legislation for special education practices supported by the U.S. Department of Education. Most states organize their special education departments along what has become known as categorical lines. A category is simply a name assigned to a particular type of disability or group of related disabilities. Although the names of the categories vary slightly from state to state, special education is generally provided for children who have any type of disability that affects their educational needs. For example,

specific learning disabilities (SLD)

speech or language impairments (SLI)

mental retardation (MR)

emotional disturbance (ED)

multiple disabilities (MD)

hearing impairments (HI)

orthopedic impairments (OI)

other health impairments (OHI)

visual impairments (VI)

autism

deaf-blindness (DB)

traumatic brain injury (TBI)

developmental delay (DD)

Every student with a disability who receives special education must have an *individualized education program* (IEP). Developing an IEP creates an opportunity for teachers, parents, school administrators, related services personnel, and students (when appropriate) to work together to improve educational experiences for students with disabilities. The IEP is the foundation of a quality education for each child with a disability, and it is an important part of efforts to make inclusion work.

By law, the IEP must include certain information about the child and the educational program designed to meet his or her unique needs. You should be very familiar with this information if students with disabilities are included in your classroom:

- Current levels of educational performance
- Measurable goals and measurable objectives or benchmarks
- Special education and related services
- The extent of participation of children without disabilities
- A statement of how the child's progress will be measured and how parents will be informed of that progress
- The extent of modification of participation in state- and district-wide tests
- The dates and location of services to be provided
- Beginning at age 16 (or younger), a statement of transition services the student will need to reach post-school goals
- Beginning at age 16 (or younger), a statement of transition services to help the child prepare for leaving school
- Beginning at least one year before the child reaches the age of maturity, a statement that the student has been told of any rights that will transfer to him or her

You will be expected to make every effort to ensure that each annual goal and short-term objective are directly related to the statement of the student's present level of performance. In this way, annual goals and objectives are based on assessment data and not on beliefs about programs thought to be beneficial to the student, regardless of assessments and other information used in developing the IEP.

In planning interventions, the IEP team needs to take into account the student's current skill level, the teacher's skill, the resources, and the likelihood that the intervention will be implemented. This last factor often depends on (a) the effectiveness of the intervention, (b) the length of time and skill required for the intervention, and (c) the significance of the student's needs.

The IEP must be reviewed at least annually, and goals and objectives are modified as the student continues to demonstrate mastery. The attainment of the stated objectives is measured by daily performance as determined by your records and frequent objective measures of the student's ability to perform the skills needed to attain the goal.

Learning to teach students with disabilities is often part of a specialized teacher preparation program. Most school districts provide assistance to teachers who have general education teaching credentials. Sometimes, this assistance is offered by outside agencies or professionals. More typically, general and special education teachers share the responsibilities. Regardless of how students with disabilities received special education, here are a few of basics that all teachers should know.

KNOW THE LAWS

Both federal and state laws address special education programs. Be sure you know them and you understand your role as a teacher in supporting them. The Council for Exceptional Children is a great resource for information about laws and public policies affecting individuals with disabilities (http://www.cec.sped.org/pp/).

MEMORIZE THE LABELS

If you haven't figured it out yet, the special education world uses lots of abbreviations. Sometimes, common sense can help you figure them out. But when it comes to special education, there is no room for error. As soon as possible, get your hands on a list of those abbreviations that are used in your state or district. They may be very similar to the federal names and categories, but there also may be differences that you will need to know.

MEET THE DEPARTMENT CHAIR OR EXCEPTIONAL CHILDREN'S CONTACT IN YOUR SCHOOL

Find out who is in charge of special education at your school. Take time out of your day to introduce yourself to him or her. This person will provide you with the list of students within your school who are qualified for services and will also assist you in any way you may need, whether it be contacting parents, adjusting classroom instruction, or simply supporting you in discipline or instructional matters. You will also be working with special education professionals when a student's IEP is reviewed. It is important for you to be skilled in following guidelines and documenting behavior and performance.

CREATE A "CHEAT SHEET" OF STUDENTS WITH THEIR RESPECTIVE MODIFICATIONS

You are likely to have more than one student who requires modification; you will probably have many. Don't expect to remember which students received extended test time and which ones had read-aloud tests. One way to keep everything straight is to make a simple chart with all the modifications and then list the students who receive each of them (see Survival Guide). The list will be a great asset for you.

YOU CAN DEFINE PREFERENTIAL SEATING

A very popular modification is preferential seating. You may have more students who need this than you have front-and-center seats. Remember that you can decide what is preferred and best for each student. Look at the list of students and then your seating chart. For example, you may have one student with a visual impairment who definitely needs to be front and center. A student with epilepsy may also need a front-row seat. You may have three boys who have *behavioral and emotional handicaps*, and each has the potential to be violent; they stay up front. Once all the front-row seats are filled, use you best judgment on where to place the remaining students. For example, you might place students with learning disabilities next to buddies so they can ask questions if they didn't understand or follow an example if they are unclear as to what the directions were. This way, they learn to solve problems and challenges on their own, which can help to build their self-confidence.

MODIFICATIONS 101

In addition, you sometimes have to be creative in the area of modifications. Please understand that at no time can you shortchange a student because of the challenge he or she may pose to you. Remember, students with disabilities are legally guaranteed these modifications, and your goal is to provide the best education possible for all students. These are simple suggestions to help implement some of the most popular modifications in a way that helps you and the student. If you have questions about how to adjust to other specific modifications, just *ask* a mentor teacher or one of your special education teacher colleagues. Your state will also probably have a list of acceptable modifications on its Web site.

- *Abbreviated assignments:* Students can do even- or odd-numbered questions. Students can choose which 10 questions to answer (when returning the graded paper, be sure to complete the answers to the omitted questions if they are necessary to understanding the lesson). Students may opt not to respond in complete sentences, or students are allowed to write on a worksheet or in the book. Also use this modification for tests and quizzes. Give the student the exact same number of questions, but modify the answer choices; for example, instead of having four choices, eliminate two or make the "distractors" more obvious.

- *Extended time:* This modification has to be established based on the type of assignment, and it needs to be emphasized as confidential between you and the student (another lesson learned by my mistake). For example, on projects, give 1½ the amount of time other students get. So if others have a week to complete the project, a student with this modification is allowed a week and a half. If a student is unable to complete quizzes and tests within the assigned time, make special arrangements for a time when it can be done (after school, during a study hall/skills class).

- *Copy of notes:* Easy! Just find some triplicate paper (there should be some at your school), and have the student with the neatest handwriting use it; then, give a copy to the student who needs it. Also make a copy of any overheads that are used, "whiting out" words to be filled in as you go through it. Be sure you have established a system of organization for these students as well.

- *Study guide:* Take a copy of the test, erase the answer choices, and then write the page number in the book or the page of notes where the answer can be found. Before the test, check the study guide to be sure everything is correct. For bigger tests, such as a midterm or unit test, create a detailed outline that contains all of the crucial information on it that needs to be studied. This is great for all students, not just those with modifications. You can adjust it according to the ability levels within your classroom.

ALWAYS REMEMBER TEST ACCOMMODATIONS

In the world of high-stakes standardized testing, this is the biggie. You need to research how this is done in your school, system, or state. In most states, any standardized assessment, whether it be quarter, semester, or end of the year, must be administered according to a student's IEP—no exceptions. Modifications for teacher-generated tests are optional, based on parent/student preferences, but must be consistent all year. This means that if you have students with a read-aloud modification, they *may* have their teacher-made test read to them, but they *must* have a standardized test read to them. If they have one read-aloud for a chapter test at the beginning of the year, they must have a read-aloud for every chapter test after that. It is best to consult with the parent and the special education teacher prior to your first test to be sure you are all on the same page. Remember, it is very important to get the testing accommodations right. Your state or system may have a different way of doing this. Be sure you know it and do it. For more information, check the National Center on Educational Outcomes (education.umn.edu/NCEO/default.html). To become familiar with effective teaching methods for students with learning disabilities, check the Council for Exceptional Children Web site (www.cec.sped.org) and other Internet resources (www.teachingld.org).

CHAPTER NINE

Oh, I Almost Forgot, the "Teacher" Part

Most teachers would agree that the actual teaching part of their jobs is easier than all other aspects. If you are organized, well-planned, prepared and can get the attention and respect of your students, the teaching will come. You cannot expect everyone to learn everything you teach them, although your goal is to be as effective as possible.

You will find that the more interesting you make your lessons, and the more excited you appear about the material, the more students learn. You will also find that by using a "hook," students are more likely to learn. Hooks are something that gets their attention right away such as funny or unusual stories, intriguing questions, a video clip or song, or an artifact. Once you get them hooked, then you will not be fighting for their attention.

Lesson planning and curriculum vary by school systems, schedules, and grade levels. You will need to know the requirements and make them work for you. Remember, you will have a variety of students in those desks: Some are auditory learners, some are visual learners, some will be tough to teach, and some will be very easy. Plan your lessons with diversity in mind. Try not to lecture too often and try to balance the time spent on group work and individual work. It will take a little more time to plan this way, but the results will be well worth the effort.

Here are a few ideas and strategies that may help you. They can be adapted to any subject or grade level. You will also develop your own strategies and learn from other teachers and your own reading and professional development opportunities. Share and borrow as much as you can!

COOPERATIVE LEARNING IDEAS

Don't be mistaken; this is not simply pairing up partners for assignments. Cooperative learning is very beneficial when done correctly. Groups of students should be put together based on their abilities, their interpersonal skills, and the material to be learned. Sometimes, I make groups according to ability, and other times, I mix students of different abilities. Sometimes, I assign roles, and other times, I allow students to assign roles within their groups. I use the privilege of letting them pick their groups as an incentive for good behavior (this was huge in middle school). I recommend that you get to know your students before you group them together. You never want to set students up to fail by putting them with someone with whom they can't successfully work for whatever reason.

SOCRATIC SEMINARS

There are lots of books and workshops out there that will help you learn how to have these seminars according to your grade level and your content. In a Socratic seminar, students use references to an assigned text (an article, poem, or journal entry) to ask and answer thought-provoking questions. In the process, students explore new ideas and gain insight into the understanding of their classmates. Socratic seminars can be formal or informal; the students are usually in a circle or other arrangement that allows them to see each other, and the teacher serves as a facilitator (meaning you are out of the conversation—students talk to each other, not you). This is a great exercise for allowing your quietest, most reserved student the chance to speak up and be heard by all. There is sure to be one expert on this in your school, just *ask* around.

DEBATES

Teachers generally love debates. More important, students love to argue, and so they love debates. When you have a classroom debate, the most important thing is to establish clear rules and high expectations. With higher ability classes, you can give them a topic and tell them to research both sides of the issue and then take a stand. When it comes time to debate, assign a position to each group rather than letting them select the side they agree with or like. By doing this, they are prepared for both sides, and they see the debate as more of an educational experience. You also get to see some of your shyest students really come out of their shells. Any topic can be made "debate-able" with a little creativity.

EXPERIENTIAL EXERCISES

Experiential lessons can be done in any subject. An experiential exercise is a lesson in which the students re-create an event or process. For example, you might have students re-enact battles (two-front war, trench warfare, the surrender at Yorktown). Assign each student a country that was involved in the war. Then, have students set up in the positions that the countries would have held and, with safe weapons like foam or plastic balls and paper wads, order the attack. The students love it, and they have to know what to do based on the actual events and the geography of the war. You can also set up processes or simulations. You can do an assembly line, the Underground Railroad, the Greensboro sit-ins, and the stock market crash. Science teachers could do the solar system (let some students be planets, some be stars, and have them orbit and rotate around the room) or mitosis and have them divide accordingly. Some programs create these exercises based on subjects, but if you can't find them or afford them, just use your imagination.

ALTERNATIVE/ENHANCED LECTURES

You were probably told somewhere in your teacher preparation program that lectures were not effective means of instruction, but lectures can be good if used in moderation and supplemented with visual or auditory aids. Find songs that you can adapt to your lesson. For example, you can give notes on the causes of the American Revolution and then listen to songs from School House Rocks to reiterate the information. The students are engaged the entire time, and you have addressed different learning styles. Use giant maps, beach ball globes, and fun posters to keep students interested in the lesson. Video clips are great sources of information if you have your students take notes while watching. Let them listen to important historical speeches, and whenever possible, try to find an artifact of the era you are using for your lessons. The Internet is a great resource for teaching materials for lessons that involve students. If you make your students a part of the lesson, your teaching can be very effective.

GRAPHIC ORGANIZERS

Graphic organizers are some of the most effective teaching tools you can use, and they are easy. See the Survival Guide for a variety of graphic organizers. Using graphic organizers will help visual learners to arrange information spatially, helping them to remember it. Organizers can be simple or as complicated as the content of your lesson. You can even get a little fancier and create your own graphic organizers with a theme. For example, use a train to teach about westward expansion, a car to teach about industrialization, a boat to teach about exploration, and so on. You could use a heart for poetry, a mountain for slope, or a magnifying glass for atoms. When you use symbols that are creative or have meaning, your students will be interested in writing the information on them. Just don't go overboard: It's what's inside the organizer that matters.

FOLDABLES

These are cool little ways of getting mass amounts of information in an organized way. There are actually books full of foldable ideas for all subjects and ancillary materials that come with textbooks with foldable lessons, too. You can use foldables for vocabulary, categories (like Congress, three branches of government), or unit/chapter reviews. Books and videos are full of great foldable lessons. One simple way to create a foldable is to simply fold a piece of construction paper in half like a book. Insert notebook paper and staple the "spine." Have the students cut the construction paper to create tabs that open up. On the construction paper, they write the topic or vocabulary word, and on the notebook paper underneath, they write the information or definition. These make a very easy lesson, and using them improves students' ability to listen and follow directions. Be sure that you have made one first to provide an example, and bring a lot of patience to class with you that day!

PAPER DOLLS

These can be historical figures, scientists, authors, or characters from a novel. Have the students cut the dolls from a pattern. Have them decorate the dolls with a face, hair, and clothing, and make an index card with information about the person the doll represents. Higher ability students can put one or two symbolic items in the hands of the doll (the Declaration of Independence for Jefferson, an apple for Newton); students can also work together on their dolls. Although it may seem childish, this works great for middle school and high school students. There is a pattern in the Survival Guide; feel free to change the size or shape or whatever works for you.

PUPPET SHOWS, QUICK SKITS, AND PLAYS

These are self-explanatory. One suggestion is to videotape the plays, skits, or puppet shows so you can show them as a review or a reward.

Kids love to see themselves on TV. Puppets can be made from just about anything—socks, Popsicle sticks, paper towel holders, old dolls. Skits can be scripted or improvised, depending on the age of your students. They can use simple costumes or props or just be themselves. Some students learn best when they are doing something. So pretending to be a puppet will help them to understand the characteristics associated with their role.

GAMES

Any game you can create, students will play. You make the rules and explain them twice, and then, let the games begin! Kids learn amazingly well when they are being competitive, having fun, and not thinking about learning.

Basketball	Twenty Questions	I Spy
Baseball	Scavenger Hunts	Charades
Bowling	Dice Games	Pictionary
Football	Family Feud	20 Questions
BINGO	Hangman	50/50
Tic-Tac-Toe	Wheel of Fortune	Bluff
Concentration	Jeopardy	Four Corners

HUMAN TIME LINES OR DIAGRAMS

Use signs or labels and make the students order themselves appropriately. You can make it a little more difficult by timing each group or by not allowing the students to talk. Consider any modification that will make the lesson more effective.

CUBES OF KNOWLEDGE

Have students create cubes out of construction paper. Explain what information each student needs to put on each face of the cube. They can use scenes from a story, formulas in math, shapes in geometry, states of matter, chemical reactions, reports of countries, systems within the human body, or anything else to cover the faces of the cube. Basically, these are three-dimensional graphic organizers that look very cool hanging from the ceiling or on a window.

MINI-BIOGRAPHIES

Mini-biographies can be in the form of a poem, symbolic speech, poster, headstone, song, skit, children's book, or regular paper, and they work well in any grade or subject. Have students briefly describe the details of the life of an important figure. Mini-biographies can serve as a review or even as an alternate form of assessment. They are also a great way to integrate writing across the curriculum.

CARTOONS

Students can make these as funny or serious as they want. Be sure to explain that it is not necessarily artistic ability that makes a cartoon funny, it is the content. Use current examples of political cartoons to let them get the hang of it. These make a great bulletin board, especially in the high school classroom.

BROCHURES, PAMPHLETS, OR TRAVEL GUIDES

Design your own, and have students share. Computers and magazines are great sources of cool pictures. Students can use a brochure to provide information on a specific place, a type of government, or regions within a state. Pamphlets can be used to describe a leader, an era, or a major topic. Travel guides are great ways of reinforcing geography themes or a historical period.

COMMERCIALS

Whether they are for the radio or TV, students will have a blast creating their own commercials. Let them advertise for an event, invention, product, or travel destination. Students will amaze you with the quality of work they produce. Do not forget to record these for reviews or rewards.

WANTED POSTERS

A teacher we know used the movie, *The Good, the Bad, and the Ugly,* to help students design a poster including historical figures and themes of the Wild West. Literature teachers can create posters for authors, heroes, or villains. Posters are easy to create and fun to look at; students can really get into these.

INTERVIEWS

You may have an Oprah, Barbara, or Montel in the making. Be sure to help students with writing the script, and encourage a serious approach. You can even have the rest of the class "rate" the show.

MAGAZINE COVERS

These are simple and effective. Depending on the subject, have each student create a cover that reflects some information that you have taught. You can use the solar system, shapes, parts of speech, integers, and so on. Hold a cover contest in which you reward "Most Popular," "Best Seller," "Most Colorful," and so on.

ABC, HOW TO, OR COUNTING BOOKS

Use each of the 26 letters to begin a word related to your subject—maybe cities in Europe, elements from the periodic table, or types of trees. You can bind the books, using either your library's book binder or rings and yarn. When the books are finished, you can mail them home to parents, display them in a case somewhere in your building, share them with another grade or class, or use them throughout the year.

MOBILES

Parents are more than willing to donate wire hangers, and yarn is cheap. Mobiles help students to classify and organize information. They also look great displayed, but be sure to check your plans with a building supervisor to make sure the mobiles won't interfere with the alarm system if they move and sway when the heat turns on at night.

TECHNOLOGY

Find out what technology resources are available in your school. Game systems, Smart Boards, projectors, or laptops will make learning fun. When you take away pencil and paper, you can make learning more fun for your students (and you). Most textbooks come with their own Web sites, which often provide links to other social studies sites. Web-based lessons have been especially designed to help students use the Internet to research a question. Some software programs are related to specific content (U.S. presidents, the Middle Ages, etc.). Some of these must be purchased; if so, don't spend your own money until you have to do so. Ask your administrator, parents, parent-teacher organization, a local educational sponsor, or curriculum specialists, or write a mini-grant. When all else fails, then reach into your own wallet.

CHAPTER TEN

Do's and Don'ts

A Little List of Teaching Tips

We hope that by the time you've reached this point in the book, you haven't changed your mind about teaching. We love teaching. We would do it for half the money and double the time, if we had to . . . well, maybe. We think that teaching is the most rewarding of any profession. We rank teachers right up there with doctors and firemen when it comes to changing lives. In fact, we wouldn't have doctors and firemen if we didn't have teachers. We wrote this book to prepare you for the worst, but we are hoping for nothing but the best for you! To end our mission, we want to share a few do's and don'ts.

- Do know that you are doing the most important job in the world.
- Don't forget that you are doing one of the hardest jobs in the world.
- Do smile during the first week.
- Don't try to be their friend.
- Do tell them that you care.
- Don't give them your home phone number unless they ask for it.
- Do plan the perfect lesson.
- Don't expect the perfect lesson to always work.
- Do make time for yourself and your life outside of school.
- Don't bring your life into the classroom (especially on a bad day).
- Do take pride in your work.
- Don't take criticism personally.
- Do aim for perfection.
- Don't forget that this is the first time you've done this! We all fell when learning to walk and crashed when learning to ride a bike, so you will mess up when it comes to teaching, and that's OK.
- Do make note of your mistakes.
- Don't make the same mistake twice.
- Do start everyday with a clean piece of paper.
- Don't hold grudges.

- Do seek out teachers in your school that you'd like to model yourself after.
- Don't hang out with the teachers who are unhappy with what they do for a living.
- Do play the numbers (meaning teach to the greatest number of kids first, then review with the ones you lost while the ones who got it are doing something else).
- Don't isolate your lower-skilled kids or bore your higher-level ones.
- Do relax.
- Don't be caught off guard.
- Do demand respect.
- Don't forget to give respect.
- Do be ready for challenges.
- Don't run from difficult situations.
- Do expect not to know all of the answers.
- Don't pretend to know something you don't.
- Do remember what it felt like to be a kid.
- Don't act like a kid.

Now think of the best teacher you ever had and go out and be a little bit better!

Appendix: Survival Guide

Document Text Cross-Reference Page

Contact Book Form

Date	Name and Contact Information	Context, What He/She Said, Resource

Professional Development Log

Date	Activity	Location	Presenter	Summary

Résumé

STACEY JARVIS
1234 East West Street
Charlotte, NC 28888
704-555-8888
sjarvis@sjarvis.edu

PROFESSIONAL PHILOSOPHY AND PERSONAL STATEMENT

As a teacher, I am worried about the future of my profession. A school can only be as strong as its weakest teacher. Students deserve good teachers, and in order to do something well, you have to practice and learn from your experiences. Too many teachers leave the classroom after only a few years. Many new teachers come into the classroom with a distorted view of reality, and when the true picture of public education becomes clear, they leave. If we are going to change the high teacher turnover rate, we have to start by helping those teachers who are the most likely to leave. We must prepare them for the challenges they will face, assure them of the importance of their job, provide them with situations they can be successful in, and congratulate them for the little accomplishments made everyday. I believe the best way to do this is by serving as a model for new teachers.

EDUCATION AND PROFESSIONAL CREDENTIALS

High School   A.C. Reynolds High School, Asheville, NC 1996

BA in History   University of North Carolina at Wilmington, Wilmington, NC, 2000.

MEd (enrolled)   Secondary Education, University of North Carolina at Charlotte, Charlotte, NC (anticipated graduation Spring 2006)

North Carolina Certification, Social Studies Grades 6–12

National Board Certified Teacher

Advanced Placement (AP) Certified Teacher

PROFESSIONAL EXPERIENCE

2002–current
   High School Social Studies Teacher
   • *Varsity softball coach.*
2000–2002
   Middle Grades Social Studies Teacher
   • *Piloted new supplemental curriculum program across the state.*
   • *Social committee chair.*

- *Member of the School Improvement Team.*
- *Softball coach.*

2001–current
  Presenter at the North Carolina Teaching Fellows Senior Conference
2000–current
  North Carolina Teaching Fellows Regional Screening Committee Member

RELATED EXPERIENCE

New Hanover County School System	1998–2000	Substitute Teacher
University of North Carolina at Wilmington	2000–2003	Academic Tutor, All Ages

SPECIAL AREAS OF INTEREST

- New Teacher Mentoring Programs
- Building Effective High School Web Sites
- Future Teachers of America Program/Teacher Cadet Program

OTHER RELEVANT INFORMATION

- Certified in CPR and Emergency First-Aid
- Proficient in Microsoft Office Applications, including FrontPage and PowerPoint
- Dean's and Academic Honors Lists

REFERENCES

University of North Carolina
  at Wilmington
Credential and Placement
  Office
Wilmington, NC 28999
343-343-3434
www.uncw.edu
placement@uncw.edu

Dr. Frank Jefferson
Bayside High School
33345 East Jones Street
Charlotte, NC 28293

Dr. Harrison Holmes
Secondary Education
UNC Wilmington
Wilmington, NC 28999

Dr. Mary Louise Thompkins
Middle and Secondary Education
UNC Charlotte
Charlotte, NC 28282

Dr. Marvin Mattersmore
Middle and Secondary Education
UNC Charlotte
Charlotte, NC 28282

Meeting Schedule

Month of _____

	Monday	Tuesday	Wednesday	Thursday	Friday
Meeting Time Place					
Meeting Time Place					
Meeting Time Place					
Meeting Time Place					
Meeting Time Place					

Student Information
Meet the Student

Fill in the blank with the best word that would make the statement true.

1. I am _____ years old.

2. I have _____ brothers and _____ sisters.

3. My favorite food is _____ and my least favorite is _____.

4. I am very good at _____ and I would like to be better at _____.

5. My favorite subject in school is _____.

6. I _____ to read.

7. A person I really admire is _____.

8. If I had a million dollars I would _____.

9. If I could go anywhere in the world I would go to _____.

10. My favorite sport is _____ and I pull for the _____.

11. I _____ to dance and _____ to sing.

12. My favorite music is   _____.

13. I have _____ pet(s) named _____.

14. My favorite thing to do outside is _____ and inside I like to _____.

15. My first impression of Ms. Jarvis is _____.

Student Interest Survey

In order for me to teach you most effectively, I need to know some things about you. Please answer these questions honestly; no one else will ever see them.

1. What is your favorite subject in school?

2. What is your least favorite subject in school?

3. Who has been your favorite teacher? Why?

4. If you could go anywhere in the world, where would you go? Why?

5. Have you thought about what you want to be when you grow up? What?

6. If you could travel back in time to any era in history, what era would you go back to?

7. What is one thing you'd like to learn more about this year?

8. What are your favorite in-class activities?

9. Do you enjoy reading? Why or why not?

10. Is there anything you'd like to know about me?

Name: _____

Student Questionnaire

1. What are your hobbies/interests/talents/pastimes?

2. What do you enjoy reading?

3. What are three of your favorite movies?

4. Tell me about your family (please be specific).

5. Who is the most influential person in your life? Why?

6. What motivates you?

7. What is your favorite subject in school? Least favorite? Why?

8. Who is your favorite all-time teacher? What did he/she do that inspired you to learn?

9. What is your favorite era in world history?

10. What would you like to learn more about this year in world history?

Special Education Modification Chart

Modification	Students

Rubrics

Written Report

Area	Quality Indicator		
	2	*1*	*0*
Topic	Topic of the report is clearly stated.	Topic of the report is unclear.	Topic of the report is not provided.
Structure	Introduction, supporting details, and summary are clearly stated.	Introduction, supporting details, and summary are unclear.	Introduction, supporting details, or summary is not provided.
Mechanics	Spelling, punctuation, and grammar are excellent.	Spelling, punctuation, and grammar are average.	Spelling, punctuation, and grammar are poor.
Overall Rating	Exceptional	Average	Poor

Book Report

Criteria	Rating		
	5	*3*	*0*
Introduction	Engaging	Boring	No beginning
Genre	Clearly specified	Not sure, unclear	Didn't mention it
Main Character or Topic	Character or topic clearly described	Not sure, unclear	Nothing about character or topic
Detail	Who, what, where, when, why, and how	Not sure, not clear	Litter or no detail
Integration	Linked content to current area of study	Not sure, not clear	None
Oral Presentation	Clear, strong, engaging style	Difficult to understand	Dull, boring
Overall Rating	Excellent	Good	Poor

Cooperative Group Rubric

Student Name _____   Date _____

	Rating			
Expectation	Beginning 1	Developing 2	Focused 3	Exemplary 4
Punctuality	Doesn't hand in assignments.	Hand in many assignments late.	Hands in most assignments on time.	Hands in all assignments on time.
Research Information	Does not collect information.	Contributes little information.	Contributes information that mainly relates.	Contributes a good deal of relevant information.
Shares Information	Keeps information to self and doesn't share with group.	Shares some information with the group.	Shares important information with the group.	Communicates and shares all information with the group.
Cooperates with group members	Never cooperates.	Seldom cooperates.	Usually cooperates.	Always cooperates.
Listens to group members	Always talking and never allows others to speak.	Talks much of the time and rarely allows others to speak.	Talks too much at times but usually is a good listener.	Balances listening and speaking well.
Makes fair decisions	Always wants things their way.	Often sides with friends and doesn't consider all viewpoints.	Usually considers all viewpoints.	Total team player.
Fulfills duties	Does not perform any duties.	Performs very little in way of duties.	Performs nearly all duties.	Performs all duties.
Shares responsibility	Always relies on others to do work.	Rarely does work–needs constant reminding.	Usually does the work–seldom need reminding.	Always does assigned work without being reminded.

Source: http://www.zianet.com/cjcox/edutech4learning/cincorubric.html

Parent Contact Log

Date	Parent's Name	Student's Name	Method of Contact	Reason for Contact	Outcome

Graphic Organizers

Bubble Map

Describe Using Adjectives

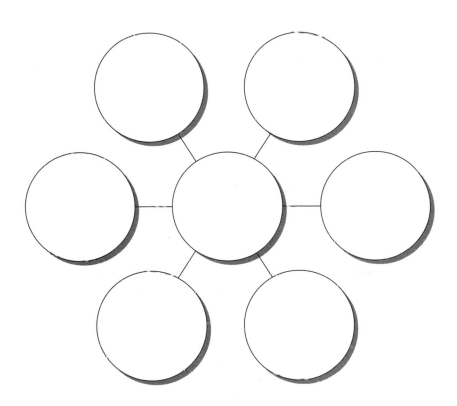

Chain of Events

Process, Tell a Story, Time Period, Monitoring Change

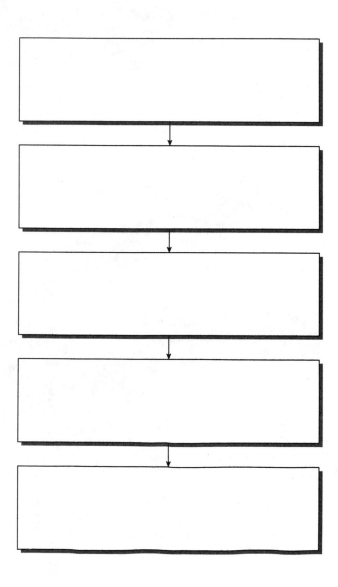

Coat of Arms

Five Aspects of a Topic

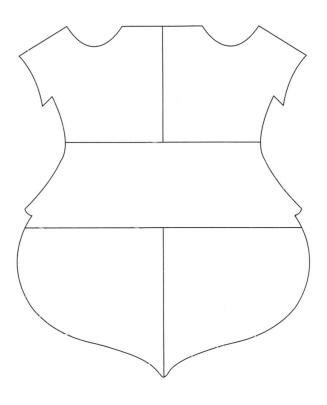

Comparison Chart

In-Depth Critique of a concept, Detailed Analysis

```
┌─────────────────────────────────────┐
│                                     │
└─────────────────────────────────────┘

        ┌─────────────────┐
        │   SIMILARITIES  │
        └─────────────────┘

┌─────────────────────────────────────────┐
│                                         │
│                                         │
└─────────────────────────────────────────┘

        ┌─────────────────┐
        │   DIFFERENCES   │
        └─────────────────┘
```

Double Bubble Map

Compare/Contrast

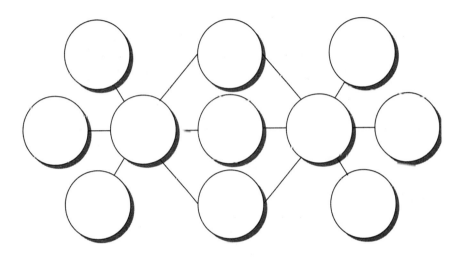

Flow Chart

Sequence of Events, Outline of a Story,
Steps in solving a problem, Scientific Process

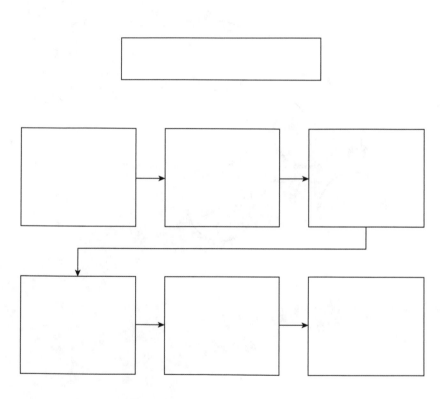

Multiple Causes & Effects

Analysis of an Events Causes And Effects

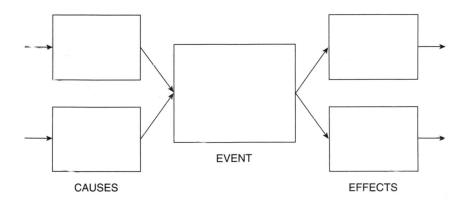

CAUSES   EVENT   EFFECTS

Tree Map

Classify, Group, Main Idea with Supporting Details

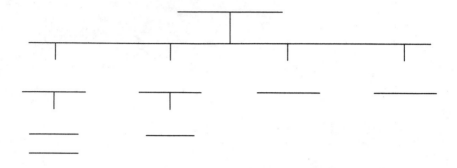

Venn Diagram

Compare Contrast

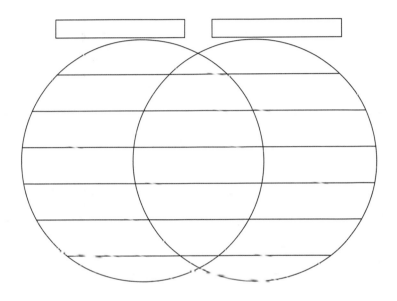

Vocabulary Activity I

Word	Think?	Means	Sketch

Vocabulary Activity II

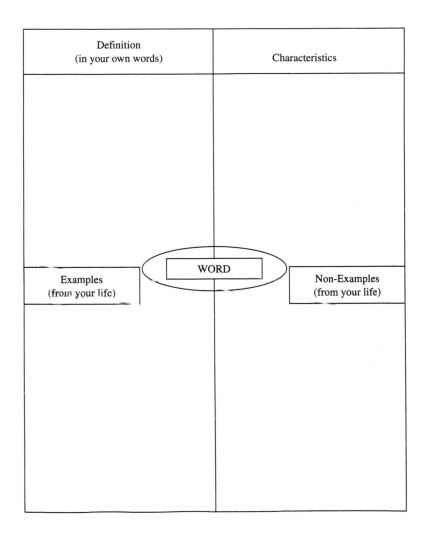

Web Chart

Catagories, Subgroups, Classify Information

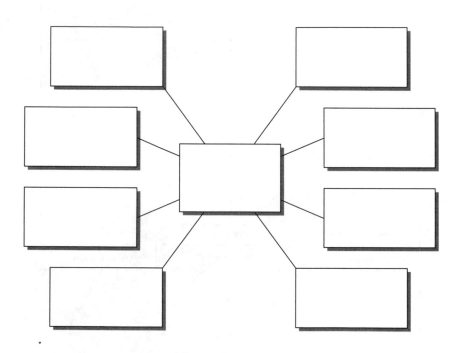

Paper Doll

Biography

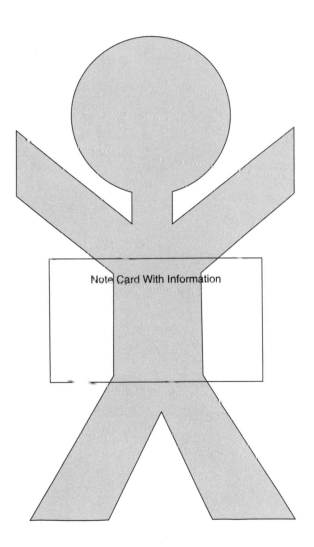

Index

**CORWIN
PRESS**

The Corwin Press logo—a raven striding across an open book—represents the union of courage and learning. Corwin Press is committed to improving education for all learners by publishing books and other professional development resources for those serving the field of PreK–12 education. By providing practical, hands-on materials, Corwin Press continues to carry out the promise of its motto: **"Helping Educators Do Their Work Better."**

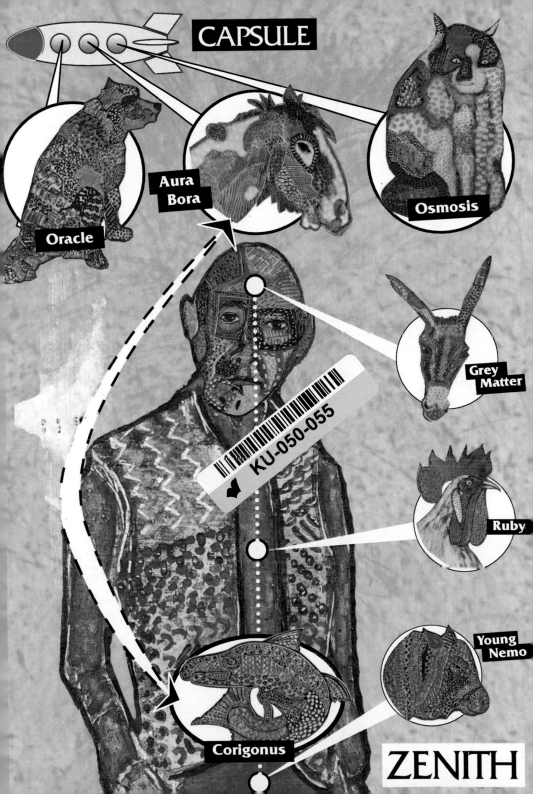

CAPSULE

Oracle

Aura Bora

Osmosis

Grey Matter

KU-050-055

Ruby

Young Nemo

Corigonus

ZENITH

THE WISDOM OF
ORACLES
BY JOHN RYAN

POETRY BY
JAMES DANIEL RYAN

Boyne Art Studio
Publishing

Copyright © John Ryan 2011

johnryanmeath@gmail.com

First published in Ireland in 2011
by
Boyne Art Studio
Clady, Old Trim Road,Navan,
Co. Meath, Ireland.

John Ryan asserts the right to be identified as the author of this book and The right of James Daniel Ryan to be identified as the poet of the works contained within this book is likewise asserted.

Distributed by
Boyne Art Studio Publishing
boyneartstudio@gmail.com
Ph +353 85 120 24 52

Cover Design by
ART NOWGALLERY
Bective, Navan, Co. Meath.

Promotional photos by
MB NOW INTERNATIONAL

ISBN 978-0-9569461-0-2

THE WISDOM OF ORACLES
BY JOHN RYAN

Forward by Kate O'Neill R.P.N.- R.M.- M.A. Psychology

This book is first of all a book of hope for it is confident in the ability of the human race to change for the better. It guides us through a maze of our own misunderstandings, our misconceived intentions and our misguided behaviours through to the core of our own truth. It explores what is truth, what is love and what is creation and makes a clear distinction between for example honesty and truth, emotion and feeling and construction and creation.

The very language of the book brings us on a new journey and we engage in a way that encourages us to think from a different angle so that our old automatic reactions are not readily available. We are directed to contemplate the information and its meaning from a new perspective.

The book is a strong and sometimes uncompromising comment on our accepted value systems and the manner is which we use them. There is an understanding of how we got to where we are as a race and developed into our current state.

The assertion that illness is an unnecessary part of the human condition surely deserves attention. It is certainly worth the risk of increasing awareness of oneself and the happenings to oneself in order to find out the truth behind this interesting theory.

There is a challenge to let go of the long trusted structures we have organized to help us understand and make sense of the world in which we live.

In the final analysis this book is an invitation to live life simply and with peace of mind. Getting there presents an interesting challenge. We are shown in a step by-step approach how to get in touch with our innate selves, the basis for developing a fuller understanding not alone of our own human nature but of the universe.

The exercises in the book make it useful in practical terms for soulful workshops orientated toward self-discovery and innate development.

THE WISDOM OF ORACLES
BY JOHN RYAN

DEDICATION

This book is dedicated to the lost explorers of this world.
May they one day realize their unique role in the world
and their important place in the universe.

THE WISDOM OF ORACLES
BY JOHN RYAN

NOTES

It is recommended that you read the book from cover to cover rather than taking out sections at a time. If you find that the first 60 pages are not fueling your imagination then this book may not be for you. The characters, the language and terms of reference are written in a particular style so that the reader does not immediately associate with references in other books of this kind and thus, get caught up in making assumptions around already used, misused and taken for granted terminology that may get in the way of the message of the book. For this reason it may at first be more difficult to engage however, your persistence I guarantee will pay off.

It is not necessary to know or learn all the characters and their functions at first because the information is repeated several times throughout the book and will gradually sink in through the process of osmosis. However, you can also refer back to the illustrations at the beginning of the book and the character descriptions in chapters 1,5,7 and 10 until you get used to them.

The message in the book is repeated for good reason, so that it absorbs gradually into your psyche to help counteract everyday messages mostly through media that we hear and see on a regular basis, messages that can have a subtle but destructive impact on our lives.

The book is designed to make you **question your attitudes and values** and if necessary to change them. For this reason you may resist the message it holds and your brain in particular may present a barrier to protect you from the information. Such words as unnecessary, silly, stupid, and ridiculous may present themselves and your body may even experience boredom, inability to concentrate or tiredness. This is your brain trying to protect you from information that it considers harmful to your already learned attitudes and values. You may need to talk to your brain several times during your reading of the book to reassure it you are not in any danger.

If you do not question your values and attitudes, question their beginnings and the reasons why you continually engage them and change those that are found questionable how can you expect the rest of the world to change? You have the power within you to change the world around you. Likewise, by staying as you are, the power you have is to ensure that the world around you stays as it is. This is a clear choice and you engage that choice every second of every day.

What each individual does on a personal level affects the world. When groups of people are engaged in a similar activity this has a much more potent effect. When we as a civilization engage the acceptance of poverty in others, of war, of abuse, of separation in its many forms we encourage the existence of those very behaviours. Why do we accept war as a way of dealing with perceived difference? Why is poverty acceptable when it doesn't affect us directly? Why is untruthfulness accepted as a way of life? By accepting these behaviours we support them and encourage our world to be misguided.

The purpose of the book is to encourage you to question your personal safety zone where you, unknown to yourself, accept and encourage dangerous behaviours in yourself and others.

The book is designed to bring you past what is called the thinking ability of the brain, past the emotions of the heart and past the physicality of the body to a place where you begin to engage the world through the **awareness of your own innateness**. From this place real thought is engaged, likewise real feelings and real creativity. You will see how and why you engage the world as you do, how you can change any dangerous patterns you may have unknowingly developed and in the process change your existence to a meaningful, healthy and fulfilling life.

THE WISDOM OF ORACLES
BY JOHN RYAN

INTRODUCTION

Balanced

Despite the fact that most people in the world are well meaning and caring we as a race find ourselves in the position that we are destroying our own planet. With the best of intentions we have placed ourselves in the unenviable position of being precariously balanced between survival and annihilation.

Take Action

Clearly what we have been doing up to now has to change and **our attitudes and values toward our world have to take a dramatic turn** if we are going to survive as a race. The time for talking is over we need to take action now not tomorrow or the next day. But what action can we take, where do we start and how do we know our actions will effect the changes necessary to offset the inevitable danger knocking at our front door?

New Solutions

The problems we are facing are new problems. We need therefore, to seek new solutions and not to be dependent on past experience for the answers to our current situation. We are going on a new journey our old maps won't serve us in this new terrain

Two Elements

The first thing we must realize is that the human race has been operating up to now through misguided and false perceptions. The larger the population gets the more this fact impacts on us and the more protective we become of our individual place in the scheme of things. There are two main false perceptions of the world that most people share:

1. **We are each individual and therefore separate from one another** and

2. **There is not enough to go around so we each must take what we can to survive**.

Change

Until we change these two misperceptions nothing will shift. What we need to do is

1. **Realize that each individual is equally important. This means that every body in the world is entitled to equal opportunity and an equal share of the world's resources,** and

2. **There are enough resources in the world for everybody and for anybody to take more than their fair share is the cause of unnecessary suffering to others as a result.**

Deeper Level

In almost all aspects of modern life our egos are massaged to think in terms of separation, the individual is encouraged to venture forward as a separate entity battling against the world. We need to seek uniqueness not through separation but through participation on a **deeper level of understanding** adding to the awareness of human **exploration and creativity rather than emphasis on survival.**

New Direction

At the moment our social structure is not designed to support the awareness needed to have a more equal distribution of the world's wealth so, at this stage it is enough to know that these changes need to be realized. As more people realize the necessity for change **society will embrace the new direction** we need to face. The faster people take up the call the quicker will be the response.

Turning Point

We are at a turning point in our evolution. It is necessary for us to **completely change our attitudes and values** so that we can put in place our **creative** needs. Our current set of values will not serve us well in the coming years. We need to prepare on not alone a personal level but collectively. So, now more than ever we need to realize our connection to everybody else to move from an egocentric outlook.

Response

This book is an introduction to the first steps toward this response how to get from the crawling stage to standing up. Beyond this there is walking and running then jumping and flying after which there is exploring in space. Clearly there are exciting times ahead as we explore the planet with our new understanding of life.

Newborn

However, nobody explores space without first learning how to crawl. At the moment in our world we are back-peddling trying to preserve that which has already been exhausted. We need to come to a stop and face forward to the new life that's in front of us **rather than looking back toward blame and retribution**. We are like a newborn clambering back into the warm womb from whence we came and closing our eyes to what's coming. It's too late for that.

How

This book shows us how we can face the future with confidence and the things we need to be doing on an individual basis to change the dangerous attitudes we hold so dear that keep us bound to the womb. It shows us how we have become disconnected from our innate selves, how

to remake that vital re-connection and to embrace the beginning of an exciting future in a new universe waiting to be discovered.

THE STORY

The Explorer

This is the story of **the explorer** who has become disconnected from his Capsule, the reasons why he has become disconnected and the process he goes through to make that vital reconnection.

Capsule

There are many Capsules at different levels of understanding throughout the Cosmos. From time to time a Capsule comes in contact with the planet earth and may decide to explore life on the planet for the benefit of further knowledge. One or more explorers are sent from each Capsule at various times to explore creativity on earth and to carry back information to Capsule. Although explorers from the same Capsule can connect with one another on earth they may not always realize their Capsule origin.

Core Connector

The explorer takes on a body that is suitable for living on the planet. The body is equipped with a Core connector to receive and send messages to Capsule. When the mission is complete the explorer is absorbed back into Capsule and the assumed body is left behind to decompose.

Survival

At times the explorer loses contact with his Capsule. He may eventually become totally disconnected and lose his identity.

In the absence of purposeful guidance, the lost explorer's planet life now becomes the focus of attention and he assumes a new role.

This new role transforms his outlook from one of exploration and creativity to one of survival and preservation. This is the condition of the vast majority of explorers on this planet.

Messages

Occasionally, a rescue operation is put into place to retrieve lost explorers. Messages are sent by Capsule to help retrain lost explorers into remembering their initial mission. *This book is a message from Capsule*.

Generators

The explorer's assumed human body contains three generators which, when linked with the Core connector, also in the body, are used to transfer vital information to and from Capsule. The **generators** are the main **storehouses of information** within the earth body of the explorer and are intended for use **only** in conjunction with Capsule. With the explorer's disconnection from Capsule his generators now assume a new role, that of **total control of explorer's functions**. They now direct the lost explorer through his new life as **survivor** rather than explorer, **even though they are not equipped to take on the task.**

The Vast Majority

The vast majority of people on this planet experience the lost explorer at regular stages in their lives. A large proportion of these people live their lives almost totally as lost explorers. This means they live almost totally under the **control** of their generators instead of under **guidance** from their Capsules. This has a profound effect on the world and its inhabitants and completely alters the personal attitudes and values of the explorer and his mission on earth.

It is the single largest contributor to the world's problems.

THE WISDOM OF ORACLES
BY JOHN RYAN

CHAPTER 1

DESCRIPTIONS OF THE TWO HUMANS AND THEIR MAIN CHARACTERISTICS

Zenith

Zenith **is** the human earth **explorer**. Known as enlightened and connected because he is connected to his innate self. He is identified by his intuitive, inventive, imaginative, inspirational and creative, easygoing approach to life.

Meme

Meme started out as the human earth explorer Zenith but has chosen instead to become the human **survivor** by connecting to earth matters. Meme is inclined toward intelligence and logic, emotion and reaction because he depends more on his three generators, the brain, heart and reproductive system. Meme may have a regimented, unimaginative, emotional, reactionary and somewhat repetitive approach to life.

The Three Generators

(See Meme Diagram at the front of the book)
The Generators are the three internal energy centers within Zenith and Meme namely Grey Matter, Ruby and Young Nemo. They are connected to one another through Corigonus, the central connector.

The three generators in Meme assume total responsibility for his welfare and thus, don't make use of Corigonus. However, the generators in Zenith don't take on the same responsibility. His innate or Capsule self motivates Zenith. Thus, his generators, by keeping in touch with Capsule, make constant use of his central connector Corigonus.

Grey Matter

Grey Matter is the first generator of Zenith and Meme, is located in the human brain and is the memory store for and activator of **information and logic** pertinent to their brains.

Ruby

Ruby is the second generator of Zenith and Meme, is located in the human heart and is the memory store for and activator of their **emotions**.

Young Nemo

Young Nemo is the third generator of Zenith and Meme, is located in the human reproductive system and is the memory store for and activator of their ***physicality and sexuality***.

Corigonus

Corigonus is located in the human's Core (just below the belly button, sometimes recognized as butterflies in the stomach) and plays a vital role in Zenith's life as the Core connector between his innate self in Capsule and his three generators. Meme is controlled by his generators and as such does not use the link at Corigonus.

The generator's link to Corigonus can be temporary, sporadic or more permanent depending on the individual's awareness and as a result a person may be almost permanently in one or other mode or sometimes in Zenith mode and other times in Meme mode. ***The ideal situation is to be totally in Zenith mode***.

THE WISDOM OF ORACLES
BY JOHN RYAN

CHAPTER 2

ATTITUDES AND VALUES

**No man a highland
No woman a sea
No parent an island
No baby a tragedy.** *pil*

Personal Attitude

One of the most important elements to an individual, that which makes life safe or threatening, is his own personal attitude. Through personal attitude we engage the world and the world is reflected back to us in the manner in which it is perceived. If we have an arrogant personal attitude to the world we will experience arrogant feedback. If on the other hand we have a caring attitude to the world we will experience caring feedback, for arrogance attracts arrogance and cannot attract caring and caring attracts caring and cannot attract arrogance.

Mixed Attitudes

Most people in the world have mixed attitudes consisting of loving and unloving elements. The subjects they have a loving attitude toward will respond lovingly while the subject they have an unloving attitude toward will respond un-lovingly. As a result most people experience a mix of loving and unloving feedback from the world.

Confused

Within each individual subject there can be a mix of attitudes some caring and some uncaring and when these subjects are mixed the result can be a very mixed attitude which can result in very mixed feedback to such an extent that attitudes can appear crisscrossed over one another. This system of attitudes can become very confused and confusing and thus, the world's response or feedback can be seen as confused and confusing.

Different

It stands to reason if personal attitudes are confused and complicated the world's response can be seen as equally confused and complicated. **Our perception of the world dictates how we react to the world or act in the world.** The world an individual presents to himself through his attitudes will be a totally different world to that which his neighbour presents to himself, simply because both will have a completely different set of personal attitudes, for no two people view the world in exactly the same way. Two people viewing the same event will perceive the event differently according to their individual attitudes.

Personal Attitudes

Personal attitudes are made up of ones **belief system and aims** in life whether we are aware or unaware of them. These in turn provide the various choices we make that ultimately produce individual values. These values are influenced by our interpretation of life, our attitudes and the meanings we take from life. **Our fears, pains and any seemingly unhealthy experiences** contribute to our attitudes, as do **seemingly healthy experiences**.

Understanding

The persistence our brain has of trying to understand the structure of the world and the whole universe is ultimately self-defeating. Our brain cannot know from a purely human perspective that which is an innate issue. For our brains to learn anything **original** we must **enter the innate world.** It is not possible to enter innate understanding from **a purely** human perspective. Even our current knowledge of the human race would not have been possible without the innate awareness of a few enlightened people at various stages of development in human understanding.

Different Worlds

We cannot develop an understanding of timelessness, of consciousness, of limitlessness or of divinity from a single human viewpoint because these elements are outside the human ability of understanding, for these are innate values. Nor do we have an understanding of innate values such as intuition, inspiration, invention, imagination, creativity, forethought etc. from a purely human perspective. It would be like asking a flea to develop an understanding of a dog. While the flea might live on the dog, they won't share the same understanding of life. They both live in totally different worlds of understanding.

Develop Traits

When a person is consistently promised or seduced into thinking positively about a set of circumstances, which in turn are not delivered as promised, for example with advertising, the person develops an attitude of eventually accepting this set of circumstances as normal behaviour just because it is continuously repeated on television or other media. The result can be one of disappointment with what is accepted as normal or everyday outlets. The individual may seek satisfaction in other outlets that are not everyday to most people and thus, develop traits not normally accepted by

society. These traits may then be accepted into his value system. He may not see these traits and attitudes as misguided, but as an accepted natural part of his developed personality and value system.

Normal Behaviour

In extreme cases as in murder, theft, sex offence etc. the perpetrator will justify his acts rationally, will accept his own behaviour as normal for him, and will be unable to see where he has become misguided. Law abiding people also do this all the time. However, their actions are less noticeable or may even be considered by society as normal behaviour. Their behaviour is considered normal when most other people accept the behaviour as normal. There are different levels of acceptability and sometimes the line between what is acceptable and what is not and the reasons why can be gray areas.

Mixed Messages

Most current entertainment in the form of T.V., computer games, videos, newspapers, magazines, promotional literature, books etc., through their mixed messages continuously give promise without delivery. This type of promotion is hypnotizing society into an expectation the delivery of which is continually not being realized. This contributes greatly to **the programming of destructive habits** and behaviours that become a normal **accepted part of societies attitudes and of our value system**.

Unhealthy Attitudes

Our bodies carry these destructive behaviours in the form of illness, frustration, anxiety, dissatisfaction, anger, resentment and innumerable unhealthy attitudes. These unhealthy attitudes contribute to the makeup of our belief system and become the basis of our value system. We may blame society or others for our condition. However, we are responsible for our own condition, our own behaviour, our own attitudes, whether they be healthy or not. Ultimately people make themselves healthy or unhealthy, happy or unhappy, aware or unaware, there is **nobody to blame, not even one's self**, as we shall see later.

Seduced

The simple truth is if we engage unhealthy input we will focus on unhealthy output and if we engage healthy input we will focus on healthy output. The fact is we as a society in the western world are being seduced continuously and we don't even realize that truth. We remain unconscious or mesmerized into submission continuously by undelivered promises that feed us the message that we are not good enough. There is a standard to which we all must apply and comply and when we do apply and comply the rug is pulled out from under us by ourselves. **We are seducing ourselves.**

Values

Ultimately our attitudes depend on our personal values and when we allow our values to become degraded, we have now reduced the value of our values. By being unaware of reducing our value system we invariably disable ourselves. We have thus, pulled out the watchdog's teeth and scolded him for barking. In doing so, **we have reduced our own level of awareness and of consciousness**.

Dangerous Behaviour

Left to its own devices the brain lacks the ability to differentiate between unhealthy input and healthy input. **All input is equally acceptable to brain.** Thus, dangerous behaviour can continue to go unchecked. Even though on an intellectual level we may know we are causing our own problems**, we somehow seem unable or unwilling to actually do anything about the causes.**

I was on holiday in Barcelona and on the streets were various street entertainers who performed for the passing tourists, one in particular caught my attention. He was obviously very practiced as he played the minute waltz on his violin for he played brilliantly and with great speed and clarity. However, nobody gave him any money and he walked away dejected and even though everybody else knew this happened to him continuously, he still looked surprised by it.

The problem was he was not a true musician and the reason everybody else knew and he didn't was his instrument over the years had gradually become out of tune and so the tune he heard was not the same tune everybody else heard. *His brain registered the original tone* and didn't register the gradual alteration. Had he been a real musician he would have checked his instrument regularly.

Likewise**, information we initially register in our brain is thereafter taken for granted by the brain unless we make a point of updating the information.** This is the reason why when as an adult we take up drawing or painting for instance, the initial attempts are childlike because our brains information hasn't been updated. **The brain is only capable of regurgitation it is not actually capable of thinking.**

Life Of Struggle

Most people in the western world, whether consciously or unconsciously, realize they are living a life that is out of control and are **generated purely through their brains, their hearts and their reproductive systems**, thus ensuring a life of struggle. All three generators seem to be **taking different directions** that seem to put more pressure on the perceived struggle. The mere fact that people have to put such an effort into controlling life speaks for itself. The more one struggles with life the more integrity and values are challenged and the more indignant one becomes in defense of values.

Self Deception

The fact that the brain, **without its innate connection**, cannot detect a false statement and differentiate it from a statement that is true means the brain is open to being seduced and self-deceived. All apparent facts engaged by the brain and all information are lumped together and accepted as actual fact by most people.

Even where the information is questioned, it is the brain that is engaged to make the clarification and while it may appear to be astute its findings are still questionable. There is little or no filtering out, so what one reads in a newspaper, or sees on T.V., or reads in books or reports or magazines, or is told by parents or teachers etc. is either accepted or questioned as fact even though the supposed facts may be fictitious. **Brain can discern only from a brain viewpoint and not from an innate perspective**.

Naive

Herein lies one of the problems associated with disconnection from one's innate self. People are in fact easily brain washed when they are disconnected. Meme is the person disconnected from his innateness and is thus naive and incapable of discerning falsehood. The main reason for this is that Meme, instead of being motivated through his innate self is in fact generated by **his three generators, 1 Grey Matter, 2 Ruby, and 3 Young Nemo.**

So, if Meme sometimes suspects on a deeper level that he may be being duped, his generators will be unable to pinpoint any indiscretion and simply accept the information or question its honesty but will be unable to see the truth. Repeated encounters, particularly with advertising media, contribute to the feeling of being subdued or being self-defeated. This contributes to the feeling of being intellectually and emotionally seduced continually and repeatedly.

That's Entertainment

Initially, there may be no intention toward deception by any of the media. However, their individual interests can take first place. So, while a T.V. show sets out to entertain, and this may be its main objective, any information given out may be taken by the viewer as fact. The viewer, even when discerning, may engage in accepting the information as relevant and true even if it's a soap opera, a chat show, a period play, the news, advertising or even cartoons.

All fiction or fact can be taken on an equal basis. All are credible, thus a murder report on the news can have the same effect on the viewer as a killing in a cartoon. The same can be said of all media, newspapers, radio, T.V., videos, C.Ds., computers, books, magazines, etc. All can be taken with an open trust by the three *naive* generators **because generators are not designed to be discerning and have no way of filtering out or distinguishing between healthy and unhealthy programming.**

Fraternities
The bleeding-heart's Fraternities
Are small, and very snug
They irritate your armpits
And prickle like a bug.

The bleeding-heart's Fraternities
Are mostly male, m'dears
They all adore Conformities
They all have flapping ears.

They overhear your small affairs
And turn 'em inside out
And, having pawed 'em once or twice
Dismiss 'em with a clout.

They're even on the Radio
Maybee TV, too
The bleeding-heart's Fraternities
Die hard, but damage do. *pil*

Mindless
The three generators **Grey Matter, Ruby and Young Nemo** contain large banks of information and are designed to accept, to store and to regurgitate at will. They are not inbuilt with **intuition, discernment, truth, forethought, imagination, inspiration, consciousness, mindfulness, creativity, infinite knowledge, wisdom, thought, or timelessness etc** for these are **innate** values. These values are not an intrinsic part of Zenith (who is connected to his innate self) or Meme (who is not connected) and are thus, not part of the three generators.

Although one's innate self is accessible through Zenith's Corigonus (the connector located just below the belly button- this will be discussed later on in the book), more often than not it is shut out by Meme's acceptance of **mindless** behaviour. As was mentioned earlier, Zenith transforms into Meme when he decides to **not** use his innate connection. The large majority of people in the world unknowingly and unwittingly shut out access to their innate selves through mindless behaviour. So, the large majority of Zeniths have become Memes.

For the three generators to have access to innate values, Meme needs to alter his perception from mindless Meme activity.

The Three Generators

Rightful Communication

There are three generators in Zenith which when operating efficiently are in full support and co-operation with his innate self. However, although this is rightful communication, Meme most often lives his life solely through his generators **without** the aid of his innateness thus ensuring a life of struggle as *the survivor*.

Generator 1, Grey Matter is responsible for informational intelligence and logic. Generator 2, Ruby is responsible for emotion and emotional intelligence. Generator 3, Young Nemo is responsible for physical intelligence, sexual and physical actions and reactions.

Rounded Decisions

We constantly put off what we know we need to be doing in our lives and in place occupy our time with activities that are of little benefit to our bodies or minds. When we are not connected to our innate selves, our well-intentioned generators with the limited intelligence they possess direct us into the areas and activities they **assume** are appropriate for us. However, they more often than not are incorrect in their directions because they lack the overview needed to make these decisions. Generators need to be connected to Zenith's innateness to be able to make rounded decisions.

No Imagination

Generators can base their assumptions on past findings related to the individual very accurately. However, they have no facility to delve into the present or future to see what may actually be the possibilities in a particular case. Also, **they don't possess the imagination, inspiration, wisdom or truth needed to make wise decisions.** For example, Meme's romantic relationships nearly always seem to follow the same path and end in similar circumstances after a predictable lifespan even though the intention may be to change, for instance, a person who always chooses a seemingly understanding partner and is surprised to find that they are in face abusive.

Nagging Questions

More often than not Meme is left in a position where everything doesn't quite match up. This sets the stage for an unhappy set of circumstances. He may feel displaced and this displacement is a major contributory factor in unhealthy experiences that follow. For example, he may wonder why his relationships never seem to work out as he wishes but can't seem to pinpoint the reasons with his logic and so stumbles through his relationships hoping they will work out.

Compromised Generators

By allowing his generators to take on the total responsibility of his innate self, Meme compromises his three generators unwittingly and places an unnecessary burden on his brain, heart and reproductive system. Now the generators are being called upon to come up with the answers to circumstances with which they were never intended to deal.

The generators in turn are always willing and enthusiastic to assist in whatever way they can and so they come up with answers and solutions to the best of their abilities.

However, they will not be imaginative answers and no matter how much effort they put in, and they will exert an enormous amount of effort to satisfy the request, they cannot match Zenith's innate knowledge or wisdom acquired through his connection at Corigonus (this is discussed later in the book). The generators will invariably come up with incomplete answers. For example Meme's relationships become more complicated through his thinking and emoting and actions. The more he tries to exert his influence on a problem the further away the solution gets from him.

Awesome

The ability of the generators to carry responsibility for that which was never intended is courageous, dynamic, forthright, energized, hardworking, persistent and giving. With the correct alignment these abilities are indeed awesome to witness and feel.

Innate Feed

When the generators are called upon to act without input from Zenith's innate self they act in an uncharacteristic manner. They put Meme under strain without realizing it. Generators depend on the innate feed for correct direction to be realized. When the Generators are deprived of this guidance *they self generate and act independently of Zenith's innate self and also act independently of one another.*

Under Pressure

With most people the innate connection is only occasionally called upon to motivate and feed the generators. Usually this is an unconscious act where Meme is oblivious to the involvement of his innate connection. The generators are sporadically fed which means they are more often than not under pressure to perform without innate guidance.

The Devil You Know

If for example, Meme is working in a job he doesn't like but doesn't want to leave because he's afraid of the possible consequences (the devil you know is better than the devil you don't know), his generators are working overtime to keep him on top of the situation. If along side this work situation he has an unhappy home life, his generators are working double shift on overtime to keep him going.

Occasionally Meme may go on a holiday or a break and renew his generators by doing something in which he *freely* wants to be involved. This allows his innate self to feed the generators and return him to Zenith.

Familiar Life

So, Meme is mostly unhappy but putting up with it because logically, emotionally or re-actively he sees that this is the only option open to him. On his holiday breaks, because he's relaxed, he explores his imagination and gets ideas of what he would like to be doing, motivated by his innate self (whom Meme has temporarily let take the lead bringing him back to Zenith). For example, he may see imaginative ways to change his routine that allow more time for pleasant activities.

However, on his return home Meme stores all these ideas in the back of his brain so he can get back to his familiar safe life and be under pressure once more. Perhaps next year or when he retires he can begin to listen to his innate self and return to Zenith, that is if he makes it to retiring age or even to next year.

THE WISDOM OF ORACLES
BY JOHN RYAN

CHAPTER 3

EGO

Love Life
The nights are slow to go
And nothing much else matters
He knows it's truly so
Cos his love life is in tatters.

He sips on cups of tea
Cushiontops he batters
His ego's gone for free
Now his love life is in tatters.

His scalp is scaly now
Dandruff dry it scatters
He sits with furrowed brow
Cos his love life is in tatters.

His number's all but up
Fickle Fate he flatters
Swill and slop he'll sup
'Cos his love life is in tatters. *pil*

The Self

Ego is self-esteem, the self of an individual person. One cannot have self-esteem without consideration of self in relation to surroundings. Judgement is an opinion reached after what is considered thoughtful or emotional. In other words it's a Grey Matter or Ruby issue. To have self-esteem is one thing. To have self-esteem based on judgements and observations purely from Grey Matter or Ruby is quite another. It is in the consideration of Meme through generators that the problems arise. Consideration of self-esteem from an innate perspective and including Grey Matter has a completely different outlook and has a totally different set of values to that of a purely Grey Matter perspective.

Separating

A value system based on judgement is separating and therefore dangerous to oneself and to society. The judgements are usually made from a generated standpoint. I went to a garden center to enquire if they sold an organic weed killer. The owner said that there was one on the market but that he didn't stock it. When I enquired why, he spat out this explanation. 'It's a con' he said 'sure it's only made of vinegar and salt'. So what he was saying is, although this product works well, does no damage to the environment and keeps the weeds down he is not prepared to stock it because its made from easily accessible materials. However, he does stock the non-organic weed killer because it is made from harsh chemicals and is therefore not a con. This from a man who sells plants, trees, and vegetable and flower seeds but has a judgement based on brain and heart generated fixed attitudes and a tunnel vision value system.

Authority

Trusting in ones innate self is one of the most difficult things to do coming from a Meme perspective. It **requires changing the hold we have on our learned value system. It is particularly difficult for somebody in authority for the system supports their attitude and their value system is based on an authority** that is more likely to be separating because authorities tend to be brain generated rather than innate.

They lack true compassion because they are emotional rather than feeling, brain generated rather than thinking and constructing rather than creative. As individuals, professionals, in our families, our workplaces, our organizations, our countries, our race, we need to change our attitudes particularly concerning our interaction with others.

Generated Viewpoint

A person with a generated viewpoint would **rather be right in his own convictions than face the truth.** He will see his opinion as protective in the face of what is perceived as an attack. Anything that throws doubt on his value system may be unacceptable. Generated people are **attached** to their generated opinions and become **self-righteous, emotional and forceful** in defending them. The same can be said of some people who are **extreme** in innate awareness. A balanced view is an appreciation of innateness and **the rightful use** of generators.

Considerations

From a Zenith perspective one's innateness is considered, whereas from a generated Meme perspective Grey Matter, Ruby and Young Nemo are the **only** considerations. The consideration of ego from a generated point of view can only result in a disfigurement of ego. **It is the consideration of the world from the perspective of disfigured egos that has the world in its present misguided state.** The idea of ego from this disfigured perspective allows individuals to view themselves as separate entities, encourages self-righteousness and thus, the **separation** of individuals. Where there is separation there you'll find opposites. Where there are opposites there is discrimination and with that are the problems experienced in the world both personal and collectively. For example, our acceptance of poverty and the need for war in the world.

Different

Once Meme sees himself as different from anybody else he sets himself and everybody around him up for an unhappy life. This perception of difference gives him permission to engage in the most horrific activities in the name of personal principal, country, religion and any disfigured cause he cares deeply about through Ruby, thinks righteously about through Grey Matter and forces physically through Young Nemo.

Paradox

Uniqueness we all have, but difference we do not and this is the paradox and this is what we need to understand. As long as one individual sees himself as different and thus, separate from everybody else he and those around him will have problems. Where the vast majority of people are ego hunting the world becomes a playground for every convoluted dance in which Meme engages.

Separation

This single issue of separation of ego is a main cause of the world's problems. It gives us permission to go to war, to accept inequality of opportunity, to accept poverty and starvation in others, to accept discrimination as long as we're not affected and to stand back from our own abuses of ourselves and of our world and observe whilst our fellow man suffers indignity because of our ignorance.

Refuse

The word ignorance sums it up, ignorance means lacking knowledge or rude through lack of knowledge of good manners. It's derived from the word ignore which means to refuse to notice or to deliberately disregard. A misguided ego allows us to be adamant in our refusal and arrogant in our disregard.

THE WISDOM OF ORACLES
BY JOHN RYAN

CHAPTER 4

FEAR

Trouble in the distance
Trouble in the air
Trouble all around me
Trouble, most unfair.

Trouble in the future
Trouble in the past
Trouble in the present
Trouble here to last.

Trouble seems tied up with me
Every where I go
Trouble that I never see
What a So-and-So.

Trouble in the distance
Trouble on the way
Trouble all around me
Trouble, grim and grey. *pil*

Invention

Meme believes in fear and because the appearance of fear has been with him through his life he is convinced beyond all doubt that a thing such as fear exists. Fear does not exist in Zenith awareness. It only **appears** to exist in Meme awareness. When his generators are in a state of misalignment he is thus fearful, this is also the state of non-reality.

The word fear is an invention of Grey Matter. In the absence of a logical explanation for the confusion that takes place in Meme because of generator disorientation a word to describe the confusion must be found.

Fear is the word invented by Grey Matter that describes the experience in Meme during discord between the generators. Fear

in fact is not possible when the generators are in alignment for fear does not exist in Zenith's world, in other words in reality.

Not A Feeling

The emotion of fear is a false state of being. Actually it's a false state not of being, but of human Meme. He logically assumes it is a feeling, for out of proportion emotions result in **perceived** fear in the absence of real feelings.

Straight To Core

Feelings can be only healthy and only come from one's innate self. If Meme is experiencing perceived unhealthy feelings, he is actually experiencing unhealthy **misalignment**. There are no unhealthy feelings. Straight away, in this situation, he must realize his generators are misaligned. At the slightest unhealthy thought, emotion or action Meme could realize he is a danger to himself and quickly change his set of circumstances by going straight to Corigonus and contacting his innate self. The generators perceived fear would then disappear (connecting to Corigonus is covered later on in the book).

Fear

This is one of the areas where logic runs into problems. Discord within the generators does not register with the individual generator. They each individually register a separate response. Grey Matter registers **danger,** Ruby registers **distress** and Young Nemo's registered response is **alarm.** In Meme mode, the three generators operate independently, unaware of the responses of the other two generators.

The combination of responses from the three generators puts Meme in a confused state. The confusion in him is perceived as fear even though fear does not exist, it is only confusion caused by misaligned generators.

Enemy

Grey Matter now registers this state as fear and since there is no obvious explanation, for each generator is unaware of the other two generator responses, a hidden **enemy** within the camp is perceived. The perceived enemy within Meme comes in many guises- bad, evil, devil, boogey man, ghost, wrong, ego, etc. each of which comes with a Grey Matter perceived fear condition with a corresponding Ruby emotion and Young Nemo physical response.

Monitored

There are many combinations of perceived fear and equally as many combinations of responses from the three generators, with a multiple of Grey Matter identities all perceived by Meme to be of personal danger to his body self and all of which need to be constantly monitored. **Thus, Meme spends his life monitoring conditions that in reality do not exist instead of living his life creatively**. Meme now sets himself up to receive a combination of different **illnesses all induced by a perception of that which does not exist,** when what is really happening is simply generator misalignment.

Progresses

Unease can be an early symptom of illness that manifests in the body. Because the unease is not recognized for what it is and is given power to disturb the body, through further and continuous acknowledgment of this power the unease may quickly progress to ill-at

-ease, the ill-at -ease progresses to dis-ease, and dis-ease progresses to disease or illness.

As with fear, illness does not exist but is a misperception brought on by misaligned or misconceived generators only evident in Meme. Zenith in his true state does not experience illness.

Falsehood

Confusion and lack of communication between the generators through lack of rightful connection with one's innate self is the original cause of perceived disease and illness. There is no other reason for disease and **there is no other reason for illness**.

A Thrashing

All of the discord experienced by Meme is self-induced. There are no enemies within him yet he perceives there to be an enemy within. Even though it is untrue he still has the experience of discord. Meme wants to do things his own way without guidance from his innate self, the loner with no partners and in the process he is getting a thrashing from his generators and what's more it's totally unintentional and totally unnecessary.

Experts

With the best intentions, the generators are serving Meme as well as they are able, but their continued misalignment is causing him the most horrendous problems. He tries to get help from the experts. Those are the experts in Meme world.

Meme has an abundance of experts in every field of misery and misalignment, who do everything in their generated abilities to bring him back to a complete person. **But Meme is already complete and even the experts don't realize it, for they are experts in the physical body and not in innateness.**

So, Meme gets treated predictably as an ill person, but not as a misaligned Zenith with an innate disconnection. Only Meme's body gets treatment by the experts. So, even if he makes a recovery that appears complete the likelihood of a relapse is almost inevitable.

Doubt
The Hack
He's the sorta guy
Who wonders why the sky
Remains in place each day
And never goes away.

He's a kinda fellow
Who's more than slightly yellow
Who isn't strict or strong
And finds life very long.
He's a mainly minor turd
But he's a certain knack
For making do with things absurd
From this he gets some craic.

He's not up to very much
But what he's got is plain
An appitude for scribbling such
As lines his purse with gain. *pil*

Destruction
Because he operates through his generators, according to Meme there is no such thing as innateness. By placing Meme on the oracle throne he has condemned himself to a life of illness, of ill logic and ill assumption, of ill information and ill intelligence, of ill emotion and ill reaction. He has developed in himself a Meme weapon of destruction.

Meme Understanding
One of the reasons why Meme uses such a small percentage of his brain is because he can only exist in a small percentage of the brain in Grey Matter. The rest of the brain is waiting to be discovered in the innate zone. There are many theories particularly in the areas of medicine, education, psychotherapy, religion, economics, politics, science, art etc. that, because they are mostly brain generated theories, merely add to the ignorance and confusion rather than promote a more complete understanding of the universe and of humanity.

A Golf Ball
The method of trying to understand the universe from a Meme perspective is like trying to understand how to play the game of golf by dissecting a golf ball. It's simply not possible to gain insight into what is an innate matter from Meme's limited perspective. It's like the flea trying to get inside the dog's world.

Greater Benefit
When the individual and institutional Meme eventually move out of Meme world and into the innate zone they will begin to develop their natural abilities in the larger percentage of their brains and be of greater benefit to humanity. Only then will we as a race come out of the dark ages. Only then will we begin to develop the structures in societies to place mankind on a safer footing for the future.

THE WISDOM OF ORACLES
BY JOHN RYAN

CHAPTER 5

STATES OF ZENITH AND MEME

No Opposites

In this 'Meme' orientated world we readily and incorrectly accept the notion that there are opposites. For instance, right and wrong, good and bad. However, there are no opposites in Zenith existance although there are consequences. There are no opposites of the sun, the stars, the planets, the moon or the earth. There is no opposite of the sky, the sea, the land, trees, grass, plants, weather, people, animals or insects. There are no opposites of time, wisdom, power, enlightenment, intuition, imagination, invention or inspiration etc. all of which are available to Zenith through his innate connection.

Primary States

Zenith can access enlightenment, intuition, imagination, invention and inspiration through each of the three primary states 1 thought, 2 feeling, 3 creative expression and these primary states are accessed through the three generators only when they are connected to Corigonus. Meme on the other hand is disconnected from Corigonus so his three generators are cut off from the primary states and he therefore cannot access true thought, true feeling or true creativity.

Secondary States

Meme without Corigonus cannot produce the primary states of thought, feeling and creativity. Meme alone can only produce the secondary states of 1 siftings, 2 emotions and 3 constructions through the three generators Grey Matter, Ruby and Young Nemo respectively.

Mix Of Secondary States

Zenith is open to his innate self so his three generators have access through Corigonus and thus, can engage the creative wisdom, knowledge and truth of Capsule. So, sifting can be truly thoughtful, emotion can reflect true feeling and action or reaction can take the form of true expression.

Without innate contact Meme is a mix of secondary states, which means that he can be, 1 acting emotional sifting, 2 sifting active emotions, 3 sifting emotional actions, 4 acting sifting emotions, 5 emotionally acting siftings or 6 emotionally sifting actions. This depends on which generator is leading at a given time. All of these conditions are thought-less, feeling-less and creation-less. In other words they are mindless because they do not include input from the innate Mind.

Fruits of Knowledge

By excluding his innate self, Meme is now living his life as was never intended. Even Adam and Eve were told this when they were warned to 'beware of the fruits of knowledge.' The fruits of knowledge are the stored information in all three generators combined. They are not coming from the innate and so cannot be innate knowledge, wisdom or truth. **Acceptance of the fruit of knowledge (rather than knowledge itself) or generator information alone is what keeps Meme away from the truth.** Where Meme directly engages Grey Matter, Ruby or Young Nemo before Corigonus he closes off access to his innate self and thus, to knowledge and this is the warning.

Rightful Access

Rightful access to the three generators comes from his innate self to Corigonus to Generator in that order. If through lack of awareness one of the generators, say Grey Matter is engaged before Corigonus, Grey Matter kicks into automatic and provides a generated or driven response for Meme without the aid of or guidance from his innate self.

A Happening

There is no malice intended by Grey Matter. It is not brain's fault it has been engaged first. There is in fact nobody to blame. It is not even a mistake; it is but a happening. The happening occurs when Zenith or Meme engages Grey Matter before engaging Corigonus. Zenith's innate self will not override brain, nor is brain trying to override Zenith. There is no conflict (although Meme may surmise conflict) for both have free will.

The What? Question

There are many ways of engaging Grey Matter before Corigonus, for instance, when a What? question, is asked. For example, 'What do you do for a living?' Zenith's innate self is not concerned with What? questions because What? questions take **only** the bodies needs into consideration. **Zenith or Meme can easily overlook this issue, however, it's an extremely important issue.** The What? question has become such an acceptable part of everyday life that to question its use may in fact seem ridiculous. It has become part of our accepted unquestioned value system even though it emphasizes the separation from one's innate self.

The Who? Question

One's innate self is concerned with Who? questions, for example Who are you in relation to your work? The emphasis is **personal and inclusive of Zenith's innateness.** The field of interest is broadened with the Who? question to include all of Zenith and not simply confined to Meme issues. The What? question by implication is non inclusive. (The What? and Who? questions are covered in more detail later in the book).

Other Option

When Grey Matter tries to engage Corigonus with a What? question Zenith's innateness will not and cannot answer the question. The only other option left open is for Grey Matter to come up with an answer. Grey Matter roots around in the store of information and comes up with an answer. The answer is the best available to brain under the circumstances. The answer will be logical, factual and honest and will be given with the best of intentions because brain is honest and factual.

So, the answer appears to Meme as honest even though it may be untrue, as correct even though it may be inaccurate, as clever even though it may contain no wisdom and as fact even though it may be fictitious. This occurs when Zenith loses contact with his innate self and Grey Matter takes over responsibility for Zenith decisions and thus, Meme is born. Since most people are disconnected from their innate selves, most situations fall into this category but it doesn't need to be that way.

Free Will

The reason Corigonus does not take the What? question is because Zenith, **simply by asking the question What?, has placed** himself within the singular concerns of the body without consideration of his innate self. His innate self realizes that Zenith has gone outside his innate domain with the question but cannot and will not interfere, for Zenith has free will to do as he chooses. There may appear to be a delicate balance at play here however this is not the case. If Zenith wants to look for answers elsewhere and transform into Meme so be it. His innate self will offer to help and remain open for guidance but cannot and will not interfere.

Clear Message

The fact is there is never a need for Zenith to ask a What? question. By asking a What? question he is sending a clear message to his innate self saying, 'It's O.K. I'll field this question on my own.' He uses his free will to answer the question blindly even though his innate self can bring knowledge, truth and wisdom into the answer instead of the information, honesty and cleverness that Meme alone is capable of answering. This is the clear choice Zenith in Meme mode makes for almost all his questions, and there are hundreds of questions asked by him every day on this bases. For example, What will you have for dinner?

Where Meme engages in taking over for an innate responsibility he sets himself up on a path that is totally contradictory to Zenith's nature and introduces willful mistrust of his innate self. By believing his generators are the best judges of a given situation he introduces a blinkered approach and unknowingly bullies his own innate self.

Engaged The Body

The What? question is just one obvious example where **Zenith unthinkingly transforms to Meme and misguides himself into everyday problem situations instead of utilizing the guidance of his innate self.**

The body is on earth to experience the world from an innate perspective as well as a physical perspective but when the body becomes absorbed in world-only issues Meme automatically disengages his innateness and goes with his physicality alone. He now reverses his role on earth from **explorer** for knowledge to that of **survivor** of self-inflicted dangers.

Big Trouble

Eventually Meme becomes totally involved in world only issues and totally dependent on the three generators for his survival. **This is the very reason he has so many varied problems.** He is trying to live life through his generators. That means he's in big trouble and doesn't know where to turn. **Even if he realizes his situation, he has become so out of touch that he forgets how to contact his Corigonus.**

The Generators

Grey Matter

The brain lives in the past. It draws on past experience and events for its information and logic. For example, my mother when she was in her 70s applied for a new passport. One of the questions asked the colour of her hair to which she answered 'brown'. Although she had snow-white hair, she still saw it as brown because her brain still registered the original colour and what her eyes saw still didn't alter the brains misinformation.

Grey Matter has no capacity to deal with present or future events. Anything that has ever happened in the world every major minor and mediocre event is in the stored information of the brain bank. It's an enormous bank of information and very often misinformation.

The World Grey Matter Bank is a record of everything that happened throughout history and prehistory. Everybody has access to the bank for personal use. The brain's great capacity to remember past events is its strength, but this ironically is also its weakness.

Ruby

The heart likewise lives in the past. Ruby remembers past delights and hurts. Ruby holds onto them in its bank of emotion. When a new situation is encountered the heart searches its emotional memory bank to see how to deal with the new situation.

If it recognizes a pattern in the new situation, Ruby develops a relationship with what is already familiar. So, the heart's reaction to the new situation is a reaction to a past recognized or familiar situation.

Familiar Pattern

In other words, the new situation for which Ruby may not have a reference is examined from a familiar perspective or from the stored information already in the heart. The heart picks out the aspects of the new situation that are familiar and bases its answers or conclusions on its findings from these past experiences.

Like Grey Matter, Ruby has no capacity to look into either the present or the future. Its strength is in its ability to remember past events. This is also its weakness.

Young Nemo

Young Nemo like the heart and the brain depends on its stored bank of information. Young Nemo is born during adolescence. At this stage, it has no information in the storage bank and must begin to accumulate information. This may be one reason why teenagers are often in troubled situations. They are building up their store of information into their Young Nemo and this takes time to build up.

At the early stages there are few references. So, mistakes are made and teenagers learn from the mistakes and thus build up the store of information. Like the heart and brain, the reproductive system has no capacity to search the present or the future. Its strength is in its ability to learn from past mistakes and successes. This is also its weakness.

Work Tirelessly

Grey Matter, Ruby and Young Nemo are the three generators of Zenith and Meme. It is from these three centers all decisions are taken for Meme's welfare but not for Zenith who is connected to his innate self. The three generators are superb at their jobs. All three generators work tirelessly to bring the best results to Meme.

Characteristics Of The Three Generators

The three generators are very hard working, are remarkably honest, are grounded, possess a huge memory storage bank, are ultra persistent, selfless, open, very trusting, positive, hungry for information, absorbing and have excellent integrity. **Generators possess no unhealthy qualities.**

Their qualities include an aptitude for manifesting, storing and analyzing of intelligences, problem solving, assimilation, association, belief, trust, coherence, communication, character comprehension, concentration, response, authority, analysis, logic, sense, control, conversion, correlation, curiosity, determination, learning, memory, display, aspiration, integration, perception, habit, structure, literality, generation, pattern, reference, philosophy, arousal, and recovery etc. Their own individual specialist abilities are in each of the three generators whilst possessing all of the above qualities.

Grey Matter

Grey Matter is the brain and as such is the largest store of intelligence, of logic and of information in the body. Grey Matter itself **does not think and is incapable of thought for it is not mindful and does not initiate knowledge.** All aspects of Zenith's body have their own individual specialized memories that can link into the three generators.

The special qualities of Grey Matter are in its ability to access the store of information and use its intelligence and logic. These qualities manifest in the form of information. They include the gathering of information, assessment of complex formulae and complex situations, storing information, past memory, recovery of information in a split second for present use, ability to search and find lost information of past events, calculating, measurement, dimensional understanding, monitoring current intellectual states, assessment, investigation, investment in intelligent output etc.

Grey Matter has a remarkable memory bank and has the ability to store and arrange data; can gain access to any of its stored information within a split second; and can access very old information in a short space of time.

Grey Matter has remarkable investigative and logical abilities, can comprehend complex formulae, isolate and synchronize intelligence, juxtapose complicated patterns and arrive at logical, conclusive provable evidence. Grey Matter is the intellectual protector, provider and producer for Zenith.

Ruby

Ruby is the heart and as such is the emotive center of Zenith. Ruby has a large bank of stored information pertinent to the emotions of Zenith. Its qualities manifest in the form of emotional intelligence. They include the storage of emotions from past events, memory of feelings, recovery of emotional information in a fraction of a second, ability to find and search emotions in relation to past feelings, calculation of emotion, measurement of emotion, assessment and investigation of emotional situations, monitoring emotional states, investment of emotional output etc.

Ruby *does not create feelings* (this is not to say that it does not have feelings) but is the instigator of emotions activated by feelings from Zenith. It can recall the *memory* of feelings experienced and express the appropriate emotions that Meme often assumes are in fact feelings.

Ruby is the emotive protector, producer and provider for Zenith.

Young Nemo

Young Nemo's qualities manifest in the bodies physical outlets in the form of physical expression. They include the storage and gathering of information concerning physical activities from the past, past actions, past reactions, past physical encounters, assessment of complex actions, dexterity, movement, coordination, precision, physical manipulation, balance, physical strength, maneuverability, investment in physical, sexual activity and fitness etc.

Young Nemo is the reproductive center of Zenith and does not create expression but is the activator of Zenith's physicality and can recall the memory of learned expressiveness and can activate and reactivate physical action and reaction. Young Nemo is the producer, provider and protector for Zenith's physicality and sexuality.

Children

As a child Zenith does not have a Young Nemo and so has not developed expression through this generator. Children are born with their Grey Matter and Ruby and use these two generators in response to life from a very early age. Their physicality develops naturally without the aid of a generator during the early years. Through early experimentation under the direct guidance of their innate selves, children develop a physical understanding and knowledge of their new world and its surroundings. The introduction of Young Nemo occurs in adolescence and the child's physicality transfers over to the generator during this time.

The World Grey Matter Bank

The World Grey Matter Bank of information is the total of the world information stored in books, libraries, educational institutions, computers, peoples brains, newspapers, magazines, T V, videos, C.D's, etc. Grey Matter does not have direct access to universal wisdom or universal knowledge without connection to Corigonus. **Grey Matter can only gain access to truth, wisdom and knowledge through Corigonus**. The Grey Matter Bank can and does store contradictory and untrue information that can be confusing to Zenith thus, contributing to the arrogance experienced in Meme.

THE WISDOM OF ORACLES
BY JOHN RYAN

CHAPTER 6

MODERN LIFE

Mindless World

The problems humanity faced at the beginning of time are exactly the same problems Meme faces today except that the world is more modern. There are also a lot more people who are under a lot more pressure. Basically though it's still the same age-old problem. Meme is living life through 'the fruits of knowledge'. Grey Matter has taken the place of his innate knowledge and because of this Meme now lives in a mindless world.

Attack On Self

Many of man's modern problems occur because Meme does not understand symptoms, misinterprets perceived pressure and overreacts in ignorance. High blood pressure, ulcers and heart disease are all very late symptoms of self imposed psychological pressure. Meme incorrectly views early symptoms as a problem and with the best information available through his brain bank prescribes a logical and intelligent heart felt and physical solution and suppresses the symptoms.

But symptoms are the means employed by our innate self to defend the body against attack. By suppressing the early symptoms Meme breaks down his own defenses. In other words, he inflicts a well meaning, intelligent and logical attack on himself.

Disease

Approximately one third of all people in the western world, including men women and children, suffer hypertension. Two thirds of diseases associated with heart disease

strokes and blood pressure are common among men who are not only in their 40s and 50s, but now in their 30s and 20s.

Pressure

A person who is operating at a faster pace all of the time is putting his body under unnecessary stress. The body can cope with the pressure now and again but those continually in a hurry, and thus, nearly always under pressure, are courting an unhealthy lifestyle and unhealthy attitudes.

Warning Signal

The person who feels under pressure is feeling uncomfortable and this feeling is a message or a warning signal from his innate self through his Corigonus. Warning signals are not life threatening. They are **an important early indicator** and need to be taken seriously.

Accurate Answer

At this point Zenith needs to ask for advice from his innate self who has sent the original signal to him. He needs to ask through Corigonus a Who? question. Who is the cause of this discomfort? And he will be given an accurate answer.

Limited

Unfortunately through habit or for various other reasons Meme may ask a different question, a What? question. A What? question automatically engages Grey Matter and shuts out his innate self. Meme may even feel emotionally attached to Grey Matter answers through Ruby.

When Grey Matter takes over responsibility for what is, **considered to be** thought it searches the bank of information of past events for a cure. While Grey Matter answers honestly from the generator's stored information it is nonetheless limited and no comparison to his innate knowledge.

Ignore The Warnings

Because Grey Matter has the capacity to deal with the past but not the present or future Meme doesn't heed the early warnings because he doesn't recognize their value, so the symptoms are perceived as a minor problem and are not dealt with. Because generators are not innately aware they have no capacity for receiving innate advice except through Corigonus and when they are disconnected from Core they simply ignore the warnings or don't recognize them as such (Coreigonus is the body's connection to its innate self and is dealt with later in the book). In other words, the warnings don't even register with the generators. For example, road rage begins with slight irritations that over time build up until they are out of proportion and the driver may not even notice the gradual changes or accept he himself has any culpability.

Zenith or Meme receive warnings from their innate selves. If a warning is ignored another warning is given, and another. These warnings come in the form of symptoms. The symptoms become more exaggerated the more they are ignored until Meme finally perceives himself to be ill. He is not actually ill he has just always ignored his symptoms.

Medical Advancements

One may argue that scientific and medical advancements are made through asking the What? question. However, this is not the case. Advances are slow and laborious because the What? question must always be satisfied. The inspired people who have explored and engaged their imaginations have been first to realize major advancements. This is not a facility of Grey Matter but of one's innate self.

Several years may then be spent in proving the advancement to What? orientated Grey Matter institutions. When the institution is finally satisfied it proclaims the new knowledge as authentic. However, at this stage it is in fact past information and the original discoverer has already moved onto the next project.

A New Theory

When a new theory is discovered science and medicine intellectualize on the theory and logically make any advance only as far as the limit of the theory. Once the theory is open all the information leading up to it becomes available simply because the possibility of advancement has opened up to that measure of understanding. A broader view is not sought for Grey Matter cannot explore beyond a known limit.

Ingenious Inventors

Imagination and inspiration are perceived to be the talents of a few. Whilst this may be the case in a generated world it is not actually as it was intended by Capsule. Imagination and inspiration are gifts from our innate selves and since Zenith can work innately, with a little practice, all people can become inspirational and imaginative. All are unique and ingenious inventors derived from their individual authentic selves. The problem is Meme doesn't know how to acknowledge that fact because of his generated approach to life.

Educational System

A root problem of this situation can be found in our educational system which gears us toward **answering** questions rather than **asking** questions. **The way to further knowledge is to ask questions.** We do not need to know answers for all the answers are already available to us through our innate selves. However, our educational system doesn't seem to appreciate this fact and our generated response to lack of knowledge is to sift through regurgitated information. This exercise ensures we maintain the same level of information and make no advancements to knowledge.

The way to learn is to ask questions. The quality of the questions determines the quality of the answers to which we will be guided by our innate selves. The current exercise of employing Grey Matter to come up with answers to preset questions is futile.

Future Exploration

As always Grey Matter can only store information from past experience, knows nothing of the present or future and cannot project beyond an already suggested theory. Everything still has to be proven so Grey Matter can store the information into its past memory bank. Grey Matter has no capacity for future exploration for its not part of its brief. Only Core connection to one's innate self provides access to future exploration as well as to imagination, inspiration and invention (this is explored later in the book).

Disrupts The Process

While Zenith can automatically set about healing his own symptoms naturally through his innate self, Grey Matter with the best of intentions in the world disrupts the process with generated ideas of cure. These applications are derived from past information stored in Grey Matter rather than any current knowledge and may not consider the individual circumstances. Each individual Zenith has a uniquely different makeup to his fellow man and therefore needs separate consideration.

Prevented

In the western world today ¾ of people who die do so as a result of illness that can be prevented. Cancer, strokes, heart disease, violence and accidents are all caused by psychological problems, cigarette smoking, unhealthy eating habits, lack of exercise, alcohol consumption, drug abuse and reckless driving, all of these situations are caused through Meme not having access to his innate self.

More Aware

Meme needs to listen to his bodies warning system. He may need to become generally more aware of his body and notice any minor warning signs or symptoms. At this early stage it can take only seconds to deal with the symptoms. Later if symptoms have been ignored continuously it may take months for him to recover.

Self-defeating

The act of disengaging Corigonus to engage Grey Matter is limiting and ultimately self-defeating because it does not include one's innate connection. It fills the brain with information already known within the world. So, while it may increase information for individuals of the world to a certain extent, it does not increase knowledge or make any further wisdom of the universe available to the world. It is ultimately self-defeating and pointless and further separates Meme from his innate self.

Mindless

The act of engaging Grey Matter without first engaging Core is therefore mindless and encourages mindlessness even though Grey Matter is called mindful by generator orientated people. Engaging brain first cannot be mindful for the act doesn't engage

Mind rather it becomes an act of mindless sifting a regurgitation of past information and logic.

Knowledge Or Wisdom
The world does not in fact have knowledge or wisdom without the innate connection. Although Meme calls it knowledge it is in fact a huge bank of stored past information. Any new information or knowledge coming into the world comes from the innate connection.

How Zenith uses that knowledge and wisdom to develop is the means through which Capsule can evolve to a higher level of awareness. However, when Meme does not engage his innate self this progress is halted through lack of awareness.

 ## Ruby
Ruby stores and produces emotional intelligence. Ruby does not produce feelings. This is not to say that Ruby does not have feelings. The perceived pain felt in the Heart over a death, separation or injury of a loved one for example, is the emotional trauma felt by the singular belief in Meme.

Emotion is strongly felt in an earth bound Meme for a loved one. The pain felt deeply in the heart is often unbearable and traumatic. This pain can be further exacerbated by called up past feelings of guilt, separation, loneliness, desperation, confusion, worthlessness and a whole host of emotions all equally devastating to the sufferer.

Separation
It can sometimes take years for the sufferer to finally come to terms with the separation. This is a very natural Meme reaction to what is an overpowering situation for the body. Emotions have a strong influence and are very active in different situations throughout Meme's life. Indeed some people seem to bear an unfair, enormous and unequal amount of tragedy in their lives where their emotions are tested continuously to the limit. This is indeed tragic.

Connection To The World
Meme in this situation suffers untold pain and anxiety. The belief of complete loss, of separation, of hardship, torture and pain are a result of total connection to the world. Allied to this is a sense of purposelessness. He has lost the meaning of life. There needs to be great understanding and acceptance of Meme's circumstances in these situations.

Tragedy
This sense of disconnection is a terrible tragedy. With this separation Meme condemns himself to a life of desperate emptiness filled with disquiet, doubt and feelings of despair.

Value System
Tragedy comes to us all it's a part of life. Our belief system and values are what provide us with the means of dealing with life's problems. A value system that is built on Grey Matter foundations will be shaken in the face of tragedy and may even crumble.

Everlasting Foundation
A value and belief system whose main element is one's innate knowledge draws on universal energy as its source and thus, is an everlasting foundation. Zenith's or Meme's individual attitudes and values are ultimately what decide how each will act or react to perceived tragic circumstances.

THE WISDOM OF ORACLES
BY JOHN RYAN

CHAPTER 7

JOURNEY THROUGH THE COSMOS

The Connection

Connection to our innate selves is our natural state of being. Most people in the world fail to make this connection and when they do connect temporarily they don't recognize it for what it is.

To explain the connection, it's purpose and how it may be achieved is the object of this book. The connection is described in a journey through the cosmos. The main characters in the book are the two humans, the three innate beings in Capsule, and the three generators and Corigonus within the humans as they explore this part of the cosmic journey on earth. Each of the characters has a specific function and each is unique to the make up of the two humans.

 Cosmic
Cosmic is the manifested Universe.

Innateness

We are each made up of **four** individual beings three of which most people are unaware or refuse to acknowledge. This means most people operate through only one of their four beings and thus, have **little understanding of their (Capsule) innateness, their unique value or true purpose** in life. The four beings are Oracle, Osmosis, Aura Bora and Zenith.

Capsule

Capsule is the innate presence in all humans but not always recognized. Capsule is made up of the combination of the three innate beings Oracle, Osmosis and Aura Bora.

 Oracle
Oracle is the captain of Capsule, the first innate being. Oracle **is** the wisdom, truth and knowledge pertaining to Capsule's journey through the cosmos.

 Osmosis
Osmosis is the first mate of and the second innate being of Capsule and is **the accumulator** of wisdom, truth and knowledge. Osmosis is Capsule's advisor under Oracle.

 Aura Bora
Aura Bora is the engineer and the third innate being of Capsule and is **the instigator** of wisdom, truth and knowledge. Aura Bora is the creator of the earth explorer Zenith and is Capsule's connection to and motivator of the three generators in Zenith (see Zenith diagram at front of book).

 Corigonus
Corigonus plays a vital role in Zenith's life as the Core connector between his three generators and Aura Bora. Capsule's innate wisdom, truth and knowledge travel to Zenith via Corigonus. Vital earth information from the generators also travels back to Aura Bora via Corigonus. *Where Zenith loses contact with Aura Bora the contact is lost at Corigonus and as a result Zenith is transformed into the lost explorer Meme.*

Meme is controlled by his generators and as such does not use the link at Corigonus to gain access to Aura Bora. This loss of contact can be temporary, sporadic or more permanent depending on the individual and as a result a person may sometimes be in Zenith mode and other times in Meme mode.

Zenith

Zenith is the first of the two humans mentioned in the book. He is an earth *explorer* for Capsule and is the fourth being. He's outside of Capsule's Triune-Oracle, Osmosis and Aura Bora and is the sender of vital information from earth for this part of Capsule's journey through the cosmos. Zenith is Capsule's *activator* or creative *explorer* on earth.

Meme

Meme is the second human in the book. He is an earth *survivor* who started out as Zenith explorer but has chosen to become disconnected from his Capsule. The loss of contact with his Capsule can be described as amnesia brought on by confused connection to earth matters. Meme is one of Capsule's *lost earth explorers*.

The Problems

Everything runs smoothly when Aura Bora and Zenith are communicating. All aboard Capsule benefit from the interaction and likewise Zenith. This is the intention from the start and this is how it should be. However, Zenith's problems were first realized at the beginning of time. To examine the problems in a broad sense and to understand their beginnings we can take a quick look back to the beginning of time to see where some of Zenith's problems may have originated.

THE WISDOM OF ORACLES
BY JOHN RYAN

CHAPTER 8

THE BEGINNING

Sixth Sense
Is it true about Woman's sixth sense
Their hidden and final defense
That they got it when Eve
By the serpent took leave
To give Adam a bite in offence?

Now Cain may be Abel's bad brother
But to me one's akin to th'other
The big thing's to die
I'll never know why
Both had to have the same mother. *pil*

Adam And Eve

In the beginning Cosmic created the Cosmos including Oracles and the world and all its creatures. Oracle created Osmosis and Aura Bora and thus, Capsule contains three innate beings.

In order to explore earth, Aura Bora created Adam. Likewise Eve. There is no reason to assume Adam and Eve were adults. They may have been babies, children, adolescents or adults. If they had been babies they would not have been able to take care of themselves. The likelihood is that they were children, but old enough to look after themselves (not that these details make much difference). They both live in perfect harmony with all around them in The Garden of Eden, a perfect paradise.

The Warning

Adam and Eve spend a few years in harmony with their Oracle, Osmosis and Aura Bora communicating with Zenith. Each of their two generators, Grey Matter and Ruby are in harmony with Aura Bora and all is well. Adam and Eve are both warned by Oracle of the fruits of knowledge.

The fruits of knowledge are intelligence and logic or the apples on the tree. The warning relates to human intelligence and logic (that Zenith can access through Grey Matter), and not to universal knowledge that Zenith can access through Corigonus connection with Aura Bora.

Intelligence And Logic

The fruits of knowledge are not knowledge itself. The fruits of knowledge are what can grow from the tree, the apples or intelligence and logic that come from Grey Matter in Zenith. Capsule is the tree itself, the source. So, the warning by Oracle of the fruits of knowledge is a warning of giving power to Grey Matter's intelligence and logic over the knowledge, truth and wisdom of Capsule.

The Who? Question

So far every question asked by Grey Matter and Ruby in Adam and Eve is a Who? question; Who made the world? Who am I? Who is Oracle? etc., for Grey Matter and Ruby both know at this stage that it is only necessary to ask Who? questions of Aura Bora to gain knowledge, wisdom and truth.

All questions by Grey Matter and Ruby go directly to Corigonus and from Core to Aura Bora (see Zenith diagram at the front of the book). *The knowledgeable answers come back from Aura Bora through Core to Grey Matter or Ruby.* Who is this animal? Who is that plant? Who is that stone in relation to me? etc. The Who? question keeps

Adam and Eve in touch with Aura Bora and thus, with knowledge, truth and wisdom.

There is no need to ask any other type of question or to go anywhere else for answers. *Everything knowledgeable and wise and truthful lives in Capsule and Zenith can gain access to 'all' answers by going through Corigonus to Aura Bora.*

The New Generator

Up to now Adam and Eve as children have been living life through their Grey Matter and Ruby in Zenith connected to Aura Bora. A new generator is about to be born in Adam and in Eve that will evolve their child state into adolescents.

With the onset of puberty Young Nemo makes its appearance. Up to now activities of the body occurred as a natural development without the aid of a generator. Now for the first time Adam's and Eve's activities can transfer during adolescence and become generated through their new reproductive systems.

New Experiences

Young Nemo brings new experiences never before encountered by Adam or Eve. For the first time in their lives they become conscious of their bodies as never before and the effects of puberty. These new experiences don't present any problems because all questions go through Core to Aura Bora and are answered straight away. However, Young Nemo is new and the gradual transfer of their physicality to the generator from time to time presents Adam and Eve with new and unexpected experiences.

Symptoms

The new experiences are presented to Adam and Eve in the form of symptoms. Eventually breasts, blood, hair and pimples etc. begin to make their appearance. These symptoms are natural to puberty. Also, internally both Adam and Eve experience a shift in attitude and mood and sometimes each becomes introverted. *They experience mixed generator reactions for the first time.* Grey Matter sometimes appears to go in a different direction to Ruby that is momentarily upsetting for Zenith until contact with Corigonus restores Aura Bora's influence.

Young Nemo doesn't appear to have any boundaries and it's quite difficult sometimes for Zenith to come to grips with the feeling of being overrun by the new generator. The new generator appears to be erratic and irrational and takes time to learn its place in Zenith.

A New Question

A new set of behaviours and different symptoms are experienced in Zenith as a result of Young Nemo's introduction. Grey Matter sees them as erratic and irrational and not logical or intelligent. Ruby experiences emotional upset by the changes in Zenith who is often close to tears.

Both Generators relay the upset to Core with a Who? question, and Aura Bora puts both generators at ease once more. However, sometimes Grey Matter and Ruby are taken by surprise and ask a new question. They sometimes ask a What? question.

A What? Question

A What? question has never been asked before by either Adam or Eve. A What? question is a whole new ball game altogether to a Who? question. A Who? question is a Capsule orientated question answerable by Aura Bora. However, a What? question on the other hand is a Meme orientated *question that cannot be answered by Aura Bora because it is not a Capsule orientated question.*

A Dilemma

So, Adam and Eve, by asking a What? question, set themselves up with a dilemma which is experienced as confusion between the generators. *For the first time Zenith through his generators has asked a question which cannot be answered by Aura Bora.* The reason Aura Bora cannot and will not answer the question is the What? question gives recognition to the human condition over Capsule. The Generators for the first time perceive the symptom not to be of Capsule but of the body. *This has the effect of separating Zenith from Aura Bora and thus, creating a Meme experience.*

What Is This?

What is this pimple on my face? What is this blood? What is this hair growing on your body? What are those sensations experienced by Zenith? What is this sadness in his heart? What is this aggressive reaction? What is this euphoria in my heart? What are these breasts? What is this mixed emotion? What is this mixed logic? What is this unintelligent puzzling situation in Meme's Grey Matter? What's causing that bump in Meme's stomach? *Now suddenly for the first time Zenith*

has turned into Meme. So, though they may be seen as legitimate questions, *the manner in which they are asked* directs them toward the generators.

Closed Off

By asking a What? question power is given to Meme and thus, Aura Bora is shut out or closed off to Zenith. The question comes from one or other of the generators. When it's an intellectual or logic-orientated question it comes from Grey Matter. Where the question is emotive it comes from Ruby and if the question is of a physical nature it comes from Young Nemo.

Because Zenith experiences no confusion between the generators he knows his connection is innate. However, when Aura Bora is closed off to the generators and Zenith chooses to deal with the question through his generators, he transforms into Meme. It is a choice he more often than not makes unconsciously.

Searches The Banks

For Meme to deal with the What? question he searches the three generator banks for information on similar events up to date. The generators find the nearest corresponding situation and a related answer attached. *Meme doesn't question where the answer came from but simply accepts it as correct even though it is a generated answer.* The new answer whilst it is an honest response from the three generators *may invariably include elements of untruth* because it won't have come from Capsule.

Very Important

It is very important to grasp the fact that when Meme chooses to close off contact with Aura Bora he begins the process of setting himself up with perceived problems that affect his whole life. *This single act of choosing to close off Aura Bora is literally the only thing Meme has to do to ensure he has a life of perceived hardship. 'All' of his perceived problems stem from this single act being repeated throughout his life.*

All his problems, hardship and misery are perceived from a Meme viewpoint. They are an unnecessary purely human being perception made by a Meme who chooses to live life without Aura Bora guidance. This is not to say that Zenith doesn't experience difficulties, but the difference between them is in the way they deal with the difficulties.

Ignored

All aspects of human life are made up from Capsule. Only a small portion of this energy is manifest in physical form. The largest percentage is invisible. However, Meme relates physically to things that are earthbound, because almost all the energy he sees has physical form.

Most Memes don't look past the physical manifestations of the energy of the world. As a result Memes fail to make connection with that which is nonphysical for example electricity, sound waves, telepathy, inspiration, intuition, imagination, Capsule awareness etc. Thus, the energies that are not physical are either ignored misunderstood or taken for granted.

Power

Because most things are perceived as physical, even though they are not, nearly all Memes relate to a very small portion of life. *By doing so, they completely ignore or take for granted the aspects of life that relate to the invisible including Aura Bora.* They are in fact ignoring a very large percentage of life in the process and *living life through a minute percentage of their capabilities.*

Because everything he sees has physical form Meme assumes the What? question. What is this object? What do you do for a living? What's he thinking? What car do you drive? What are my feelings? In this way Meme gives power to the human generated world instead of to Aura Bora.

There Are No Problems

Meme is ignoring the essence of his existence, the Aura Bora world. He is replacing it with a false world of misperception and second-rate generated answers to generator manifested perceived problems.

There actually are no difficulties in life that cannot be handled. However, because Meme is mishandling his own life he firstly manifests and then perceives there to be unmanageable problems. This he does by not allowing Aura Bora to deal with the symptoms in his life.

Most Utilized

Of the three generators Grey Matter is by far the one most utilized by Meme. Because of Grey Matter's obvious intelligence and logic Meme learns eventually to field most questions through Grey Matter. Thus, Ruby and Young Nemo act mostly as backup to Grey Matter. However, where Meme is emotive Ruby leads the way and where he is physical Young Nemo is leader.

Fruits Of Knowledge

Grey Matter is considered by most people to be the important generator. After all it is Grey Matter that produces the fruits of knowledge of which Adam and Eve were warned at the beginning of time. *Man's desire for knowledge has lead instead toward misappropriating intelligence and assuming logic.* Grey Matter cannot produce knowledge without Aura Bora contact, only a simulated version filled with mistruths.

The Fall

Having failed to access Aura Bora with a What? question, it now ends up with Grey Matter who searches the bank of information for the most appropriate answer. Grey Matter gives its honest, hard worked, logical and intelligent answer. This is the best answer Grey Matter can find. Because the answer is brain generated it has not come from Aura Bora. As such it does not contain universal wisdom and falls short of the mark.

Hence, we have the fall of Adam and Eve or the biting of the apple. The tasting of the fruits of knowledge is *the acceptance of generated intelligence* over knowledge, intelligence being the fruits of knowledge.

Free Will

Aura Bora does not interfere with the process of selection by Meme. The reason Aura Bora does not interfere is because Meme has free will. Aura Bora acknowledges Meme's free will to search for answers anywhere he wishes. It would be totally uncharacteristic of Aura Bora to impose on his choice to look for an answer elsewhere.

There is no attempt on Meme's part or on Aura Bora's part or on Grey Matter's part to be in any way malicious.

All aspects of Meme and Aura Bora are acting honourably. However, Meme makes choices *out of ignorance and lack of awareness of the rightful process of thought.* It is Meme's free will to be unaware.

Don't Recognize Eden

No doubt Adam and Eve realize their mistake at a later stage and redress the balance. However, as they grow older they unwittingly ask more What? questions and gradually become more dependent upon Grey Matter answers.

Adam and Eve still reside in the Garden of Eden but at this stage they don't recognize it as such. Gradually they have lost sight of the garden and don't recognize it as Eden. They get glimpses of it now and again when they contact Aura Bora but not as much as they used to.

Develop Intellect

There are compensations. Over the years they have developed their intellect. By dealing with all those perceived problems they now have quite a large bank of information on which they have become more dependent. They have gotten out of the habit of contacting Aura Bora for knowledge.

Emotional Love

They have developed their emotional intelligence also to such an extent they call it love but emotion is to love as intelligence is to knowledge. And of course they have their bodily desires that they need to keep in check but thankfully at this stage of their lives this doesn't seem to be such a bother as it used to be. They've also learned a great deal about their physical condition. Adam and Eve have become quite intelligent and logical at this stage so much so they now place their brain's intelligence above emotions on the intelligence scale and certainly above physical desires.

Logical System

Now there is a logical ranking system to make life on earth more workable and to fit into Grey Matter's very important and neat filing system. After all Grey Matter is the most important aspect of what they now call human being as far as Meme is concerned.

The Mind Switch

There is so much fruit of knowledge growing between Adam and Eve they now see no reason to bother with the notion of Aura Bora. Grey Matter has taken over so much from Aura Bora and indeed from Capsule that all the information generated by brain is in fact now called ' mindful'.

A Mind switch has taken place in which Grey Matter now logically and intelligently replaces Capsule. Even though Capsule is not consulted all Grey Matter's logic, intelligence and information is now known to be *mindful.* As far as Grey Matter's logic is concerned Mind must exist in the brain since Grey Matter does all the sifting. *This sifting is what Grey Matter calls thinking.* But of course its not thinking because thinking is a Mind occupation.

What's It All About?

At this stage Adam and Eve are not too concerned with Who? questions. They can't remember the last time they asked a Who? question. In fact there are so many What? questions that keep going around and around they don't have time for any other kind of question.

Now and again and increasingly as time slips by they get that knowing feeling in their Cores that they over the years have managed to suppress. That knowing feeling tells them that things have not quite turned out the way they expected. And Adam asks another What? question, What's it all about?

Who? and What? questions are covered in greater detail later in the book.

THE WISDOM OF ORACLES
BY JOHN RYAN

CHAPTER 9

LOVE

Is Eagal Liom Gur Dainid Leat Mo Ghrá (I fear my love grieves you)

**I fear my love grieves you
I fear you don't love me as I love you
I fear your love is waning
And I have no peace or joy on this account.**

**I won't be happy with two thirds of your heart
I won't be happy with half, tho' it's rotten with love
Your heart and mine, together as one
'Tis that would please me and take away my sorrow.** *pil*

In Love

To be in love is a most wonderful state of being. It is not just a feeling it is a state of being when connected to Aura Bora. It is a state of **knowing** and a state of **acceptance** of what is present. it is a state of *open awareness*. *Love is not in the head, nor is it in the heart, nor is it in the reproductive system*, although most people assume it is in all three generators especially the heart.

Love is in the knowing of Aura Bora. It is not just a body feeling. The body is not an active part in the **creation** of love. Love does not come from the heart as most people assume and the creation of love has nothing to do with connection to any other person as most people also assume.

Love is within ones own Aura Bora, it is not just an emotion. It is empathy with Capsule. Zenith must be in connection with Aura Bora to experience love. This is the way Capsule knows love. This is Aura Bora love.

Perceived Love

Meme without Capsule contact has a different perspective on love and a totally different take altogether from Capsule love. Meme without the backup is not capable of love and needs somebody else to love. Left to their own devices, without guidance from Aura Bora the generators generate a sifting, emotive reacting that Meme identifies incorrectly as love. However, this is merely perceived love and not actually love. Zenith on the other hand with access to Capsule creates love, knows love and knows how to be love for Aura Bora has access to infinite love, knowledge, truth and wisdom and is not merely depending on generator intelligence to cultivate a type of simulated love.

One Reason

Generators do not know how to step back. They give all their energy all the time. In personal situations, such as perceived love, they can come on too strong. Eventually, somewhere along the line problems are caused for any number of reasons. However, the one reason that matters is that the generators are not connected to Aura Bora. Without this connection they will inevitably run into trouble even though their intentions are honourable and honest. For example, Meme may be overly affectionate to, may be in constant suspicion of and may act irrationally with his partner.

Overact

Without Aura Bora guidance Meme can be placed in a false euphoric state of perceived love. He may become highly emotional, intellectually stimulated and physically driven and this can be easily misinterpreted as love and mishandled. The effort to retain the euphoria can lead him into a false state of being.

Often a person in perceived love will intellectualize unreasonably, overact emotionally, or react uncharacteristically, or a combination of all three. This is the result of misguided over reaction to situations that are generated in the name of love.

Off Switch
Without Aura Bora guidance generators in their enthusiasm to please don't know when to pull back. Generators don't have an off switch and so need to be constantly monitored. Without Aura Bora's guidance the generators just keep going. Even when the relationship hits a problem they will continue generating more of the same energy in an effort to overcome the problem even though less may be what is needed.

Breakdown
Eventually this may lead to a breakdown. The brain has given all it can, the heart has been completely open and the reproductive system has acted to its utmost ability but still everything goes out of all proportion and ends up in a breakdown. How does the situation that started off so lovingly end up in such a mess? Every aspect of Meme is devastated. How can Meme end up hating the very person to whom so much affection was shown?

These are not easy questions to answer for a Grey Matter disconnected from Aura Bora, for a Ruby disconnected from Aura Bora and for a Young Nemo disconnected from Aura Bora. All generators, having gone into overdrive, begin to break down and a seeming depression may set into Meme.

Compromised Position
Contrary to appearances Grey Matter, Ruby and Young Nemo are not inadequate in fact they are more than adequate. They have been unwittingly placed in an impossible position and they were never designed to deal with this type of situation on their own. Meme's disconnection from Aura Bora placed the generators in a compromised position. Thus, the more they try the more likely they are to fail.

Other Environments
This is not just the case with matters of the heart this is also the case in working and other environments. Meme makes all decisions based on past experience. The three generators do not possess the ability to see into the future, nor do they possess imagination, intuition or any of the other Capsule gifts. All generated solutions to problems, whilst they may be logical, emotional and reactive, lack the foresight necessary to make rounded decisions.

Large Organizations
This can be the case in all walks of life in business, social settings, personal, large organizations, institutions, corporations and governments all can be affected with the same lack of awareness and lack of imagination. The larger the organization the larger may be the problem because there are more people involved most of whom may be unimaginative and give generated solutions to already generated problems.

Problems
The problem becomes the system and the system becomes the problem. However, it may not always have been this way. Although the original idea may have been perceived from a Capsule place over the years it can eventually become run by generator-orientated people. Without the further guidance from Aura Bora a new set of complicated problems is inevitable.

Blind

A well-intentioned system continues throughout its life with the driving force of well-intentioned Memes with well-intentioned generators.

Because they themselves are completely above board and continue to be well intentioned they are blind to the effects their generators are causing. They do not believe the system could be the cause of the problem. Even where the problems are painfully obvious Memes still remain blind to the solution.

Imagination

Imaginative solutions to problems are not sought because Grey Matter does not understand the concept of imagination, of forethought or of intuition. All generated siftings that are perceived to be imaginative or forethought are in fact gleaned from past events and are based on past experience.

The concept of forward thinking is not properly understood or believed to exist for there is no capacity for its understanding in the Grey Matter that operates without the wisdom of Aura Bora.

An Unsustainable Burden

The vast majority of organizations, large businesses, institutions, government departments and governments, that may have been originally built with Capsule intentions are now operated by mostly hard working, dedicated, well intentioned people who have become generator orientated over the years. Whilst still run by the same honourable intentions, these organizations may not however, be operating with the full awareness of their Capsule selves.

As a result solutions to problems tend to be costly and unimaginative. **In the end the very reason for their existence in the first place may become an unsustainable burden**.

Capsule Beginnings

Many organizations are started up by Zeniths and have Capsule beginnings. However as time goes by the original organizers move on and are replaced by others with different ideas and different ways of implementing their new and often generated ideas. Eventually they become unimaginative generator orientated organizations.

THE WISDOM OF ORACLES
BY JOHN RYAN

CHAPTER 10

CAPSULE

Elements of Capsule

Each Capsule is made up of three beings, Oracle, Osmosis and Aura Bora. They are the three innate persons and are everlasting. **They are the being, knowing and motivating elements of Capsule** (see Zenith Diagram at front of book).

Oracle

Oracle **is** knowledge, truth and wisdom and is the creator of Osmosis and Aura Bora. Oracle is connected to and is an intrinsic part of Cosmic, Infinity, Eternity. Oracle is **everlasting** as are all three elements of Capsule. Capsule does not depend on Zenith to exist.

Osmosis

Osmosis is the **accumulator** of wisdom, truth and knowledge and is the second important aspect of Capsule. Osmosis has a much larger body of information than the three generators combined. Not alone can it access information from past events as can the generators, but Osmosis **has access to all knowledge past, present and future from Cosmic that's pertinent to Zenith.**

Osmosis does not view past, present and future as separate but collectively for in eternity all time exists in the now. Osmosis has **a specific purpose** in passing **vital knowledge, truth and wisdom** on to Aura Bora. This in essence means that Zenith has access to Capsule's knowledge both past, present and future.

Aura Bora

Aura Bora is the **instigator** of wisdom, truth and knowledge, is the third important aspect of Capsule and is an intrinsic part of and an everlasting element of Capsule. Aura Bora is the **activating** element of the three innate persons and **does not therefore depend on Zenith for its existence.** Aura Bora has always been here with Osmosis and Oracle long before Zenith was born and will still be here as part of Capsule long after Zenith passes on, in fact, **Aura Bora is here forever.**

It is through Aura Bora that Zenith gains access to universal knowledge, wisdom and truth. In other words, Aura Bora is the go-between who **passes eternal knowledge, universal wisdom, truth, knowledge, mindfulness, timelessness, love, joy, intuition, invention, inspiration, and imagination** etc. to the three generators. Without the Aura Bora connection Zenith alone cannot access these innate functions.

Important To Note

It is important at this stage to note that Capsule (otherwise known as Mind) does NOT exist as a part of the brain. Mind is NOT located in the brain. Capsule is NOT subject to Grey Matter as most people assume. Brain is physical and Mind is the three beings of Capsule. The notion that Mind is related to brain is misguided. Mind exists without brain, is totally outside of brain and totally separate from brain. **Mind is not a brain function and brain is not a Mind function.**

Zenith

Aura Bora is the creator of Zenith. Oracle, Osmosis and Aura Bora all belong to Capsule and as such are innate and everlasting. Zenith on the other hand is born on earth, lives for a period of time and is not an innate aspect of Capsule. Zenith's information is constantly monitored through Osmosis.

Zenith is very important to the development of Capsule for it is through Zenith that Capsule evolves to the next stage of evolution and he is thus **always remembered. Aura Bora activates through Zenith on earth.**

Zenith's function is to experience life on earth so that the knowledge gained from the experience can be added to Capsule's knowledge. Zenith is really a stage in Aura Bora's life and as such does not die. In a way Zenith is like a child. As a person grows the child's physical form is no more but evolves into adolescents, then into an adult and is remembered by the adult. In the same way Aura Bora always remembers Zenith. Without the life of Zenith, Capsule would remain in its current state of evolution. It's in Capsule's best interest to take care of and to nurture Zenith.

Access

Through Aura Bora, Zenith has access to the knowledge, wisdom and truth stored in Capsule.

Corigonus - Core

Another important element in the makeup of Zenith is Corigonus or Core. The function of Corigonus is to connect Aura Bora to the three generators. Core has an important role for it is here Zenith decides, either consciously or unconsciously, whether to engage Aura Bora or to engage the generators and become Meme.

Important Link

The Core is located just below Zenith's belly button. Although Core is invisible Zenith can feel Core. When Zenith knows something is not quite right he can get an uneasy feeling in the pit of his stomach. *Core is the important link between Aura Bora and Zenith. Meme most often does not acknowledge or understand this connection although it may be felt at specific times throughout his life.*

Importance Of Core

The importance of Core needs to be fully understood for it is here Zenith makes the vital decisions through life. *It is decided at Core whether to involve Aura Bora in Zenith's life or shut out Aura Bora's involvement in his life.*

These decisions, and there are many and frequent decisions, are responsible for the direction Zenith takes in life. They set up his attitudes, assumptions and beliefs throughout his life. *In other words these decisions set up Zenith's value system or the guidelines for his life.*

True Qualities

Since the time of Adam and Eve, humans have struggled to answer the questions of life. With the best efforts through history they have insistently and consistently fought and argued against their better nature. They have fought in many wars, battered their own self-image, tried to hide their perceived imperfections, and presented a false face to cope with the onslaught of disconnection from Capsule.

Humans are truly remarkable in their adaptive abilities and in their efforts to survive. Zenith instinctively knows that this is not the way life needs to be, for equally humans have a great desire to be free, joyful, loving, expressive and above all knowing, truthful and creative. These are the true qualities of life.

This in fact is Zenith's birthright. He knows this deep inside his person. He is attracted to these qualities because they are an innate part of his authentic Capsule. Zenith resonates with these qualities.

Unhealthy Lives

Some people seem to be happy in their lives but these are the exception. Most people seem to court unhappy lives. Most people seem to live in a constant struggle. Some always worry, some are fearful, some are in turmoil, some constantly question without finding adequate answers, some are very ill, some are poor and some are starving A lot of these situations we seem to inherit from our forefathers. Others we seem to bring on ourselves but are helpless in avoiding them. Many people continuously fall into situations that are unhealthy for them.

Despite best efforts and healthy intentions Meme can find life pulls him down, keeps him in his place and ensures he is always looking over his shoulder never far from worry or trouble just waiting for the hammer to fall.

Another Way

There is another way of dealing with life a way that will eventually bring Meme the joy, fulfillment and truth that is his birthright a way that is natural, harmless, real, personal, loving, caring, does not cost anything and does not expect anything of Meme. This is a way that integrates him with his authentic

self and leads him to his true path in life. No longer will he feel like a survivor, seeking preservation on an unfamiliar dangerous life path. The other way is connection with Aura Bora.

A Full Understanding

In order to fully understand this way of discovering his authentic self, Meme may first need to take a close look at his life to see how he is thinking, feeling and creating at the moment. *He may need to examine the current situation particularly the connection he has to Aura Bora and to closely study the path in life he is taking.*

In this way he can become fully aware of all aspects of his current situation, to what degree he considers Capsule as a part of his life and of the manner in which he is dealing with his current life's circumstances. There is no need for Meme to examine the past for it is of no benefit to his present circumstances. *How Meme thinks, feels and creates in the present moment is what is important.*

Meme
The three beings of Capsule, Oracle, Osmosis and Aura Bora *are invisible to Meme and herein lies the first problem in his life.* Meme perceives himself as singularly human being with no other connections and so, does not acknowledge Aura Bora in his life. *He is totally unaware on a conscious level of any connection to Aura Bora.*

When Meme engages in life without Aura Bora he is living life only through his three generators or his human capacity and this makes life unnecessarily difficult for him. It's like cutting grass with a knife and fork while the lawnmower is in the shed. The generators are not equipped to deal with life in this way and this is not their function.

However, Meme can choose and does insist on living life the 'hard' way.

Doing The Impossible

The simple fact that Meme doesn't acknowledge Capsule and sees himself as the only aspect of being is the main reason he has problems. *This single fact manifests the large majority of his problems.*

What Meme needs to do is live life with consideration of Aura Bora. However, he has chosen to go it alone. Meme is a crewless ship in fog navigating at full speed rudderless through icebergs in the North Pole. And he wonders why he has problems. It's a miracle he has lasted this long. It's a testimony to man's endurance under impossible situations that the human race still manages to struggle on mindlessly. Meme remarkably has survived his kamikaze life style thus far. He is in fact doing the impossible.

THE WISDOM OF ORACLES
BY JOHN RYAN

CHAPTER 11

CRYING

Crescendo Decrescendo
Crescendo decrescendo
Crescendo very raw
Crescendo not cascando
Crescendo full of war.

Cascando deprecando
Cascando, in a rush
Cascando not crescendo
Cascando, then a hush. *pil*

Healthy Act
When Meme comes in contact with tragedy in his life it is not unusual for Grey Matter to generate sorrow, for Ruby to generate sadness and for Young Nemo to generate crying. Crying can be an extremely healthy act. It is recognition by Meme that the generators are in confusion. Often in a crisis one or other generator will take over complete operations.

Meme may become superbly organized, or indeed much more emotional than unusual, or sometimes overly active and fastidious in an effort to keep the pain of loss at bay. These are heightened reactions that activate the generators to a point where they are working continuously to keep things together. Sometimes, Meme just can't cope with the overload and breaks down temporarily or indeed for longer periods. It is during these periods he may even cry.

A Sense Of Peace
Very often after crying Meme receives a great sense of peace. This peace is in fact contact with Aura Bora. However, more often than not he doesn't recognize the sense of peace for what it is. The act of crying has physically pumped the Core and opened up access to Aura Bora. Ruby can open up Corigonus to Aura Bora by inducing crying or indeed laughing. The peace that is felt is the presence of Capsule in Zenith.

Lost Contact
Children do this automatically all the time. When they are upset by a fall for instance, or by hunger, or by something they don't understand, they cry. The reason a child cries is because the circumstances create confusion in the generators, so he temporarily loses contact with Aura Bora and he feels the loss. The lost contact can happen suddenly, as in a fall or other surprise, and the child can become acutely aware of his own body without the presence of Aura Bora.

The sudden impact earths the child and Aura Bora is temporarily disconnected. Although he may not be outwardly aware of it, the child's crying pumps the Core and thus, he reconnects directly with Aura Bora.

Grounded
A child may continue crying, not simply because he is hungry or hurt, but because, by the hunger or hurt, he is continually being grounded. When the child is fed and comforted and accepted he can then return to Capsule awareness. Likewise, when a child falls the parent hugs and soothes him and acknowledges the loss thus, allowing him an earlier opportunity to return to Capsule awareness.

Token
However, if the child is continuously soothed by a token such as a sweet or candy or toy for example, he becomes introduced to a substitute for Aura Bora early in his development. **Eventually he learns to value the token more than Capsule.**

A Life Of Struggle

As the child grows older his three generators move further from Capsule contact and learn over time how to generate without the aid of Aura Bora. Thus, begins a life of struggle and pain rather than a life of harmony and joy.

It is Aura Bora's desire to be present and supportive, not just during tragic circumstances, but to be present **always.** Any separation from Aura Bora inevitably means Meme's logic, emotions and reactions will be mindless and without the benefit of Capsule's wisdom.

Free Will

Aura Bora will not impose and accepts Meme's free will to choose a direction in life. Aura Bora will respond to an invitation, but will never respond to being asked What? Meme mostly only asks What? questions and by doing so keeps Aura Bora out of the picture. It's like sending an invitation to the incorrect address. Aura Bora lives at the Who? address not at the What? address.

Show The Way

So, when Meme needs help and turns to the three generators he shuts out Aura Bora who can show the way through to enlightenment, awareness and peace.

Inventive, Imaginative & Intuitive

Since they can only draw on past experience, the generators are not in a position to come up with inventive, imaginative and intuitive answers. This is where Aura Bora can be invaluable providing Meme with knowledge of the true situation particularly in times of trouble and strife.

Uphill Battle

When Meme is totally dependent on the three generators for all of life's decisions he sells himself short because they can at best create only a second-class result. Without guidance Meme is living a life of struggle, an uphill battle, unnecessarily sad, poor, unhealthy, troubled, empty and painful. However, with input from Aura Bora he can live a joyful, knowledgeable, pain free, wealthy, healthy, wise and fulfilling life.

A Living Hell

Meme in his race through life has unwittingly misinterpreted his own value system. **In its place he has put in a different set of values and attitudes.** These values and attitudes are the bedrock of his existence. He was originally intended to live peacefully and joyfully in the Garden of Eden, but instead has chosen to live dangerously and destructively in a living hell, lovingly created by his own generators.

Wise Men

Since the beginning of time man has misinterpreted his original intention and purpose in life and has been doing the same ever since. What aspects of history, if any, can we draw on to gain a better understanding of man's situation?

There have been many wise men, many leaders and prophets who have lead man out of disaster in their time Noah, Moses, Jesus Christ, Gandhi, and Mandela to name but a few.

Let us look briefly back through history to the time of Moses and examine this great leader's intentions.

THE WISDOM OF ORACLES
BY JOHN RYAN

CHAPTER 12

MOSES

Ancient Laws
Say Santa Claus
Has woolly jaws
And mittened paws. *pil*

Remembered

Moses is most remembered for transcribing The Ten Commandments. The Ten Commandments place a value system into our society at a level underlying the whole structure of western thinking. Whether we are religious or not these values have an effect on the structure of our lives. The current interpretation of the commandments is generated and as such deals with the human Meme aspect of life to the exclusion of our innate needs.

The Ten Commandments

First.
I AM THE LORD THY GOD THOU SHALT NOT HAVE STRANGE GODS BEFORE ME.

Second
THOU SHALT NOT TAKE THE NAME OF THE LORD THY GOD IN VEIN.

Third
REMEMBER TO KEEP HOLY THE SABBATH DAY.

Fourth
HONOUR THY FATHER AND THY MOTHER.

Fifth
THOU SHALT NOT KILL.

Sixth
THOU SHALT NOT COMMIT ADULTERY.

Seventh
THOU SHALT NOT STEAL.

Eight
THOU SHALT NOT BEAR FALSE WITNESS AGAINST THY NEIGHBOUR.

Ninth
THOU SHALT NOT COVET THY NEIGHBOUR'S WIFE.

Tenth
THOU SHALT NOT COVET THY NEIGHBOUR'S GOODS.

Wisest Writings

The Ten Commandments, currently in use by modern day religions, are based on the original writings of Moses. They were the wisest writings of their time, transcribed about 2,500 years ago by the wisest leader of that time. Writings such as these don't go out of date. They are intended to last. They set out the conditions whereby man can live in peace and harmony.

Stone Tablets

The original Ten Commandments were transcribed onto two stone tablets, which according to the Old Testament were broken soon after Moses descended from Mount Sinai. So, the original version of The Ten Commandments does not exist, and in its place is a version written several hundred years later.

Truths

The original version of The Ten Commandments were, in fact not commandments. They were commitments or truths, for on close examination, it's obvious there is not one word of command in any of the truths. Indeed, why would Oracle command *for Oracle is all-powerful and would have no need to command the human race?*

Human Traits

In man's efforts to understand he has given Oracle human traits. Oracle is supposed to be good, kind and loving, but at the same time can get angry, vengeful and disappointed just like any human. *It is not possible for Oracle to have just human traits*. When it is said 'man is made in the image of Oracle', what is assumed is *Oracle is made in the image of man*. Meme has completely reversed his understanding of Oracle.

So, Oracle now fits nicely into man's understanding of himself, which is really a mistruth. Meme has little or no understanding of Oracle. Small wonder the world is in chaos. The Ten Truths have been turned into Ten Commandments, man doesn't understand his place in the world, and Oracle is viewed as a happy-go-lucky terrorist, sometimes being kindly and at other times being vengeful.

Not A Religious Problem

It's clear that the present state of affairs is not due just to modern man's interpretation of life. These problems have been with us for thousands of years. This is the reason why Moses transcribed The Ten Truths in the first place long before the time of Christ. Man's inability to comprehend Oracle is not a religious problem and never was. This problem existed long before Christianity or any of the other ancient religions.

Lack Of Understanding

Man, through his misaligned generators, has been misinterpreting and mismanaging his life since time immemorial. Meme's view of Oracle is that of a vengeful Oracle, an Oracle with human attributes such as information gathering, logic, emotion and reaction. This is not only inaccurate but a complete misrepresentation and *a complete lack of understanding of Oracle in relation to man and of man in relation to Oracle*. Meme's current view is *an abuse of Oracle* where he has slotted Oracle into a convenient box that can be opened occasionally in times of need.

Reversed Values

Whilst the problem was not manifested originally by modern man, it is a problem made all the worse by modern man's ignorance and arrogance. Meme continues to add to the problem by living his life through his reversed values and attitudes. Throughout history, Meme has continually turned his back on Oracle in the name of country, principal, religion and self-righteousness in the form of wars, conflict and abuse. This is happening on a global level as well as on a personal level.

Personal Level

When we take a look at Meme on a personal level we see he has mini wars, mini conflicts and mini abuse of himself and of his neighbour. This has been the way for longer than anybody alive can remember. Our forefathers may not have been in a position to change the status quo, and although tyranny still exists modern man is more likely to find solutions with guidance from Aura Bora. Surely, modern man can make up his own Mind, that is, if he can find it.

Operating Mindlessly

This indeed is part of the problem. Both Meme and his forefathers have been operating mindlessly for so long now that he is no longer in touch with his own Mind. He has replaced his real Mind with a brain generated, self manufactured mind.

Assumes

Once Meme lost sight of his Capsule, he was destined to live a life of trial and error, of hardship and pain, of illness and misery. We may be further from our Minds than ever before. *Grey Matter has replaced Osmosis to such an extent that the brain now views itself as Mind* and Meme now assumes Osmosis is part of Grey Matter, which is certainly not the case.

Self Examination

The modern world puts a further pressure on Meme and has turned into a playground for amateur psychologists where the idea of self-examination based on past information is accepted as everyday.

Science and medicine alike examine past information in an effort to uncover what is perceived as facts, engaging Meme in the pursuit of *self-doubt*. It is questionable whether exploration based on past activity has much to do with the present and this exploration may present problems. Without appropriate innate supervision this may in fact *encourage* further illness.

No Insight

It is not possible to be mindful without engaging Osmosis through Aura Bora. Any effort to be mindful by engaging Grey Matter instead is coming from an incorrect place. While there is a wealth of information to back up Grey Matter's

abilities both personally and worldwide accumulated through history, there is no insight into the present without Aura Bora involvement.

Grey Matter, whilst a brilliant gatherer of information and superb in the areas of detection and logic and regurgitation of past information, does not in fact possess knowledge. Grey Matter is an informer of stored information called facts, which while honest, are actually questionable untruths.

Knowledge

Knowledge is acquired through inspiration, intuition, imagination and invention, none of which are created in Grey Matter but are present through contact with Aura Bora. It is therefore not possible for Grey Matter to be mindful without the input from Aura Bora.

This is one reason why the areas of medicine and science, for instance, need proof of a new discovery. The approach is the logical, intelligent, tried and tested, step-by-step, the one step forward two steps back approach on which not only these but many institutions are built.

Pressure

Grey Matter is one of Meme's most useful facilities. However, he continually misuses its talents honing Grey Matter into areas for which it was never intended. *Utilizing it in mindless activity places Grey Matter under intolerable pressure to come up with unnecessary answers to problems. This is a misuse of Grey Matter's natural talents* that are specifically designed to operate under the guidance of Aura Bora and not to operate solo.

Misguided Generators

Under the current system of abusing generators, in which the vast majority of people partake misinformation misguides Meme through a misinformed Grey Matter, a misinformed Ruby and a misinformed Young Nemo. This is why mankind is experiencing great pressure in modern times. Our misguided generators are ever increasingly moving us away from control of our world and of ourselves as a race. For example, we have starvation, poverty, pollution and overpopulation, these situations are accepted as normal situations and our acceptance of these situations is considered to be normal behaviour.

No Blame

This is not the fault of Grey Matter who indeed is forthright and honourable, hard working and exemplary in its efforts to serve Meme. No body or no part of anybody or no institution is to blame. There is no blame for there is no malicious attempt, nor was there ever any malice intended.

It is necessary to *move away from blame* toward acceptance in order to see what is really happening in the situation, to get a clear picture of the manner in which these events unfold, to get a real understanding of the state of play and to change to a more constructive approach, for example Gandhi's non-aggressive approach to British rule in India.

The Blame Game

Without this understanding it is more difficult to move forward constructively. If we instead search for blame we employ Grey Matter once more in futile activity. *Meme needs to stop investigating through Grey Matter and employ Aura Bora to come up with some real solutions to where the actual problem lies. Meme needs to put a stop to the blame game.*

Self-Imposed Problems

Meme has an insistence on being kept informed or indeed misinformed by continually asking the What? question. This insistence is the bases to a large extent of a series of self-imposed problems. Meme needs to shift from this What? question for its misuse is dangerous. What? was never intended to be used in its present form much less abused as it is today.

A New Status

An exclamation, a query for its own sake is What? It was never intended for use as a means of investigation. Meme has turned What? into a leading question in front of innumerable facts for the specific purpose of obtaining data. What? has been given a new status, an oracle, for which it was never intended.

Doubt

Of all the questions asked Where? When? How? Why? Have? Would? Is? etc. the most asked question in the world today is a question that never needs to be asked. By continuously asking What? for investigation purposes Meme places doubt in front of himself. Aura Bora never intended for him to be in doubt for he has access to mindful expression, universal wisdom and ultimate knowledge in abundance. So, why would there be any need for What or indeed for doubt?

Confident

Meme is placed on the defensive with the question What? With access to wisdom and knowledge Zenith is capable of being confident and of a loving, thoughtful, creative response in all his activities.

THE WISDOM OF ORACLES
BY JOHN RYAN

CHAPTER 13

SPEED

The Streets're in a Hurry
The streets're in a hurry
The streets're very grey
The traffic rumbles through'em
Each second of the day.

The streets're hard and level
With buildings, on the way
They wind about, and turn me out
Into the llvelong fray.

The streets have no fixed resting place
Where I can sit and stay
The streets're but a testing place
For those who wish to stray.

The streets'll never quiet down
They aren't planned that way
The streets're in a hurry
The streets're very grey. *pil*

Living In Doubt
Man is meant to be forward moving this is his natural state of being. Zenith is meant to make progress and to find new discoveries. However, if he insists on questioning and analyzing everything it is this unreasonable insistence that continuously disrupts his progress. Meme has become suspect and answerable both to himself and society for the way he apparently thinks, feels and expresses. *When Zenith is in his true mode of thinking, feeling and expressing through Aura Bora he is being true to his innate nature.*

His untrue mode as Meme of being analytical, emotive and reactionary is a generated response and is **unnatural**. In this situation he constantly needs reassurance and proof of his direction for he is living in doubt and thus, his progress is delayed. For example, he has a closet full of clothes and can't find anything to wear. The insistence on having proof to satisfy his logic and intelligence is a large contributor to the problems Meme experiences with 'speed'.

Stop-Start
The more progress is held back the more there is need for speed to make up for a perceived loss of time. There Is no real loss of time. However, when Meme always has to account to his generators for his natural actions, this places him continuously in a position of stop-start. Thus, Meme perceives a loss of time that must somehow be made up. To make up time Meme engages in speed. For instance, he's always losing his keys and feels the need to make up for the time lost searching for them.

Proper Context
Speed in the proper context is of great assistance to man. Modes of transport, for Instance have greatly reduced the time spent traveling. However, when speed is employed to make up for a perceived loss of time it has devastating consequences. This is an abuse of time and as such has an unhealthy effect on Meme's personality. It eats into his value system and changes his perception of life.

The Main Factor
Speed can take over Meme's life to such an extent that he can be very often out of control. The service of time becomes the main factor in life and everything

else is perceived as less important. Speed becomes the master without Meme even realizing it or acknowledging the fact.

Catch Up

Speed places the three generators into overdrive. Meme is constantly in a state of preparation and thus, anxiety. This affects his concentration and has the effect of catapulting him into catch-up mode rather than concentration on the present. In an effort to recover perceived lost time, he is now ahead of himself generating more speed. The satisfying of speedy solutions becomes the object of the exercise at the expense of the exercise itself.

Standard Shifts

It is impossible to go fast and give 100% concentration to the activity. Something has to give. Eventually, it gets to a stage where Meme loses contact with the exercise and its original meaning. In doing so, the standard of acceptance in his activities shifts from being paced, well executed and engaging, to fast, shoddy and anxious.

Payoff

One of the difficulties with this approach is now Meme has learned to accept shoddy work because it has been achieved with speed, even though the payoff is anxiety. The abuse of time creates a further imbalance in the three generators that he accepts as part of the payoff for gaining speed. He now experiences anxiety and this can eventually lead to illness

Thus, illness is accepted as part of the payoff for achieving speed. Or it may not be accepted in which case Meme enters the blame game and

blames the perception of not having enough time as the cause of his illness. This in turn manifests another problem, that of emoting being hard done by, that manifests another illness, anger and on it goes.

The Speed Trap

Of course all this can be prevented. Meme can stop the cycle. He can get off the not so merry merry-go-round and get out of the speed trap by becoming aware of his three generators Grey Matter, Ruby and Young Nemo. **The very act of becoming aware of what he is doing at the time he's doing it** brings Meme back to the present. Awareness has the effect of changing ones perception.

Awareness

Awareness can be the beginning of change. Chasing time is an activity that guarantees Meme's attention is on perceived future matters. By checking himself and paying attention to Aura Bora he not only becomes aware of the present but he also comes into the present. Of course as soon as he becomes aware of the present his three generators will want to reactivate him into chasing mode.

Up To Speed

The generators are not playing games or indeed trying to take over from Aura Bora. They are merely doing their best to keep Meme up to speed. The generators have been employed in this activity and wish to serve him well. So, they will continue to generate, that's what generators do for they are very giving.

Wise Thing

A way to slow the generators down is to inform them of what they are doing. **Meme needs to have an internal conversation with his generators** (this is shown later on in the book). This may seem like an odd thing to do because communication with the generators is usually allowed to happen automatically without any real effort.

But, **the generators welcome guidance and communicating with them is a very wise thing to do** because they were designed to take guidance from Aura Bora.

Protective

This communicating may not seem intelligent or logical to Meme. In fact his Grey Matter might even call it stupid, his Ruby may emote silliness or embarrassment, and his Young Nemo could react by what may appear to be contempt or aggression. These reactions are the generators natural way of protecting Meme from what appears to them as alien. This is what eventually happens when the generators have lost total contact with Aura Bora **they begin to see abnormality in the normal and normal in what is abnormal**. They do not intend to display aggression.

When Meme talks to his generators they will understand. Once they are given a reasonable, logical and intelligent explanation they will accept it. **However, they do need an explanation when Meme changes direction**. Otherwise each in turn will generate a protective response that can instantly transform an otherwise placid Zenith into a dogged, self-righteous and seemingly arrogant Meme.

Suspect

When Meme slows down to engage Aura Bora he is engaging with Capsule wisdom and knowledge. Without guidance anything outside of the generators brief may be unrecognized and thus considered alien or suspect. Such things as wisdom, knowledge, inspiration, intuition, creativity and inventiveness will be unrecognized by the generators because of their inability to engage them without Aura Bora guidance.

Grey Matter will logically and intellectually give reasons why these activities are unsuitable pursuits and will be genuinely apathetic **and will be unable to appreciate or comprehend them or include them in Meme's value system**.

Red Tape

Meme up to now has allowed his generators to take over all his intellectual activities. Grey Matter assumes the role of protector and throws suspicion on what appears to be an intrusion. This may be a reason why large institutions become unwittingly bogged down in logic, intelligence and red tape. Grey Matter by way of protection will quite literally, **intentionally and self righteously stand in the way of and visibly obstruct imaginative progress because it does not comply with Grey Matter standards**.

Role Of Protector

This is why it is necessary for Meme to engage in meaningful dialogue and to explain his intention to the three generators when he is allowing Aura Bora to guide the way. There is no malice intended from the generators for they are merely reacting to the situation. The real problem here is that Meme has up to now been misusing his generators. So, they naturally assume their everyday role of protector and of being in charge of all aspects of him.

Going It Alone

Grey Matter at this stage of life assumes brain **is mindful**, Ruby now assumes that heart is able to produce **original feelings** and Young Nemo assumes body is able to produce **original creativity**. Meme is literately going it alone without input from Aura Bora.

Dependent

Meme didn't actually plan to go it alone. Through a series of encounters with the world this regression happens over a long period of time. It takes more than one single act to disconnect Meme from Aura Bora completely. Over time, and it may take several years, Meme ever so gradually becomes more dependent on Grey Matter for answers.

Grey Matter Orientated

The world at large encourages Grey Matter solutions to problems. Many of the worlds systems and organizations are run on Grey Matter rules and regulations. Basic systems like the educational system ensures young Zeniths are honed into a Grey Matter way of life from an early age. Most religious organizations, health services, local authorities, large organizations, corporate companies and governments are Grey Matter orientated organizations run by multiple generators in large organized institutional Memes.

Unusual

Because of this Meme has grown used to the three generators taking the lead in every situation. Even though it is quite unnatural to live life without Aura Bora guidance, Meme doesn't recognize anything out of place. This is such a common occurrence that **those people who exhibit natural abilities like imagination, intuition, invention and inspiration, such as artists or musicians are deemed to be odd or unusual instead of it being the other way around**.

Available To Everybody

These natural abilities are **available to everybody** there is nothing unusual about them. With Aura Bora in the lead Zenith can, without any effort, avail of these abilities as a natural part of life.

They are not available to the three generators without Aura Bora and this is why generated Memes don't have them. However, **they are available to everybody when they are in contact with their Aura Bora**.

Full Responsibility

Grey Matter has become so accustomed to responding to Meme's every intellectual need that it assumes full responsibility for every intellectual encounter Meme experiences. Grey Matter rightfully considers itself as Mind since there is all the evidence in its intelligence bank to back up this fact. It's an honestly assessed conclusion. It doesn't register with Meme that it is also untrue.

Nobody Seems To Notice

Just as Grey Matter assumes responsibility for all intellectual matters, Ruby assumes responsibility for Meme's feelings and assesses that emotion is in fact the same as feeling. It doesn't register with Meme that it's untrue.

Young Nemo likewise assumes responsibility for his expressive actions and assesses that action and reaction are in fact creation and original expression. It doesn't register with Meme that this is untrue.

Almost nobody seems to notice the three generators are assuming responsibilities for that which they were never intended. In the absence of Aura Bora the three generators assume their intellectual, emotive reactions to be in fact knowledgeable, feeling creations.

Death Of Original Creation

The intelligence is not knowledgeable, the emotion is not feeling and the actions and reactions are not creations. The assumption that they are is the death of original creation.

Acceptance of generator manifestations is in fact the creation of illness where our attitudes and values have become somehow reversed. **The acceptance of generated misconceptions in place of original creations can only be termed as illness**. Even in the art world there is confusion as to what is considered art. Any artwork that has its roots in generated activity cannot be considered as original, inventive, inspirational or intuitive and therefore is not art.

Life Of Joy

It was never intended that Meme should be living in illness. He is supposed to live a happy, well-adjusted, healthy, successful and integrated life of joy. Instead, he has chosen a life of sickness, failure, un-coordination, discordance, misery and war.

Take Responsibility

Oracle never intended for Zeith to be miserable. To be joyful is his destiny. However, as Meme he has become so used to being ill thinking he assumes that somehow he has been set-up by Oracle for a tragic outcome. Meme fully accepts that Oracle has played a major part in his demise often even blaming Him for giving him problems. This makes no sense although it can seem to him to be the only intelligent answer.

Meme himself must take responsibility for his own life. Oracle is not responsible for him and is certainly not to blame. There is in fact nobody to blame not even Meme himself. To blame only further complicates the situation.

Do A Runner

Oracle is wisdom, knowledge, truth and infinite. Where is there space here for Oracle to be vindictive? It simply makes no sense to place Oracle in this petty position.

Of course, where Meme realizes this he takes a different angle and denies there is Oracle. This is the ultimate insult to himself, for now he is asking that if there is no Oracle how is he going to keep himself on the straight and narrow path of life?

First of all there is Oracle but He's a terrorist and secondly there is no Oracle to keep an eye on things so Meme might as well just accept that he is doomed. The implication is that Oracle used to be here but He has deceived Meme and has decided to do a runner in his hour of need. For example, where Meme experiences a loss through illness or death he may blame Oracle for his demise.

A Genuine Attempt

Strange as it may seem these are all efforts by Grey Matter to make sense of what is going on in Meme's life and in the absence of imagination, logic is applied even where it doesn't make sense and becomes illogical. This is a genuine attempt by Grey Matter to look for answers but there's nothing in the memory bank that fits.

So, Grey Matter comes up with the closest and most honest answer it can find. Once it is an honest answer, and Grey Matter will always be honest, Meme accepts the answer even though there may not be a word of truth. It's an honest generated answer to an honest generated situation in his honest generated life. Meme's value system has reached this level through years of generating his life and he sees nothing out of place. In fact, the world around him supports everything he does.

Making It Fit

Honesty is honesty and truth is truth. There are a thousand miles between them on the road to fulfilment, and one points toward ignorance and the other points toward knowing.

Meme chooses the former, even though he has difficulty making it fit, because that's all he's got. He has no other options. For instance, people offer their honest, generated opinion of a situation in which they may have little or no understanding and feel they have a perfect right to express their opinion even if it is misleading.

The Choice

Meme does not have to play the generator game. The choice to live his life in ignorance is just that, a choice. He can likewise choose to live a completely fulfilled life of knowledge and joy through Aura Bora. Instead of living a life of illness, ignorance and fear he can, not only live a healthy life he can fully embrace the life of creator, motivator, instigator and activator with joy if he so chooses.

Speed Is Essential

The need for speed is a generated need. It is a false side effect of misguided generators. To the generators speed is essential. It confirms Meme's control of life. 'It's where the buzz is at'. It gets the adrenaline going, but that's the problem. Adrenaline is a hormone secreted because Meme is under stress. This will eventually wear him down – not healthy at all. The healthy alternative is serotonin, the neurotransmitter that increases the level of activity – a natural high and very healthy for Zenith. Serotonin comes with mindful, Oracle activity and not with generated activity.

Early Warnings

The difference between generator and Aura Bora activity is in the way Meme is affected. With generator activity he is burning energy that will eventually have the effect of reducing the bodies mobility. Minor symptoms and side effects such as irritability, complaining, nit picking, arguments, impatience, feeling tired, boredom, frustration, anxiety, in fact the minor things we tend to ignore or pass off as normal, are in fact early warning signs that there may be a problem. When Meme has a problem with time he gets these early warning signs. This is also a measure of how he perceives time and the importance time has in his life.

The Problem

This may not seem like such a problem but that's the problem. The fact that Meme doesn't see these minor symptoms as a problem is in fact the problem. He accepts these early warnings as normal behaviour. However, this is not normal behaviour. This is illness and the problem is he doesn't recognize this as illness.

Take Note

Any time Meme has a generated action or reaction it can be considered as normal or acceptable behaviour by himself simply because he may not have questioned it before. This behaviour is not normal nor is it acceptable behaviour. It is a reaction by the generators that he must not ignore. It tells him all is not well with the generators. He needs to know it and deal with it straight away. The three generators are in fact misaligned and operating against one another without the guidance of Aura Bora. These are the very early warning signs and Meme must take note at this early stage so that he can reverse the situation.

Internal Problem

There is no need or indeed no point in treating the symptoms for the symptoms are a reactionary signal. There is in fact no treatment for this in itself is not an ailment. It is the symptoms of an internal problem.

Easily Rectified

At this point the misalignment can be easily rectified by focusing on Corigonus and thus, realigning the three generators with Aura Bora (this process will be discussed later). If the symptoms are ignored or not realized Meme goes deeper into the condition. What he needs to do is to become aware of the position in which he has placed himself.

Victim

By simply not recognizing the symptoms of boredom, tiredness, irritability, anxiety, impatience etc. as an unnatural state for him the symptoms have been elevated to importance in Meme's life. It is in elevating the importance of the symptoms that gives him victim status. **By giving acknowledgement to a victim status in himself he severs connection to Aura Bora**.

Imperfection

The reason this simple recognition of victim status separates Meme is because he has given power over to an earth bound status in favour of a Capsule status. By so doing, he acknowledges an imperfection in himself. **This is an untruth because there are no imperfections in him and Aura Bora knows this**.

A Very Important Point

The act of giving power to a supposed imperfection is in itself the act of separation from Aura Bora. This is a very subtle act but the consequences of the act have a devastating affect on his life. This is a very important point to understand for if he misses this point or even plays it down Meme will not recognize any future infringement.

Subtlety

Because he is **used to pressure** any subtle point may easily be overlooked. Subtlety is not Meme's strong point when operating under generator influence for he is conditioned to force and in the acceptance of force fails to realize the implications of it. The truth is if any amount of force is being used **even the minutest amount** Meme is off track no matter what the circumstances.

Gnat to Gnu.
'How d'ye do?'
Says gnat to gnu
'I trust ye don't rue
The 'g'-nip that's my due.' *pil*

'G'nip Reaction

Illness comes in many forms, not alone personal illness but illness in society. Illness in humanity exists by default. Illness and suffering, hardship of any kind, anything unhealthy, any slight upset or minute thought, or fraction of an emotion, or tiniest 'g'-nip reaction **given recognition** will take Zenith from Aura Bora. This is why he needs to be diligent in recognizing minute symptoms.

The Nub

This is the nub of the whole matter, the very basis of understanding of truth. Any slight upset **given power** brings Zenith into victim mode and thus, to earth rather than to Aura Bora. This includes even a slight feeling of sadness, the slightest recognition of any discourse, an uneasy feeling, a tense moment, slight sadness, minute irritation, a frown, a sideways glance, in fact any slight discomfort in the brain, heart or body. **This means straight away he is off track and his generators**

need to be realigned by going straight to Core so Aura Bora can regain access to Zenith.

These are the very early symptoms, not even warnings for they would be forceful. They are early truths manifesting in the body. **These symptoms are so subtle that generators don't recognize them for what they are and therefore have no reference for them.**

Manifestation

When these early symptoms are ignored or pushed aside and taken as normal behaviour then Zenith progresses automatically to the next stage. At this stage he needs to recognize the manifestation for what it is and to deal with it by going straight to Core and thus, reengaging with Aura Bora. **He needs to hand the problem over to Aura Bora** (this is dealt with in the chapter on Corigonus). When he does this he is back on track once more. **Even the slightest discomfort means Zenith is off track.**

Looking For Confirmation

A disconnected Meme at this point is searching his memory bank looking for confirmation of this truth. However, it won't be found because it is not yet there. This truth must be proven to Meme before Grey Matter will accept the input. Once Meme tries out the truth and it is proven to be correct it will become factual to Grey Matter and then it can be accepted as part of the information and logic already in the bank ready to be regurgitated at the next similar encounter.

A War

Because Meme has been operating solo up to now Grey Matter is used to referring to its own bank of information for answers. When an answer is not found in the bank Grey Matter will correctly dispute the information. Firstly this new information cannot be true because there is no fact in the bank that confirms its authenticity.

If it is not fact then Grey Matter views it to be misinformation, a falsehood, a lie, a trick, a misbehaving or a distortion of fact. Taken to extreme it may even be seen as an attack or an attempt to overthrow, a bullying, a fight, a battle or a war. Grey Matter generates whatever energy it takes in order to protect the individual or institutional Meme. Grey Matter will even go to war.

A Separate Status

Grey Matter is not capable of being mindful for mindfulness includes imagination, inspiration, forward planning, exploration, projection, investigation, invention, intuition etc. This Capsule awareness is fluid by nature. It cannot be stored in a memory bank and is outside the realm of understanding of separated generators, so its influence is treated as alien.

This alien is given a separate status outside of Grey Matter's so-called Mind, which has been assumed into existence. By doing so, Grey Matter now considers itself to be Mind because logically and intellectually Mind could not be outside the body therefore, it must reside in Grey Matter. The fact that this is not true doesn't register with Meme.

Not The Ego

There is nothing malicious about the generators protecting Meme   They are completely above board and honourable to such an extent that they will even ensure that he will fight and die for his country or religion or indeed any generated cause if needed. This is not the ego as Grey Matter leads us logically to believe. The ego in this case is a mistaken identity, which is in fact caused by disconnection from Aura Bora resulting in confusion between the three generators and their individual intentions.

Honest Assessment

All the generators are protective of Meme and serve him to the very end without question or any complaint for it is their only purpose.   The three generators are exemplary in their conduct. This is why to cast them in the roll of 'ego' while it may be an honest assessment recovered from Grey Matter's bank it's not the truth. Ego is therefore a misperception of generator energy when separated from Aura Bora. Ego without Aura Bora does not exist in reality.

Substitutes

No aspect of Zenith is constructed to or indeed can work against him. However, a separated Meme doesn't possess information in its bank concerning mindfulness. In the absence of knowledge and truth, information and honesty become the generated substitutes. **In a generated world, information rules over knowledge and honesty rules over truth. Knowledge is not teachable by Meme. Truth is not considered to be honest by Meme and he often finds truth difficult to digest.**

One Aim

Meme now plays the generator game. The three generators Grey Matter, Ruby and Young Nemo have but one aim, to serve Zenith or Meme to the best of their abilities. In doing so, the generators are absolutely honest, dedicated, precise, diligent, concentrated, utilitarian, unbending, prudent, dogged, believing, straight, categorically correct, driving, continuous, accurate etc. all of which are very useful facilities at the disposal of Meme. **All of these traits can manifest in him to extreme as a result of disconnection from Aura Bora**.

Cut Off

When the generators are cut off from the support of Aura Bora the response is catastrophic and immediately leads to discord at various levels of action, interaction and reaction. This inevitably leads to misalignment of the generators with one another. This generates Meme into a series of uncoordinated, intelligent, logical, emotional, energetic and physical manifestations instead of Aura Bora guided thoughtful, feeling and creative expression. This leads to illness, unhappiness, disillusion, speed and discord etc.

End Up Racing

The generators, although performing honourably, are unwittingly engaged in a race against one another. This is not their intention. When a generator comes up against an obstruction it simply applies more pressure to overcome the obstacle no matter what it may be.

When a second generator is the cause of the obstacle it doesn't know and simply ups the pressure. The second generator needs now to up its pressure to compensate. The individual generators don't perceive discord and in fact there is none (although Meme may experience confusion and perceive discord). There are simply obstacles to overcome. The three generators could conceivably end up racing one another without knowing anything about it.

Side Effects

Each of the generators is pulling Meme in a different direction and manifesting problems for one another without even suspecting it. The generators are each individually responding to Meme's needs. He doesn't understand what is happening to him and misreads the situation. He experiences side effects as symptoms and begins to treat the symptoms but he ignores the problem. By treating the symptoms Meme is mistreating the cause, is exacerbating the problem and is manifesting perceived illness for himself.

THE WISDOM OF ORACLES
BY JOHN RYAN

CHAPTER 14

ILLNESS

I think it'll end in th' end
Blow out and become nothing much
This foe is surely no friend
But a cripple must master his crutch.

I think I can live without crime
Don't dirty my ledger with blots
In fact I've been wrong a long time
But a leopard can live with its spots. *pil*

Never Intended

To focus on illness is to give it more power. Thus, to give time to the study of illness for its own sake is to increase it by making it acceptable. To be ill has become an acceptable way to be in the modern world. Meme does not have to accept illness and must realize it is not an innate part of man. It was never intended to be part of man and for Capsule even the thought of illness wouldn't be possible. Illness does not exist in any realm in the cosmos with the unique exception of Meme and must therefore be released. .

A Lack Of Awareness

Illness in all its guises is basically a lack of awareness. It is not an enemy. It is not incurable and is not in fact an entity in itself. The unfortunate thing is Meme has given it a name an identity in other words a What? In fact it has been given an uncountable range of different names categorized logically and intellectually in an effort to understand, that which does not need understanding.

Halls Of Fame

Everything from a sneeze to a wheeze from a cough to a cancer from an ache to a break has a What? name, a description as long as Meme's arm to firmly place it in the halls of fame in the illness industry. Every illness is separated, categorized, itemized and filed away. A wealth of information pertaining to its individual supposed causes, its effects, its possible cures and antidotes are stored in the great medical Grey Matter bank.

Body Of Work

There is such an accumulation of information so many man-hours so much blood sweat and tears over the years to painstakingly come up with cures for Meme's multiple illnesses. It's an extremely convincing body of work in fact brain boggling and Meme marvels at the ability to generate such a magnificently strong and convincing body of defense to fight the illness enemy.

Honourable Pursuit

Doctors, nurses, researchers, chemists, in fact all the dedicated people working in the medical services throughout the world devote their attention for the improvement of mankind. This is a very honourable pursuit filled with compassion and a genuine caring toward those that are perceived as ill.

Heroes Of Our Society

Charities are run by the dedication of people who devote their time and energy for the betterment of humanity. The genuine affection and understanding exhibited by these heroic people is astonishing. The health services, the charities and many other services in our communities are a measure of mans great ability to harness the genuine, intelligent, heart felt and physical energies toward the recovery of mankind.

Without these dedicated people the human race would have perished long ago. It is because of these caring people, the heroes of our society and the many more who have a genuine interest in the welfare of man, that mankind has so far survived the ravages of illness in our race. And they are heroic for very often charities and other services must deal with the inadequacies forced on them by well meaning but ineffective back up services disconnected from Aura Bora that seem to exacerbate rather than help the situation. For example, the various aspects of The Health Service can be generated by different agendas.

Little Continuity

One reason for this is that while one part of the service is generated by Ruby another part may be generated by Grey Matter and yet another by Young Nemo. Thus, there may be little continuity between the different aspects of the service, especially where one or all may be acting without guidance from Aura Bora.

Usually Grey Matter holds the power in the situation and if the other two aspects do not comply with Grey Matter logic they may be seen as putting up unnecessary resistance and will suffer the consequences. Ruby's response will be emotive and Young Nemo's will be physically active whereas Grey Matter will have a logical intellectual approach.

Each needs to realize the others approach for the backward and forward movement of this situation distracts from the original business and now the discord becomes the issue and separation is the outcome for each. For instance, there is often disconnection between government-run organizations and the services that depend on them. With connection to Aura Bora the generators would be working together and there would be no discord between them.

Different Directions

Because of misalignment in the three generators these services and others are being pulled in three different directions, 1. In the direction of Grey Matter orientated interests, which usually controls the administrative aspect of the service, 2. In the direction of Ruby orientated interests, which deals with the caring and emotional aspects of the service and 3. In the direction of Young Nemo which takes care of the practical, everyday, on the ground problems of the service

Discord

All three aspects of the service are going it alone with little or no continuity between them. This is truly a tragedy for although the three generators are well meaning and working in the interests of mankind the discord and lack of continuity between them brings about an unwanted and unasked for frustration leading to mistrust within the service.

Disconnection

This may be also true of all large organizations that experience discord and in all examples through life where there is a lack of continuity. **The only reason for discord in any individual, in any group, organization, department, government, country, group of countries or in the world is disconnection from Aura Bora** resulting in lack of coordination between the three generators. **All organizations are an extension of the individual. When the individuals within an organization realign themselves in time the whole organization can slowly realign.**

Contact The Capsule

Each organization has its own Aura Bora, present in those that run it that is not being consulted in the situation. All three generated aspects of the organization need to contact the Aura Bora of the organization to see which is the best way forward. This can happen from either one of the generators each of which has access to Aura Bora. Each individual generator will benefit from the connection and begin to set up meaningful communication with the other two generators.

Proven

Grey Matter may be gone onto overdrive at the notion that Aura Bora within an organization may need to be contacted. Instantly, Grey Matter will be able to come up with about twenty possible reasons why this could not be so. Equally, there may be about twenty seemingly valid arguments that could try to thrash this idea. The fact is that Grey Matter will not entertain the notion until it can be proven.

Capsule Qualities

The notion that Aura Bora needs to be contacted may be called arrogant, impossible, ignorant, unrealistic, unimaginable, downright ridiculous, undignified, definitely stupid, very silly, irresponsibly dangerous, unqualified, illogical and quite unintelligent. However, Grey Matter will not say it is unimaginative, uninventive, unintuitive or uninspiring because Grey Matter does not have access to these qualities. These are Capsule qualities and this notion is in fact inspirational, intuitive, inventive and imaginative.

Ignore

Meme may insist on looking at the large bank of information that's been collected over millennia. He may feel he owes it to all the dedicated people who have worked to accumulate this large body of information to not entertain such a notion as contacting Aura Bora. He may feel he owes it to the heroes of our time who dedicate their lives for the good of others to ignore this notion.

A Limit

Nevertheless, it is precisely because of these people that Meme needs to take this message seriously. Without these dedicated people we would not have come this far, we would be extinct as a race. Make no mistake about it these heroes have kept humanity alive up to now.

Now is the time to realize that this situation, this acceptance of discord cannot keep going on. There is a limit to man's endurance and we as a race have reached that limit once more in our history as we have done many times before.

ENOUGH! It is time to stop. It is time to listen to the truth. It is time to take note. It is time to take stock. It is time to change. It is time to move on in a different direction. Meme has endured the pain, he has wept for sorrow, he has suffered the illness, he has negotiated arguments, he has suffered the consequences of difference, he has battled with the enemy and he has fought the wars.

ENOUGH IS ENOUGH! THERE IS ANOTHER WAY!

The Other Way

The other way is not a trick, it is not an enemy, it is not just a promise, it is not a falsehood, it is not a temporary solution, it is not just imagined, it is not flippant, it is not ridiculously complicated, it is not intelligent, it is not heartfelt, it is not all action, it is not arrogant, it is not forceful, it is not costly.

The other way is unintelligent, unemotional, inactive, inexpensive, uncomplicated, unassuming, unsophisticated, underestimated, unpopular, undemanding, unexpected, non-expectant and not painful.

The other way is wise, knowing, inventive, intuitive, imaginative, informative, fulfilling, joyful, aware, accepting, peaceful and loving.

The other way is *Capsule truth.*

Facts:

Illness has small beginnings.
Meme causes his own illness.
There is no one to blame.
Illness is self-perpetuating.
Illness is contagious.
Illness is endemic.
Illness is a manifestation of Meme.
Illness grows
Illness is originally psychosomatic.
Illness is preventable.
Illness is self-curable.

Born With Illness

Some people are born with illness. Some say this is an affliction carried into the present life from a past life. Some say the illness takes place in the womb. Some say that the illness is passed on by one of the parents. Some say that this just happens for no apparent reason. Nevertheless, it is a manifest illness and needs no further investigation. How it came to be is of no real importance for all illness is ultimately the same from a Capsule perspective.

Small Beginnings

Almost all other illnesses have small beginnings and grow through a lack of awareness. These illnesses are caused by self and by continuously aggravating the situation or condition at an early stage. Eventually, the symptoms grow out of proportion through mismanagement. Usually at this stage the illness is recognized as such and given an identity.

Now it is truly manifest and something must be done to exterminate the offending illness. *The reason illness is not recognized at the early stage is because at the early stages it is not called illness.* Illness at the very early stages is not even called symptoms. Illness at the beginning stages is called by a collection of other names, which Meme doesn't relate to as illness but are in fact illness.

Beginnings Of Illness

Uncomfortable feelings, unfamiliar sensations, irrational thought, a reaction, arrogance, an abrasion, a broken fingernail, a bruise, a small ache etc. are all the beginnings of illness. In themselves they present no problems. Meme doesn't even class these as illnesses or as symptoms so slight are their presence. *However, these are the very beginnings of major illness and if not handled properly can have catastrophic consequences.*

Reaction

The symptoms or slight illnesses in themselves don't present a problem for Zenith. *What causes the problem is his reaction to them*. Illness begins small, very small and if he is even slightly put out by any of the above symptoms this is in fact the beginnings of illness for *in that small act of being put out, Zenith actually manifests the illness and thus transforms into Meme.*

Taken On A Responsibility

What needs to happen at this point is for Zenith to return the slight illness to Aura Bora and say 'you sort this out so I can get on with my life'. Instead of allowing Aura Bora to deal with it he chooses to take on the responsibility himself by allowing the generators first access. And this is the crunch. Zenith has taken on a responsibility unnecessarily. *This is a Capsule issue not a Meme issue, but the generators are being allowed to have first access.*

Grey Matter will put logic on it, Ruby will emote and Young Nemo will react impetuously and between the three of them they'll blow the whole situation out of all proportion.

Not Zenith's Business

It is not Zenith's business or responsibility to deal with Aura Bora issues no matter how small they may appear and once Zenith does this Aura Bora cannot now deal with the symptom. Zenith has taken on board a situation in which he has no business getting involved and given it over to Meme. *This is the very act that shuts the door on Aura Bora.* He has inadvertently ignored his Capsule in favour of Meme. This act is the beginning of Zenith's undoing. *A situation, which could easily be avoided, most often ends up completely altering his whole life's journey.*

Act Of Accepting

The more Zenith repeats this act of accepting responsibility for something that is not his responsibility the more he keeps shutting out Aura Bora. Initially the responsibility is taken on by one of the generators. If it is a physical condition like a scratch or a discomfort for example Young Nemo will take it on instead of returning it straight away to Aura Bora. If it is heartfelt like a slight disappointment or emotional hurt, it will be taken on by Ruby instead of being returned to Aura Bora. Grey Matter will deal with the responsibility if it is a slight offence or opinion or verbal arrogance instead of it being given over to Aura Bora.

Manifests Illness

It is in the act of not returning the symptom straight away to Aura Bora that Zenith through his generators manifests Meme illness. Zenith has allowed his generators to deal with the symptoms before Aura Bora.

When the generators receive the symptoms their first reaction is to send it straight to Aura Bora. However, if for any reason Zenith holds on to the symptoms and *reacts to it or acknowledges it for its own sake* that reaction is enough to send it to the generators for attention rather than Aura Bora. For instance, a driver who gives out internally about other drivers is reacting rather than allowing Aura Bora take over.

This is the initial access for illness into Meme through one of the generators. *The generators in turn could send the symptoms through Corigonus to Aura Bora but in most cases they are either not aware of this or have not been trained to respond in this way.*

Responsibility

Eventually, the acceptance of responsibility ends up with Grey Matter. Although, initially Ruby or Young Nemo may have taken it on they quickly refer it to Grey Matter who will usually assume overall responsibility for dealing with the illness, for now it becomes a medical problem.

Chain Of Events

If instead Zenith went straight to Corigonus with the symptom and dealt with it through Aura Bora all would be well. By fielding Grey Matter first in search of an answer he sets up a chain of events that result in a more serious illness.

Blocks Off Core

When Grey Matter takes on the symptoms, this causes a change in direction within the generator system. Instead of the flow of information coming upwards from Aura Bora through Corigonus it is now coming downwards from Grey Matter and thus, blocks off Core access. Now the three generators are shut off from Aura Bora and are operating in isolation.

The end result is Grey Matter acts out intelligently instead of mindfully, Ruby reacts emotionally rather than with feeling, and Young Nemo reacts irrationally rather than expressively. Now mindless reaction becomes the focus.

Pilot

The generators are now drawing on their own separate energies with the result that they are each operating without the pilot Aura Bora and are disconnected from one another. *As such they are uncoordinated in their response.*

Three Different Opinions

Meme is now being generated by three different opinions about the same condition, and while there is no discord, for all generators are operating above board and with the best intentions, nevertheless, Meme experiences confusion. Each generator sets off in its own direction without any continuity between them.

Manifests Opposites

Meme now experiences discord and perceives an enemy in the camp. Thus, he invents good and bad, right and wrong, the devil and Oracle, the ego as an entity. In other words Meme manifests opposites and entities to logically and intellectually (but not mindfully) explain the discord within.

Opposites Don't Exist

Not alone has Meme created illness he has created fear, loss, poverty, suffering, self-deception, enemies, mismanagement, anger and a whole range of unhealthy attitudes and values as well as opposites. Now we have right and wrong, good and bad, honesty and lies, left-brain and right brain, intelligence and stupidity, Oracle and devil and a whole range of other perceived opposites.

We take for granted that they always existed but as we've seen before, opposites don't exist in Cosmic reality. We only assume they exist because they've always been in Meme reality. We take for granted that they somehow belong in our lives. *We have given them rights to disrupt our lives and we don't question that right or from where it came.*

Slow Progression

We have built up institutions, organizations, sports and religions to nurture and encourage our belief in opposites. *In fact most of our everyday activities go toward the nurturing of that which does not exist.* Instead of encouraging that which can develop our lives we choose to concentrate our energy on juggling opposites. Forward movement in this situation is a slow progression.

Responsibility

All this happens first through Zenith not recognizing Aura Bora responsibility. By assuming responsibility for something that has nothing to do with him, he has inadvertently tripped himself up in life's process. *The only real responsibility Zenith has is to ensure everything goes through Corigonus.* That's it. He literally has no other responsibility to himself or to anybody else. Meme is so *conditioned to taking responsibility for everything this realization may not hit home, or indeed he may feel threatened by the implications.*

Running The Show

So now, instead of the three Capsule beings Aura Bora, Osmosis and Oracle running the show for Zenith, the three generators Grey Matter, Ruby and Young Nemo have taken over control for Meme. *This is how Zenith begins to create a life of illness and discord in all its Meme forms.*

Meme is in total control of Zenith's destiny on earth without Aura Bora intervention, he therefore could not be in any condition other than ill. *Meme is now operating mindlessly.* This is a fairly accurate description of conditions in the world today.

The Protagonist

The initial question Zenith asks to introduce illness into his body is 'What is this condition on my body?' The What? question is the protagonist in most of his disconnections from Aura Bora. Although, there can be many reasons why he would choose responsibility of a Capsule matter, the initial question of What? places Zenith firmly on the path to illness.

An Unusual Occurrence

This may appear to be an exaggeration or indeed an absurdity. It is not. Meme very likely will assume it is quite natural to expect discord in life because this has been his experience. He may have difficulty in understanding that *any discord is in fact an unusual occurrence.* Discord was not originally perceived by Capsule as part of the nature of humanity.

One Single Question

The notion that such a simple thing as a question could cause havoc may seem absurd to Grey Matter for its not logical or sensible to suggest such a thing. How could one single question be so powerful as to be one of the main causes of the destruction of mankind? This notion is not coming from a logical sensible place. This notion is coming from truth, wisdom and knowledge. In fact the word What? is given the status of an oracle.

THE WISDOM OF ORACLES
BY JOHN RYAN

CHAPTER 15

THE PLAGUE

Life Of A Flea
Wednesdays the pawnshop is shut
Tuesdays his money is low
Thursdays the PO Girl gives him his cut
Mondays there's no place to go.

Sunday morning he lies in bed late
Friday there's fish for the tea
Saturdays stew is Radio Two
-A week in the life of a Flea. *pil*

Tiny thoughts

When it finally sinks in that it is acceptance of a tiny symptom that is responsible for illness Zenith can isolate it and eliminate it out of his life. The Bubonic Plague, an epidemic that occurred in Europe in The Middle Ages, otherwise known as The Black Death, was a mystery until it was discovered that the cause of the plague was in fact a tiny flea. Once the symptom is located it can be dealt with. The cause of a deadly plague can also be a tiny thought.

Almost all Meme's plagues and illnesses are manifested from tiny thoughts. That tiny thought is the thought of imperfection. **Zenith is in fact in a perfect state** when connected to his Capsule (take a look back at the Zenith Diagram at the front of the book). Capsule in fact protects Zenith. What Meme has done is reversed the situation and placed importance on self.

Kills Off Zenith

The reason for this reversal is a deadly plague. This deadly Meme plague kills off Zenith's connection to Aura Bora and in the process **kills his knowledge, wisdom, creativity, joy, intuition, inspiration, imagination and his inventiveness** and replaces them with, sifting, emotion, reaction, illness, worry, doubt, loss and pain. Eventually Meme will kill Zenith unless he realizes the need for change.

To Core

There is one way that Meme can realize change and that is by cleansing generator siftings. Zenith must make mindful decisions about thoughts rather than Meme orientated decisions. He must eliminate Meme mode and replaced it in him.

To do this he must realize each possible thought that enters Grey Matter and bring it straight to Core instead of holding onto it in his brain. If his brain holds onto the possible thought it begins an analysis and gives it Meme importance and steers all three generators into plagued waters.

Bubonic Plague

This in fact is one of Zenith's main life problems in Meme mode he is analytical. Analysis of every thing is openly encouraged in the western world. It is a most dangerous activity particularly when used for personal analysis of conditions and perceived illnesses pertaining to Meme. Self-analysis from a Meme perspective is modern man's bubonic plague. Self-analysis from An Aura Bora perspective has a totally different outlook with a completely different intention and result.

Encourages Doubt

Zenith is perfect but Meme self-analysis encourages doubt in him and drags him into the imperfection of Meme, nit picking him to pieces. **It is a Grey Matter exercise and its continued use ensures he stays in Meme mode.** It is enabling to Meme and Meme only.

Into A Plague

The encouragement of en masse self-analysis is a most destructive past time because it assumes imperfection in Zenith. The well-meaning efforts to understand him ensure he is seen only in the role as Meme. He is thus, **never seen as his authentic self**. Grey Matter is encouraged to examine every perceived thought, related past events almost every inflection in his life down to the last flea to evaluate them and encourage expression of them into a plague.

Personal Opinion

The expression 'everybody is entitled to an opinion' is so much taken for granted that to place doubt on it may be considered outrageous but what when this opinion is purely Meme generated? 'Of course I'm entitled to my opinion,' shouts Meme. So prevalent is personal opinion that on T.V. and radio, newspapers and magazines etc. as well as in everyday conversation Meme's personal opinion is absolutely rammed down Zenith's throat.

If he could take a step back, and it may be a very large step, for just a moment and examine this phenomenon he may realize that Meme personal opinion is yet another oracle. Now not only can Meme cause a plague with his misdirected perceived thoughts, but Meme is **entitled** to cause a plague.

Opposite Ends

Meme is so good at analyzing but he doesn't see the connection between self-opinion and a plague. In fact he insists on his rights to eliminate himself and the rest of humanity's reputation in the process. If he ever discovers this plague Meme will throw his hands in the air and proclaim 'I had nothing to do with it' and he'd be correct 'I' had nothing to do with it whereas Meme had everything to do with it.

I, and Meme are situated at opposite ends of The First Truth, as we will discover later in the chapter on Truth.

THE WISDOM OF ORACLES
BY JOHN RYAN

CHAPTER 16

WHAT?

What circles d'you move in
What houses do you haunt
What faces fair d'you ensnare
With blue eyes, on your jaunt?

What characters are left awry
Once you've made your mark
What little sight'll by and by
Turn you into a shark?

What buildings do you knock up
With an intent air
What creatures do you cock up
But then, what do you care?

What circles d'you move in
What houses do you haunt
What faces fair d'you ensnare
With blue eyes, on your jaunt? *pil*

The What? Question

The What? question is any question that puts emphasis on worldly matters rather than Capsule matters, in other words the 'What' rather than the 'Who'. The question does not have to begin with the word What? however, very often it does. The What? question has helped to deform the basis of civilization in the western world.

Meme is for the most part a What? person. Almost all of his existence is based on a value system run by What? What is Meme? What does Meme have? In What house is he living? In What work is he involved? What does he earn? What's his wife like? What about his children? What dog? What pastime? What golf club? What T.V? What computer? What kind of kitchen? What suite of furniture? What store? What clothes? etc. These are some of the elements that make up the world of What?

The Yard Stick

One of the most important questions is how much money does he have? (Even though the word What? is not mentioned in this question it is still described as a What? question because the emphasis is on the material world). For this dictates what station he has in life. This is the ultimate yard stick by which everything is measured. If he has no money in the world of What? then to what good could he possibly come? The pursuit of What? is a major cause of disconnection in Meme society.

In times of recession the disconnection is more evident. Meme is like a rabbit in the headlights caught by the sudden absence of What? His whole What? world collapses in a heap and he is genuinely afraid of the consequences. What people can he blame for putting him in this position? What will Meme do now?

Virtues

The lure of What? has transfixed Meme into a driven, mindless, generated activist. The extreme What? pursues, it charges, it races, it chases, it propels, is hungry, repetitive, dogged, competitive, arrogant, demanding, over inquisitive, greedy, speedy, needy, noisy, pushy, demonstrative, relentless, continuous, cantankerous, accumulative, bossy etc.

When we look at these supposed virtues that are evident under the name of What? none of them possess a molecule of humanity. These are not virtues that propagate respect for humanity. The

What? word is a force of destruction. The pursuit of What? is one of the main forces of destruction in Meme's life. To be active in any one of these pursuits is not healthy for him. To be generated into accepting all of them sets him up on the road of destruction. In fact it's inevitable he will self-destruct.

Main Function

By pursuing What? Meme has been taken over by his three generators. He is racing ever faster, mindlessly, in a continuous overlapping of facts, emotions and reactions, solely focused on his Meme life. Generators by nature are totally absorbed in their activities whether they are connected to Aura Bora or not. This is their main function, in fact their only function in life.

Different Intelligences

When Aura Bora is not engaged to guide the energies of the three generators they self generate and present their individual reactions to life's situation. Meme is presented with three different reactions from within sending him in three different directions. They are in fact **three different Intelligences sending out three different independent uncoordinated messages on a given subject.**

The first is intellectual and generated by Grey Matter, the second emotive and generated by Ruby and the third impetuous and generated by Young Nemo. Because they are uncoordinated messages, Meme experiences confusion and he may not know how to deal with that.

Two Ways

In the end Meme has two ways to go, either, 1. He is decisive and decides to go with one of the generators. This decision may contain elements of the other two generators, or 2. He is indecisive and bounces continually between the three choices never actually coming to a decision.

Either way whether he is decisive or not the outcome will be the same, it will be inaccurate. It will be intelligent but not knowledgeable, honest but not true, constructive but unimaginative.

Personalities

This ultimately is what separates different generated personalities. Where Meme is decisive he may go straight in favour of one of the three generators. Where the emphasis is on Grey Matter he will have an intellectual personality. Where the emphasis is on Ruby he will be emotive and where he the emphasis is on Young Nemo he will favour physicality. Which generator he considers second and which third will also affect his personality.

Where Meme is indecisive he may intellectualize with one generator, emote with another and be impetuous with the third, continually changing between the three generators not quite coming to a complete conclusion. Depending on the particular mix of characteristics, he can display any of six different personality types being decisive and six more in indecisive mode a total of twelve different personality types.

Options

Where there are a large number of people for example a committee, a large organization, local authority, corporation, government etc. there can be up to twelve different opinions from twelve different personalities relating to any given situation. A lot of unnecessary effort could be saved if these twelve sets of generators were connected to their Aura Bora.

The Next Meeting

Instead of designing a world for future generations with Aura Bora guidance and with emphasis on quality, **Meme is deciding the future by past experience for current necessity with the element of What? or worldly matters the only important consideration.**

In most cases plans for the future only go as far as the next business or board meeting. There is little or no consideration for the needs of future generations. The quick fix in our fast moving world can suit What? and all its implications. We're too busy with What? to stop and think of what the consequences related to our What? orientated world are having on our actual world.

Never Intended

The question What? is that which requests for a statement to be repeated. It's an exclamation of surprise or anger or inquisition, a complete word-sentence in itself. *What? was never intended to be used and indeed abused in the multitude of areas in which it has current use.*

What? has penetrated our whole society and particularly in the past one hundred years. What? has taken on new meaning in the media, in science, in medical practice generally, in education, in religion and every other subject. The persistence with the What? question pertaining to Meme is one of the prime causes of manifesting doubt in the human race because the answer to the question is a generated answer.

Above Board

The many people working in these areas are thoroughly well intentioned and completely above board and these services are run by dedicated caring and highly qualified people with impeccable records. Most are generated by honourable intentions and with the highest qualifications gleaned from many years of hard work and study culminating in a massive bank of information.

These facts above may present the ultimate barrier to Meme's ability in recognizing truth.

This Boy

What's your number, what's your name,
What's your business, what's your game,
What's your heartache, what's your joy,
What's your answer to This Boy? *pil*

Information

The net effect of all this accumulated information, the sheer volume of evidence to back up the reputation of these institutions makes it difficult for anybody involved in the industries to see there may be another way of perceiving life. By their nature they encourage the positive application of the question What? and thus, encourage doubt in Meme as a complete person. In fact they are built almost exclusively on the word, and Meme's authenticity comes into question at the mention of the What? word.

The Challenge

The main drawback is the lack of recognition of the three aspects of Capsule; Oracle, Osmosis and Aura Bora and almost total concentration on generated Meme who may be viewed as somehow incomplete or ill. Meme is in fact complete and is not ill whether he knows it or not. Some aware practitioners are making progress, for example Candace Pert with her Aura Bora approach to science and Stanislav Grof with his approach in psychotherapy and slowly some industries are advancing toward recognizing and acknowledging the value of Capsule.

The challenge is to realize Meme in relation to Aura Bora, that he is an important aspect of life and that he would not exist without Aura Bora.

Dependent

A large part of current practice is earth bound and very much dependent on the What? question. The fact that it is held in such esteem and indeed depended upon by Meme may present a large stumbling block to the understanding of his Capsule and of truth.

By manifesting a stumbling block the purpose of investigation would be reversed. *Instead of serving mankind, as was the original intention, like so many institutions and inventions, they may in fact stand in the way of their very own original intentions and block understanding of Meme and Zenith.*

The Understanding

It is the act **of treating Meme as a separate entity** from Aura Bora that creates all his troubles. Practically all of his activities are orientated toward Meme as an entity presuming to be Capsule.

In medicine Meme's body is the main and most often the only factor taken into consideration. When several centuries ago a certain doctor began to incise human bodies for medical research, the then Pope gave permission for this research on the understanding that medicine dealt solely with the body and left Oracle matters in the hands of the church. From then on body matters and Oracle matters were dealt with as separate identities.

Today, even though there is no longer reason for it we continue this same practice because we have fallen into the pattern of it and don't question the pattern. Simply because we take it for granted, or we assume because we have no alternative way of progressing, we base most of our medical practice on a ruling that, while it may have made sense then, certainly makes no sense today.

Institutions

Now of course, there are institutions that have grown up around these rulings which copper fastens them. Now these rules form the basis of our value systems and attitudes even when they no longer make sense and we bind ourselves to them for security. It's like chaining ourselves to a slowly sinking ship out of fear instead of learning how to swim.

We have forgotten how to look for alternatives. We have become comfortable allowing not just these but many of our institutions make What? decisions for us and when these decisions are not working, other What? compensations keep us trapped. For example, where a drug free policy could be an effective means of reducing drug addiction, a government's use of methadone as a supposed treatment for heroin addicts ensures profit for the manufacturer at the expense of the life of the addict.

When an institution becomes fearful of change it has lost its effectiveness and becomes protective and self-serving. **Almost all our institutions are suffocating under the weight of their generated rules and misguided values, struggling to survive and at the same time keeping a firm thumb down on change.**

Individuals

All institutions are made up of individuals. Each individual is responsible for keeping institutions alive. Ultimately, it is the collective individuals who decide to either support or not support an institution but fear of change is binding. Awareness of Capsule begins with the individual. It is from individual awareness that awareness on a larger scale takes place and eventually impacts to make the necessary changes.

Different Systems

As with different institutions Meme is catered for by different systems. The systems are designed to take care of his needs, for example the educational system is responsible for Grey Matter, the sports system for his Young Nemo, whilst the religious system is seen at least on the outside as being responsible for Oracle matters.

Special Status

Grey Matter is considered to be the most important of the three generators. Meme has truly fixed his fate with special attention to his brain for not only has he divided himself from his **mindful** Capsule he has now placed his Grey Matter in a class of its own and dedicated a whole education system to its development and care. Almost all of the subjects taught in schools and colleges are orientated toward the practical application of world only matters or What? Meme interests. There is little or no emphasis or indeed understanding on Capsule matters in our everyday subjects.

Searches His Brain

In an attempt to find his Mind, Meme searches his brain, fully convinced when he finds it there he will be able to exert control over its unethical practices. He has even narrowed the playing field to one side of his brain in an attempt to find it adamant it couldn't be anywhere else.

It's like the joke about the guy who lost money on the street at nighttime and was searching under the streetlight. When eventually he was asked whether he was sure he dropped the money here he answered, 'no I dropped the money over there but there's no light over there'.

Control Of The Species

Grey Matter is considered the most important of the three generators Ruby is considered the second and Young Nemo the third most important. This ranking system creates a separate set of problems.

Since most men are Grey Matter orientated they have most control over the species. Woman is ranked second because of her connection to heart in Ruby and adolescents third because of their connection to Young Nemo. Since children have only two generators they are seen as disadvantaged and are lowest in the ranking system in western society.

Reversed

Adults have little or no regard for children's intellectual capabilities, for children are considered too young and inexperienced. From a Capsule perspective this whole system is reversed for not alone are children in contact with Capsule, but as a result, they are truthful, knowledgeable and wiser than most adult. But when adults play the generator game such talents take second place. Most women are naturally more open to Capsule connection than most men since they are closer to their emotions and more often operate Ruby.

Children are naturally connected to Capsule and it's this understanding that adults need to tap into.

Meme Logic

Meme has worked out that Capsule must be part of Grey Matter and as such can be governed by logic. Meme religions make no distinction between Cosmic and Oracle viewing them together as the one and only God. Grey Matter goes a step further with its logic and works out that Cosmic/Oracle is a 'Him' and is to be feared at worst. However, if Meme adores Him enough he won't be punished much for his sins. So, Cosmic/Oracle or God Is suspected as being a kindly but somewhat manipulative terrorist. This is the state of our collective value system.

THE WISDOM OF ORACLES
BY JOHN RYAN

CHAPTER 17

SEPARATION TO UNITY

Nothing is a Nobody
Nothing is a nobody
Nothing's ever blue
Nothing isn't anything
Nothing isn't U.

Nothing was what Something is
And Nothing doesn't do
Nothing never ever sees
That Nothing isn't true.

Nothing isn't red or green
And Nothing's neither, either
Nothing's one and only is
To be the indecider. *pil*

Separate Aspect

One of the major problems in Meme's world is that he is seen as a **complete entity in himself**, as a separate aspect to his Capsule. From the point of view of institutions he is a body without an innate value. Oracle and Cosmic are a religion issue and Grey Matter is an education issue.

Meaningful Change

Even with this separation a further complication arises where the emphasis is almost exclusively on generator intelligences. **There is little or no input into Cosmic and Capsule matters**. Even religion is heavily orientated toward generator intelligence rather than Cosmic/Oracle knowledge as will be seen later in the chapter on Truth.

The possibility of viewing Meme from a Capsule context is therefore minimal and in most cases it just doesn't happen. It follows that **any development toward meaningful change must begin with Meme himself**.

Institutions are so heavily ingrained in their current ways and by nature they are somewhat inflexible. It would take a huge shift of awareness for them to make the most minimal change. For example, the primary and secondary education system supports the teaching of many subjects often useless to the student during and after leaving school at the expense of practical everyday and Capsule orientated subjects.

Protection

Furthermore, because institutions are mostly brain generated they would come up with every logical generated reason to dispute any new findings, for they are built to protect the generated interests of the institution. This would not be an attempt to undermine the new findings, rather it would be intended as a protection of Meme. Generators take their work very seriously and are exemplary in their efforts to keep Meme safe from what appears to them as unwelcome outside intrusion.

Protect The Work

This action is often misconstrued as an attempt to undermine new research especially in the medical and science areas. However, this is largely untrue. Dedicated people in both these areas and in other institutions work hard to maintain a high standard and it's understandable that they would want to protect the work and indeed what they see as the invaluable research in their possession.

Proving

It is a logical progression that generated institutions would insist that their generated criterion be met. This often entails the proving of every last detail so they can be considered as a valid part of the already stored information. This is a very necessary part of the process of generated intelligence, generated emotion and generated activity, and indeed necessary for the preservation of generated institutions.

Watertight

Any individual who wishes their information, their research, new findings or discoveries to be included in the generated institution must accompany their findings with extensive proof of their validity.

This process guarantees watertight protection of the institution involved and the generator-orientated principals employed. **It also guarantees that the institutional world as we know it may take some time to realize the truth of its own existence**.

Disconnection

Grey Matter orientated organizations reinforce disconnection by always placing doubt in front of Meme who was never intended to be in doubt. It is the disconnection from Aura Bora that puts him in doubt. It is the disconnection or separation of institutions and organizations from their own Aura Bora that puts them in doubt and leads them in the direction of proof searching.

No Need For Illness

There is no need for proof in Aura Bora world. There is no need for fearful action, there is no need for doubt, there is no need for discord, no need for illusion, no need for anger, no need for mistrust, for frustration, for pain, anxiety, illness, fighting, hunger, poverty, war or any other disconnection in the human condition. **These are all symptoms of separation only seen in Meme humanity**.

Meaningful Development

Capsule's initial intention for Zenith was different from the way it has turned out in Meme. The current attitudes and values he holds dear and in turn the institutions built on these self same separating values and attitudes, **stand in the way of progress toward a meaningful development**. Meme measures his interaction with the world by his values and **where separation is a major part of his value system, interaction and indeed life in general is made much more difficult**.

Value System

The value system Zenith employs is ultimately what protects him or exposes him on his journey through life. It forms the basis for his principals and attitudes and his connection to others. Families, communities, organizations, religions, institutions, leaders, politicians, governments, countries etc., each have their own set of values to which Meme looks for reassurance in the formation of his own personal value system.

Collective Values

These collective values never the less are made up from combined individual values for what is seen to be the greater good of society. **It is the individual that is ultimately responsible** for family, community, organization's, government department's, leader's, government's and country's values, **and it is the individual who will ultimately change collective values** when they are found to be working against Zenith's best interests.

Unity

Slowly but surely as each Meme recognizes his own individuality in connection to everybody else the outlook of the world can gradually change to one of unity and to solidarity, instead of separate intentions, to a single goal, to health instead of illness, to wealth instead of poverty, to joy instead of misery, to peace instead of war, to confidence instead of fear and to unity of purpose instead of separation. This indeed is our birthright. This indeed was Capsule's original intention for the people of this world. **This is indeed possible to achieve**. Without unity we will continue to live as we have done in the past, playing the generator game.

Awareness

The future of humanity the future of the world and the future of each Meme in the world depends on one thing - Awareness. Meme must become aware, aware of the precarious position toward which he is speeding, aware it is not necessary to continue heading in this direction, aware of the immediate need to alter course, aware that by altering course he will benefit greatly, aware that with the benefits there are no compromising paybacks, aware that he can place his future on a safe footing. Awareness eliminates separation and brings unity.

One Unit

Meme can come together with his Capsule as one unit and in the process realize the true meaning of life through his Grey Matter intelligence, his Ruby emotions and his Young Nemo actions. He can achieve this without victims, without illness, without symptoms. He does not have to put up a fight for fighting of itself does not achieve anything. There will be no need for him to try to convince, for this would be forceful. There is no need for any kind of discord.

The only true way is to live life through Aura Bora to be in constant contact with Aura Bora to embrace the truth, to live the way and in the process **accept every other way as it wishes to be**. There is need for encouraging and for caring, for actively embracing the new way **without argument, without blame, without strife, without fight, without separation**.

Togetherness can be achieved with **acceptance and active unity** of purpose.

THE WISDOM OF ORACLES
BY JOHN RYAN

CHAPTER 18

TIME

The Measure Of Time
In a world where time is the measure of our existence such a notion as timelessness may seem impossible. The measure of time seems to be of utmost importance to Meme. He has measured time in seconds as the 1/60th part of a minute, minutes as 1/60th part of an hour, hours the 1/24th part of a day, days the approximate 1/30th part of a month and month 1/12th part of the year. Even the years are numbered so Meme can look back and remember precisely when a particular event from the past happened, so tied up is he in the past.

Record Of Existence
Meme can pin down any event, any achievement, any record or information to the time and date that it happened. The purpose of this is to reinforce his knowledge of himself. The effect of this is to firmly place Meme on terra firma, to ensure his record of existence in the world. It is by this record he measures his progress through the ages up to present day.

Rituals
Mans knowledge and rituals in the past were deeply rooted in the earth, the awareness of Cosmic and of the natural passage of time. The rituals of the day and the natural seasons were in themselves the basis of Zenith's existence. His rituals were what kept him in touch with his Capsule. The Aura Boras of his forefathers were remembered and each Zenith was part of Cosmic the great collective consciousness of all that existed.

Oneness
There was in fact a sense of timelessness, of belonging, of being, a deep satisfying awareness of oneness with all of life. The naturalness of pace was taken as a normal phenomenon, not questioned, just accepted.

The Time
With the introduction of industrialization Zenith's idea of time changed radically. The time clock was introduced into the workplace and thus, every second became a measure. **What had been a natural flow almost overnight switched into a second by second recorder of life**. Meme became watchful of time for its own sake and time became and was eventually accepted as the new strange oracle.

The Ultimate Oracle
Time is no longer a strange oracle. Time has become a very acceptable oracle. In fact this is an oracle that Meme has learned not to be able to live without. He even carries a measure of time on his person so every second of every day can be called up at will. Records of time breaking are now the measure of success. The new oracle has a new status and **time breaking is now the ultimate oracle of modern man**.

Adores Time
Today's value of time and the monitoring of time is to a large extent an abuse of time. It compels people to be involved in the constant measure of time and in the racing against time. It encourages the desire to be ahead of time. The prizes for being ahead of time are treasured. Time is it. Time is the ultimate. But time is a double-edged sword. The more time Meme gives to time the less time he has. The more he adores time the

less time has for him so the more he must adore it.

Catch 22

This is like the dog chasing his own tail not realizing it's attached. The faster the dog chases his tail the faster he has to chase it, for it's running away from him at the same speed he is chasing it. This is the ultimate catch 22 where Meme is caught in a trap of his own making. For instance, where he is so caught up spending all his valuable time in work to make excessive amounts of money he may even lose his family to divorce.

Abuse Of Time

Time was never intended to be treated in this manner but try to change the status quo and straight away there would be an outcry. It is not time itself Meme needs to eliminate *it is the abuse of time*. The abuse of time has brought him to his current state of being. Meme in the western world is almost exclusively concerned with time and its management.

Higher

The effect of this self-afflicted abuse is taking its toll on Meme for he is now a slave to time. When the ultimate oracle, time, cracks its whip Meme jumps higher and higher each time in response. When time oracle calls Meme comes running faster each time. The higher he jumps and the faster he runs the less this intolerant oracle appreciates him. However, he is too engrossed in jumping and racing to notice that looking after his time oracle has turned him into a time abuser.

Abuser

All abusers have good excuses, convincing arguments, logical sounding reasons, it's what abusers do best, and time abusers are no different. Time is a substance like any other. When it is abused by Meme time can take control. Handled carefully though it can be a wonderful gift.

Abuse Of Time

The abuse of time is evident in all walks of life. In cities especially, the pace of life is exaggerated. People walk at a fast pace with the next appointment foremost in their awareness and with scant attention to their immediate surroundings. Public transport is crammed with people whose only objective is reaching their destination on time, so they can spend work time concentrating on how fast they can get through work to get back home and crash out in front of T.V. On our roads certain drivers rarely keep the speed limit. Many of our children are forced into adulthood sooner than is necessary. Attention seems to be constantly focused on the future at the expense of present activity.

A Mask

On the surface everything seems to be working smoothly. However, a look beneath the surface shows a completely different picture. Meme sees nothing out of place on the surface because he is satisfied most of the time. If he does notice something out of place he usually is too preoccupied with time to give it recognition. He doesn't really want to notice anything out of place, this would put him in a position of responsibility and he really can't afford the time to deal with anything but his hurried life.

So, Meme puts on a mask and he uses the mask to hide him from the world. The mask he wears is very subtle and of course it's not called mask. It's called suit, or uniform, designer clothes, flash car, brief case, mobile phone, makeup, lunch appointment, important meeting, working late etc. *A lot of hiding can go on behind a suit*. In fact **mask** can hide him behind so many useful and acceptable guises it's difficult to distinguish the mask from the real thing or if indeed there exists a real thing. For instance, a cleric involved in sexual abuse, or a respectable business man who owes a lot of money.

Ride Roughshod

Whilst wearing the mask Meme can assume he has permission to abuse not alone himself but also others. The abuse of time is not called abuse nor is the abuse of self or of others. Make no mistake, that's what it is. When Meme needs to get things done faster and he needs to jump higher a whole range of issues can be taken for granted because no time has been given to them. As a result he may ride roughshod over most of **life and his values and attitudes can take on a whole new dimension.**

THE WISDOM OF ORACLES
BY JOHN RYAN

CHAPTER 19

SPEEDING THROUGH TIME

Quick, jump to it, don't be slow
(I've cracked my li'l whip, you know)
Everything's up to the mark
When I'm not left in the dark.

Step it out, there isn't any
Reason, you're just one of many
Waiting on the Big Cheese – me
To see what only he can see.

And so again I'll say it loud
And clear to you, on your cloud
That I'm the Business, you're my prop
-If I roar, you're heart will stop.

Quick, jump to it, don't be slow
(I've cracked my li'l whip, you know)
Everything's up to the mark
When I'm not left in the dark. *pil*

First Consideration

Speedy solutions now take first place to that which was once of utmost importance to Meme. For example, many fast food outlets ensure their customers don't stay too long eating. To achieve an aim with speed is one thing, to go so far as to completely change the value of the experience and to get caught up in that is quite another. There is a tendency to be always racing, constantly primed up to speed without realizing the consequences. Speed then becomes the first consideration over the importance of the activity.

Second Place

Speed is abused when the quality of the activity suffers as a result of it, when the race against time becomes the first consideration. The main activity then takes second place to the achievement of speed and suffers as a result. For instance, a tradesman whose main aim is to finish the job may very well take short cuts at the expense of the quality of the work.

Acceptable Norm

One of the problems is Meme's lack of awareness of his own actions. Once racing becomes the focus awareness of the important issues becomes lessened. With less awareness standards begin to slide and what once may have been unacceptable now is seen in a different light.

Now the unacceptable becomes the norm and the norm becomes acceptable. The unacceptable hasn't upped the standard to be acceptable but simply became known as acceptable and has become an everyday occurrence. For example, many processed foods often lack the real taste of the original product and are artificially enhanced but are quicker to cook.

Meme gets used to a lowered standard being around and a lower standard becomes the acceptable norm. He may grumble about it but may also do nothing about it, justifying his acceptance by his own lowered standard.

Shifted Focus

One of the problems here is Meme has shifted his focus from the standard of the activity to the standard of the speed. He is satisfied with the speed and once the standard of the activity is close enough it is accepted for what it is because it was quick. The more this happens the lower go the standards.

Knock On Effect
This has a knock on effect across all walks of life. It affects productivity in the work place, standard of workmanship, standards of products, standards of behaviour, standards of etiquette, of entertainment, of food, of services, of institutions, of governments, of T.V., of advertising. It allows us to accept abuse at all levels.

A Compromise
In the work place anything that adds to the speed in which a job can be completed may be taken on board even to the detriment of the job itself. New equipment may be installed on the basis that it can get the job done quicker. A poor second to this can be the question of standard. The standard may not be what it was before but a compromise is made for the sake of speed. For instance, fresh fruit and vegetables are artificially fertilized at the expense of taste and quality to the point where it is acceptable to slowly poison the consumer who pays through ill health for the privilege.

The Standard
This is not to say that all things achieved with speed have a lower standard. Often the standard is improved as well as speed. This will only happen where the standard is the first consideration.

Speed
There is a need for greater awareness around the issue of speed. The tendency for Meme to accept the abuse of speed is linked with his dependency to the three generators. Generators by their nature will activate at a faster speed when they come up against a perceived obstacle for they do not have a reverse gear.

However, a generator's emphasis is always toward rightful action, even though it may appear to sometimes be the opposite and may even seem to be working against common sense. They don't know how to be anything else but generators and have no knowledge about opposition since they never in themselves experience opposition. They simply serve Meme to the best of their individual abilities.

Addicted
Meme is going through life disconnected from Aura Bora and as a result has no concept of timelessness. He is not just orientated toward time he is addicted to racing with time. He can't live without it and has no understanding for others who don't share his enthusiasm for racing through life at top speed.

Little Irritations
Meme doesn't always feel good about himself. He often gets symptoms, but that's okay, these are all part of life in the fast lane and he can expect that. Besides, they're not really symptoms he tells himself, they're so slight, just little irritations, mostly caused by other people who are just not as fast as or as high an achiever as himself. People who hold him back from getting the job finished and out of the way fast.

Life In The Fast Lane
Meme has quite a lot of friends who act just like he does and this reinforces his opinion on how right he really is to be the aggressive go-getter. The fact that he has to drive over some slower people to get where he's going is incidental, a part of life in the fast lane.

Exhausted

The little irritations he experiences don't really go away unless Meme deals with them. But he's too busy getting ahead to be concerned about small matters like uneasy feelings, confused thinking or the occasional headache. He takes care of the headaches with the little packet of pills he always carries just in case he needs it.

The odd brandy he used to take just at the weekends now comes in handy at the end of a hard working day. The sleeping tablets are great for making sure he gets a bit of shut-eye. Mind you, he shouldn't really have a problem sleeping so exhausted is he after a hard day, so it just takes one small tablet each night to settle him.

Serious Encounter

Meme used never smoke, well just an odd one with the brandy, but he finds it helps him to unwind especially after a serious encounter with a slow client.

The Buzz

Meme takes a cup of coffee in the morning, no breakfast because he's never hungry in the morning. Even at lunchtime he's not hungry so he just grabs a sandwich, there's really not much time for more. Besides, two or three cups of coffee with a lot of sugar during the day, is just what he really needs. They really hit the spot, they give him that extra edge, it's just the buzz he needs.

Unwind

Meme doesn't overeat he's good like that. He really eats just once a day. He has dinner before the brandy later on at night about an hour before he goes to bed. He's better able to unwind at that time. The dinner and brandy in front of the T.V. they put him right back on target.

Unreasonable Demands

Meme changed companies last year. His boss was always on his back making unreasonable demands, so he decided he'd had enough and moved. The problem is this new boss turns out to be exactly the same as the old one, he's always complaining about the standard of work. He gets his work in before anybody else, but his boss is still not happy. He doesn't like Meme's ideas either, says their not original, there's just no pleasing him.

The boss is always telling him to slow down, he just doesn't understand Meme has a reputation for speed he prides himself on getting the job done. He's not one of those team workers he likes to take things to the edge himself he's that kind of guy.

Confused

There are a lot of similar Memes in the world hard working, motivated, energized, good and honest workers with plenty of drive and enthusiasm in their generators. The problem is their generators are operating without their Aura Bora. Their intentions are excellent but their direction is confused and uncoordinated.

Runaway Train

Without Aura Bora contact Meme is like a runaway train with just one destination, disaster. He's real problem is he doesn't see a problem. He's in the generator game and doesn't realize there is another way. He is steadily becoming less happy each day but doesn't even notice. He knows there's a problem but can't quite pin it down.

Occasionally, Meme stops for a break, takes a holiday and relaxes with the family. He promises himself he'll do this more often but within a couple of weeks he's back on the treadmill plugging away at it again.

Don't Give Up

Meme is getting older at this stage and quite tired of this running around. His health is not the best but since he's had the triple bye-pass he feels the urge to go at it again. Those generators just don't give up in fact they just keep going to the very end. Usually its an earlier end than was originally planned, but that's generators for you, they give it everything, always working for the best result, each generator to its own calling, each one able to overcome the many disruptions to its progress by going faster each time.

Under Pressure

What Meme doesn't understand is that there is no need for him to put in such a huge effort. There are other elements available to him just waiting to give a hand. Whilst he is actually killing himself in a hurry by putting himself under so much pressure, Aura Bora is waiting patiently in the wings willing to take part in his life, but he doesn't see that and he just doesn't really get what its all about. He's too busy or scared to stop and take stock of what he is actually doing and so he's blinkered.

Free Will

Aura Bora is fully aware of where Meme is heading but won't interfere because he has free will. He's so busy fighting the world all the way it doesn't occur to him there might be another way of getting through life. What he has done is to ensure for himself an unhappy life with guaranteed multiple illnesses in a large cocktail of troubles, a conglomeration of brain games, a bunch of emotional trauma and a variety of excessive activities *all of which are preventable by engaging Aura Bora through Core*. Meme could be living a life of complete harmony with a totally healthy disposition, a life of joy, of peace, of tranquility and of coordination with time.

A Welcome Companion

Whenever Aura Bora comes back into his life he is able to let go control of time and his life comes back into focus. Aura Bora was always meant to be available to him, for time under the guidance of Aura Bora is a totally different set of circumstances.

Now time can take its rightful place in Meme's life and rather than controlling every aspect it's now just another element of his life. Time is no longer the unforgiving oracle it used to be. Now it is a welcome companion on the journey through life.

The Important Factor

Instead of being always at it's beck and call, Meme can use time sensibly. Instead of trying to save time now he can give time freely. It is not the act of saving time that is important in life it *is the act of giving time* that is the important factor. To take away time is to steal a valuable asset, to give time is to give an invaluable gift.

THE WISDOM OF ORACLES
BY JOHN RYAN

CHAPTER 20

GIVING TIME

Beneficial
The act of just giving time freely is most beneficial to any activity. The Meme who doesn't have enough time is the one losing out on life. Giving time freely is a most rewarding act one which guarantees joy for all concerned particularly the giver of time. Of all the things modern man can do for his fellow man the act of giving time is very valuable particularly in this day and age.

Giving
By giving time Meme is showing he is not too busy to deal with the seemingly trivial things in life. **When time is given to the smallest problem this is the very thing that keeps Zenith in contact with Aura Bora**. It is the smallest act that is the important one. From small acts grow larger acts, from larger acts grow big acts and from big acts grow enormously important acts. In fact, the act of giving small amounts of time is hugely important and is the act of engagement and of appreciation of one's fellow man, for instance, giving a person the small courtesy of opening a door for them or just slowing down to let a fellow driver go first.

Small Acts
Great achievements can begin with small acts. For Meme to be aware of the smallest ill feeling in his body, the slightest discord, the minutest ill thought or the tiniest misplaced action is the beginning of living a joyful life filled with healthy attitudes..

Something Small
When one person meets another, even if there may have been no connection up to that, it is an opportunity to give. **Meme can look on every encounter as an opportunity to give**.

To begin, he can focus on ways he can give to others. It doesn't have to be anything big, something small, in fact the smallest thing he can imagine. A kind gesture like a wink, a kindly look, a short smile, making eye contact, a handshake, tap on the shoulder or any simple gesture is enough. The other person doesn't even have to know they're being given anything. It could be a kind thought toward him, a quick prayer for his welfare, a sympathetic gesture or a kind wish for his situation.

Behind The Facade
It is not the size of the giving that matters, and this is an important factor, it's the gesture of kindness that goes with the act of giving that matters. By giving even the slightest kindness Meme is doing something he may not have done in a long time. **He is acknowledging the Capsule of the other person and by so doing is giving recognition to his own Capsule**. This is the beginning of recognition of Aura Bora not alone in himself but in others. The beginning of recognition of Aura Bora is in fact Meme coming out from behind the facade.

One of Meme's biggest mistakes when not in recognition of Aura Bora is coveting time. So, time is what he most needs to give. **By freely giving away his most valued asset Meme is connecting with his Aura Bora**. It doesn't have to be large amounts of time **just small amounts and frequently** is fine.

In Touch

Once he becomes aware that these small acts of kindness put him in touch with his Capsule he will in turn realize the joy these acts can bring to him and to others. *The presence of Aura Bora in his life will alter his perspective on life*. These brief encounters can be repeated throughout the day until they become effortless. There is no need for magic formulae, there is no need for outside intervention, *Meme can handle this on his own, at his own pace and as often as he chooses*

Practices

There is no catch. The more he practices the better will Meme become at accessing his Capsule. **The more he contacts Aura Bora the more he will realize his connection to other Aura Boras**. He will begin to see other people in a different light. Now they will not alone be just other people, but people with Capsules. If he keeps practicing later he will realize that they are not just people with Capsules, but in fact they are Capsules with people. He will become aware that he himself also has a Capsule.

Different Set Of Values

Meme now realizes something else, as he begins to acknowledge his Aura Bora his attitude toward life gradually begins to change. **The values he once considered important gradually over time begin to fall away and he starts to replace them with a different set of values.** Meme's new attitude will gradually encourage a new direction toward Zenith awareness.

Give It Time

Meme will no longer be crashing through life at breakneck speed. Gradually, he will become more mindful, thoughtful, contemplative, considerate, accepting and allowing. As Zenith he will naturally develop his inventiveness, become aware of his own intuition, even become imaginative and inspirational. He will experience greater insight and may begin to come up with answers to questions he never before considered possible.

A new world awaits Meme, a Zenith world. What he has to do is to **give it time**.

THE WISDOM OF ORACLES
BY JOHN RYAN

CHAPTER 21

MEME / ZENITH

Little Me
Now he'll mumble, now he'll bump
Now he'll grumble, now he'll thump
Now he'll be a Little Me
Now we'll see what we shall see. *pil*

The Meme Condition
Most people live in the Meme condition having lost contact with their Capsule. **Most people hardly know Capsule exists and if they do they don't realize or value the connection, their view on life is Meme orientated**. When Zenith becomes Meme orientated he becomes not only lost to Capsule but also mindless. That's how simple it is, and at the same time that's how complication exists in Meme world.

A Quagmire
The combination of Capsule and Zenith is uncomplicated whereas the singularity of human Meme is hugely and unnecessarily complicated and is in fact the only reason for complication in the world. Meme insists on complication and difficulty. His life can be compared to a blind man insisting on trudging through a quagmire on a soggy wet day wearing no wellies, pushing a loaded flat-wheeled wheelbarrow. He's the essence of struggle.

Who? Question
The Who? question is a Capsule question. It's inclusive, for example, who is this woman in relation to the situation she is in? The Who? question is consideration of Aura Bora as against the What? question that is consideration of Meme only, for example, what can I get out of this meeting?

Simplicity
The Who? question brings simplicity because Aura Bora brings truth, knowledge, love, creativity and wisdom with the answer. The What? question brings complication because the three generators bring their individual, uncoordinated, separated honesty, sifting, emotion and impetuousness with the answer. For example, what will I wear to this party? Grey Matter may suggest the black suit whilst Ruby's choice could be the red striped top and Young Nemo might have a preference for jeans. Likewise, any other question that goes in a Meme direction is likely to be answered with complication and confusion.

Any question that goes to Capsule will be phrased differently and is answered with simplicity. How should I dress for the most interesting effect? The answer comes straight from the top. Wear the suit jacket with the striped top over the jeans. In fact this is often the measure of whether Zenith is in a Capsule place or a Meme place, the simplicity of the question or the complication of the question and the simplicity of the answer or the complication of the answer. Zenith is simple Meme is complex.

Experience Confusion

By considering Who? before What? a person opens up Aura Bora. By considering What? before Who? he closes down the connection again. In this way a person may sometimes seem connected and sometimes not. **When Zenith is connected he gets glimpses of real insight and the next moment it all disappears because he's jumped back into Meme mode.**

Grey Matter is usually the generator that intervenes and pulls him back into line with the generators. This is one reason why he may experience confusion, for sometimes he is connected to Aura Bora and sometimes he seems disconnected.

Values

Let us return to attitudes and values. Are Meme's attitudes to life inclusive? How does he value his life? Are his values based on What? principals or are they based on Who? principals, or indeed are they a mixture of both What? and Who? When he is totally in What? mode he is always in Meme mode. When he is half and half he is sometimes in Zenith and other times in Meme mode. When he is totally in the Who? mode Zenith is one with Capsule.

In Who? Or In What?

When a person is in Who? he is living a simple, joyful, healthy, wealthy, fulfilling, aware, wise, knowledgeable and truthful life motivated by Aura Bora. In What? he is mindless and living a complicated Meme orientated life, an unsure, unhappy, ill, poverty conscious, disruptive, time chasing, unfulfilled, lost, sifting, emotional and reactive generated life.

Difficulties

All the problematic difficulties in a person's life are experienced in the Meme mode. When he's connected in Zenith he doesn't experiences any difficulties he can't handle. Everybody experiences difficulties in life, however, with his attitude coming from a Zenith place they won't be viewed as problems but as opportunities to achieve meaningful solutions.

Sometimes, when I am working out I meet Peter, a regular visitor to the gym. Peter needs to be helped onto some of the machines to do his workout for he has polio in both legs and some other physical disadvantages that would disable even the strongest will and its obvious he is sometimes in great pain. He always has a smile on his face and a quick wit to match the best of them. I often wondered what it was that kept him positive in his attitude.

One day after his workout we were in the dressing room and he said to me 'I love the craic'. I said 'what craic (fun) do you mean, we're only in the dressing room there's not much craic here'. What he said next made me stop in my tracks. He said 'everything, I love it all'.

In other words this man who has every reason to moan chooses instead to love his circumstances. I once saw him on the top of a tall ladder trimming the 10' high hedge outside his parent's home. As I drove past he craned his head around 180 degrees and offered me his trademark smile and a broad wave, his bright eyes dancing in his head, he was just loving it.

The Driving Seat

That Zenith deals easily with difficulties in life is a measure of his awareness. It is Aura Bora contact that puts him in the driving seat. To be specific it puts Aura Bora in the driving seat, now the real driver is there and he is not depending on the generators to do the driving.

Dangerous Terrain

The problem with Meme mode is that Aura Bora is never in the driving seat, he's tied up in the back of the truck while the generators drive. Where a person is sometimes Zenith and sometimes Meme orientated, occasionally he chooses to let Aura Bora drive the truck but the three generators also get their turn to drive. So, he gets temporarily back on the route, but as soon as everything is going smoothly Meme invites the three generators back in and very soon he's in fog, driving blindly through dangerous terrain again. For example, a footballer that plays brilliantly during the training sessions because he's relaxed suddenly gets worried and can't seem to get his act together for the game.

Zenith Values

Zenith values come from Aura Bora and are thus mindful. They will have the overall welfare of the universe considered from a true, wise, timeless place involving imagination, invention and intuition motivated in a knowledgeable, feeling and creative expressiveness. They will be joyful, aware, considerate, loving and wise.

Mixed Values

A person's mixed values come from a mix of Aura Bora and generated values and may have a certain amount of care for the universe and a certain amount of consideration for worldly matters considered sometimes from a wise place and sometimes from an intellectual perspective.

A person with mixed values may sometimes have bursts of imaginative, inventive or intuitive output and at other times be logical, emotional and reactive. He may have a reasonably comfortable lifestyle and reasonably well in control with some doubts about his existence but overall content. He may be somewhat aware, considerate but careful, loving but cautious, intelligent and logical, somewhat emotive and somewhat reactive. For instance, the somewhat unreasonable boss may also be involved in an artistic pursuit for a hobby or give some of his free time to a local charity.

Meme's Values

Meme's values are mindless and may have little or no bursts of imagination, invention or intuition, may express little or no knowledge, feeling or creativity. On the other hand Meme may be intelligent, heartfelt and industrious and will be true to himself and his fellow Memes as long as it benefits him. He may have no doubts about his integrity for he firmly believes in Meme values and attitudes.

He may pursue these values and attitudes to the end for his own benefit, for he views himself as a person motivated to the best intentions. Meme can be unhappy, self orientated, ill, greedy, unhealthy, fast, envious, worried, logical, intelligent, emotive, reactive, shallow, bossy, unimaginative etc. or any combination of these whilst he may on the surface appear to other Memes to be content, wealthy, successful, happy, healthy and well adjusted.

Generated

Meme is not motivated, but rather he is generated although he may call it motivation. He has chosen to be generated. He is not capable of motivation for that takes imagination through Aura Bora. He would need to learn how to contact Aura Bora to become imaginative.

Let Go

For Meme to connect to Aura Bora he needs to let go of generator driving force. To do this he could take a little step back, or even just stop for a moment to consider someone else's needs before his own. This other person need only be considered for a moment for the Zenith in him to be noticed. It is from this small beginning that Meme can look toward changing his attitudes and values into Zenith expression.

First Three Steps

1   Realization of the need for change is the first step in letting go of Meme generated activity.
2   The act of recognition of another person is the second step.
3   Showing tiny deliberate acts of kindness toward another person is the third step toward awareness of Zenith self.

Straight away without much effort Meme can achieve the first three steps of the journey to fulfillment, to understanding, peace, joy, knowledge, feeling, expression, timelessness and fulfilling creativity.

Connection

The ultimate aim is for Meme to connect meaningfully to his innate Zenith. The end effect is recognition of the connection to all other people that is the basis of understanding for him.   It is through this individual understanding that he lifts the level of understanding of the whole human race. By initiating awareness of his fellow humans Meme has taken the first three steps toward a lasting peace not only in his own life but also in the lives of those around him.

Discoveries

The journey from Meme to Zenith awareness is a rewarding, painless, joyful journey filled with new discoveries. These discoveries will make it possible for him to continue the journey and will be the motivating energy behind his realization toward a mindful and meaningful life.

The object of the exercise is to become genuinely interested in making connection with Zenith for the sheer sake of being connected. Where a person sees connection there will be connection, where he sees separation there will be separation. Zenith sees that separation does not actually exist but Meme's individual perception is that of separation.

THE WISDOM OF ORACLES
BY JOHN RYAN

CHAPTER 22

BLAME

It isn't really your concern
To tell me what I shouldn't do
Nor is it for you to discern
Injustice in each separate cue.

What isn't fully my belief
I hesitate to act upon
If you desist, to my relief
I'm sure, together, we'll come on. *pil*

The Blame Game

There is no situation to which blame can be rightfully apportioned. No matter what value system or attitudes Meme adopts, when they are the result of separation or disconnection from Aura Bora, they will result in him blaming and seeking further separation. Meme need not enter the blame game for there are absolutely no advantages to it.

Opposites

To apportion blame is to believe in right and wrong and in Capsule world there are no opposites. Opposites occur only where there is misalignment of generators. When generators are misaligned Meme perceives right and its opposite wrong. When he looks at both he realizes they are tied up in opinion. What is perceived wrong to one Meme may in fact be perceived as right to another.

Separation

The right/wrong argument in any situation can lead to only one conclusion, that of separation. Meme only very rarely changes his opinions when another person disagrees with him for his opinions are based on his value system. **It takes a lot for Meme to change any aspect of his value system** because his values are the result of a lifetime of carefully collected information and logic. He has a large investment in his values and he has righteously lived by them to the best of his ability.

This large investment ensures that even if Meme seems wildly off the mark to everybody else he will still consider himself right. No matter what opinion either party holds, as long as they are generated opinions they will be equally mindless and disconnected from Capsule.

Blame Game

The blame game solves no arguments. Blame breaths arguments, righteousness, judgement, anger, hatred, separation, discord, anxiety, resentment, frustration, disconnection, opposition, guilt and force. It generates war and defense. Blame places barriers between people, between families, neighbours, states and countries. Blame is mindless and thus, outside of Capsule and places humanity in the unique position in the universe as the race that experiences separation in Meme.

This in fact is one of humanities major problems, the acceptance of separation from self and separation from one another and each individual's separation from all that exists. If instead each individual were to realize his connection to Capsule, to one another and to Cosmic and act on that realization, humanity would experience a complete reversal in its values and its attitudes.

A Victim

Blame also reinforces the belief in victim mode. Where there is blame there must be a victim. For one to consider himself as victim there must also be consideration of right and wrong.

Not alone is the perceived perpetrator seen as wrong by most people and right by others but the perceived sufferer may be seen as either right or wrong **depending on the set of values of the individual judging the situation**. This situation places people in opposition to one another all based on **the generated presumption that right and wrong need to be given an importance**. From a Capsule perspective there are in fact no victims because there is no right and so therefore there is no wrong.

Perceived Perpetrator

Lets take a closer look at the cause of these most unfortunate attitudes and values. Both parties are under the influence of generator misalignment. The perceived perpetrator in this situation sees himself and his connection to the other with **a completely different set of values to that of the perceived sufferer**. These are values, which have been adopted by him throughout his misaligned generated life and he categorically believes in them. There is no doubt that while his Grey Matter is over intellectualizing, his Ruby is also being excessively emotive and his Young Nemo is likewise over reactive. Not only are the three generators out of coordination they are **excessively** uncoordinated.

Exaggerated

Meme may become over exaggerated in his three generated reactions. Although generators themselves cannot be conflicting, because they are taking separate directions they will seem to be in conflict with one another. The perceived perpetrator may be sifting in one direction, emoting in the opposite direction and reacting physically in a third unrelated direction.

No Obvious Connection

The perceived sufferer may also be going through a mixture of irrational generated behaviours and while he does not invite the attack **both parties may be experiencing similar types of misalignment with their generators**. So, while there may be no obvious connection between the two, they may in fact be experiencing similar generator misalignment, although one may be at a much more heightened level of conflicted misalignment than the other.

Crossing The Line

Meme ends up crossing the line with his three generators Grey Matter in an attempt to educate by forceful instruction, Ruby in an attempt to be overtly emotive and Young Nemo in an attempt to be active by becoming violent. None of the advances were invited, however, the misaligned generators of both parties are **paradoxically and unintentionally cross matched, for example, in the case of a mugging, a robbery or any attack.**

Generators by their nature never intend harm and are there for the express good of Meme who can still justify his actions with logic, emotion and reaction. Even when he himself has crossed the line his actions will seem perfectly logical to him and he will still be able to justify the situation.

Justified

The perceived perpetrator most certainly has crossed the line. However, he may on some level seem justified, for each individual generator, whether misaligned or not, never intend harm, but their motivation is toward blindly producing the best results for Meme. He has been subjected to a series of discordant generator overreactions resulting in exaggerated generator activity, which appear knowledgeable to Grey Matter, feeling to Ruby and creative to Young Nemo.

However, these are only appearances and the generators have been acting without connection to Aura Bora in which case they **could not be knowledgeable, feeling or creative**. All activity is generating Meme to extreme mindless, logical, emotive and reactive responses.

Overdrive

One reason generator activity may reach the point of excess is because they have been racing unwittingly in an effort to overcome what appears as obstacles, and as one generator overtakes another they naturally generate faster. When they are not in contact with Aura Bora they appear to present obstacles to one another and hence go into overdrive, even though there are in fact no obstacles.

Above Board

Once the generators go into overdrive Meme's value system alters and**, without him being consciously aware**, his value system over time becomes thwarted. To him his behaviour is **natural and right** because it is an extension of his value system. It is also a natural extension of the three generators who after all are serving Meme to the best of their abilities. Generators are honest, faithful, hardworking, open, absolutely above board and trusting. In fact the idea of hurting a fellow human being would never occur to them.

The Crux

However, they don't have a Mind and this is the crux of the matter. While all generators have the virtues of a saint, they are operating mindlessly, for they are operating without the guidance of Aura Bora. Meme is completely disconnected from his Capsule and as perceived perpetrator he is the extreme version of Meme.

Justified

The different **levels** of perceived crime depend on the levels of intellect, emotion and reaction. The different **types** of perceived crime depends on which of the generators is more prominent and in which order of importance or influence to him are the other two generators.

Meme may know intellectually he is breaking the law of the land but may emotionally and reactively be justified. He may be emotionally upset about breaking the law but the actions he takes may be logical. Young Nemo may physically go against the grain for Meme but intellectually and emotionally he will be able to justify his actions. So, on some level within, while one of his generators may not concur with the perceived crime the other two generators will be able to justify it.

No Right And Wrong

The generators act in accordance with Meme's values and attitudes and don't question them. So, Meme generators only consider what are his needs and when they see the opportunity to serve his values they do it to the best of their individual abilities. If Meme breaks the law that is not the generators concern, for them there is no right and wrong, there is only serving Meme.

Horrendous Crimes

Meme commits a perceived crime fully convinced his generators have acted honourably. While it is called breaking the law, to Meme *the law is perceived to be wrong*. He can argue he is right. To the distorted, misaligned generators in Meme this is in fact honourable activity. *This is how people can be honourable while at the same time committing the most horrendous crimes against humanity.*

Thus war, poverty, starvation, prejudice, separation and the abuse of our plant can be justified rationally. From a Capsule perspective there is no difference between a petty crime, serious crime, organized crime or going to war for all four subscribe to separation.

Harmful Encounters

When two people are in Meme mode they can make contact even where they appear on the surface to have nothing in common. *Meme orientated activity can put any person in the line of perceived danger and opens up the possibility of harmful encounters with others who may have different agendas.* The less he is in Meme mode the less will be the opportunities for unsavory encounters.

Does Not Answer

The perceived sufferer is in Meme mode and goes to his three generators for a response. The generators, even if they could go to Aura Bora with the question they only ask the What? question as in, What is happening? Aura Bora does not answer What? questions and so the generators are left to answer the question themselves.

Drawing A Blank

The generators are now left to deal with the question on their own. They have no experience of this new type of situation and therefore no information in their banks and end up drawing a blank. Never before has Meme been subjected to physical abuse and he becomes confused, because the generators are looking in three blank banks and cannot make any response. Meme cannot logically, emotionally or physically react and the net effect is for him to provide what is perceived as no response, which is a blank response. In other words Meme goes into what is called shock.

Disconnected

Because the generators are disconnected from Capsule they are not coordinated to respond in a meaningful manner. The inability to respond effectively throws the perceived sufferer further into Meme mode and thus, further from the ability to respond effectively.

Working Overtime

The three generators are working hard to come up with a response and because they can't find either logical, emotive or reactive response Meme goes into blame mode because this is the only logical answer for him in the absence of a mindful, Capsule answer.

Blame

Firstly the perceived perpetrator is blamed, then perceived sufferer goes into blaming self for being in the situation, for that is the obvious conclusion in the light of no mindful intervention. *There is no one to blame*. This is a generator misalignment. What needs to happen is for *Meme to contact Aura Bora for a meaningful answer and to respond mindfully*.

Inadequate

Meme is in a confused state for none of the generators can respond effectively. It is then incorrectly assumed by Meme that he is mentally, emotionally and reactively inadequate in the situation. The conclusion he arrives at is that he is stupid, fearful and cowardly, however this is not the case.

Working Overtime

The three generators are being intelligent, emotive and reactive in their constant search for answers and are doing their best to come up with a solution to the problem. This is why Meme keeps going over and over the event.

Survival Under Attack

The situation is further exacerbated if the attack is repeated and the sufferer undergoes attack regularly. At this stage a completely new set of circumstances takes over. Meme is subjected to repeated assaults and still cannot respond effectively. The generators, having the experience of the first attack, conclude that in this set of circumstances Meme has survived by going into the mode of perceived stupidity in Grey Matter, fear in Ruby and immobility in Young Nemo. So, the generators apply the same logic again as they prescribed for 'survival under attack'.

Surrender

The perceived inability to respond to attacks is not in fact an inability. It is the deliberate responsive action of the three generators in their stored information concerning similar incidents. When Meme is under attack the three generators throw Meme wholeheartedly into surrender as a means of protection for survival.

Reflecting

The question of Meme's action in response to attack does not happen at the time of the attack. The questioning of the response actions comes at a later stage when he is reflecting on the event. It is then that he feels inadequate. At the time of the attack Meme is not reflecting on the attack, his generators are busy taking calculated defensive action to ensure his safety and survival.

Realistic Reflection

It is on reflection that the calculated action is seen as inaction because Meme seemed to not respond. However, even this reflection is a generated reaction. Even though it may not appear to be the case, it is the definite manner in which he does react that is the calculated and logical action.

When Meme in Zenith is connected to Capsule *a realistic reflection* can take place. He now can gain access to Aura Bora through Core and discover his true placing in this situation (connecting through Core is looked at later on in the book).

The Blame Game

These encounters of abuse and attack lead Meme into reflection through Ruby that leads to judgement resulting in the blame game. Not only does the perceived sufferer blame the perceived attacker but he also blames himself and carries the experiences through his life. *Carrying blame, no matter in what form can manifest in illness, and a series of illnesses can manifest in Meme as a direct result of giving power to the memory of attack in the form of blame*. The act of blame now turns perceived sufferer into perceived victim. The sufferer in Meme causes his own victimization by introducing blame.

As a perceived sufferer of an attack Zenith *can recover through Capsule intervention*. As a perceived victim Meme chooses to have a much more difficult time.

THE WISDOM OF ORACLES
BY JOHN RYAN

CHAPTER 23

ABUSE

**Mind your business, keep your place,
Watch your step, don't foul that face
Hold the chin up where you go
Remember what you cannot know.**

**Rip a page from Mother's Book
And learn to leap after you look
Be as cool as you can be
That's the ticket, now, you see**. *pil*

Not Recognized

The general abuse of children is very much a similar situation to that of adult abuse except that the sufferer is smaller and does not have the generator Young Nemo. The child Zenith is living life through the two generators Grey Matter and Ruby with a strong connection to his Capsule. One of the problems is **that parents are more likely to be the abuser and unwittingly place their children in dangerous situations more than anybody else**.

In western society small symptoms are not recognized for what they are. As such they become an accepted part of life. This mean that **peoples perception of abuse is in fact a symptom at a very advanced stage of abuse**. By the time the abuse is recognized it is already out of all proportion. The constant debate around the subject of abuse, without seeking **meaningful** solutions, is a generated response to a symptom filled society. As a result, what in Capsule terms could not be acceptable behaviour in generator terms is taken as a normal everyday event. **In other words Capsule values are different from generator values**.

Responsible

In a world where Meme opinion dominates society Zenith takes second place. It stands to reason that children that are Zenith connected are going to be considered less important than anybody else. The only way this can change is for parents to become responsible not just to their children, but to their own place in the world. Becoming responsible really means discovering Capsule connection.

The Same Examples

The child learns from the adult and if the adult is ill he is used to unconsciously abusing self and others. It follows that the child may also eventually become ill having followed the same examples as the adult. Depending on which adults he encounters through his early life the extent, the degree and the outcome of his illness will be determined by their influence on him and his reactions to the influence.

These encounters help to set up the child's value system and his adopted Meme values, attitudes and opinions that will serve him throughout his life. Where these values are filled with perceived discord the child will take these on board as well as any other generated messages. Eventually he may perceive illness on various levels.

Doesn't Call It Abuse

Of course Meme can blame society, but as we've seen earlier **blame only encourages further abuse** of self. Also, society is made up of individuals. Blaming society is like blaming self. There is really no point to being blaming, that attitude is helpful to nobody. Parents in a Meme state are going to abuse their children, just as Meme abuses himself and everybody else. It's inevitable. Of course Meme doesn't call it abuse for his main objective is to look after and take care of his children and not to abuse them.

Meme perceived perpetrator is an extreme version of Meme parent. In a society where people are predominately Meme orientated there will be an abundance of Meme perceived perpetrators ready to home in on the children of Meme parents, even if the children are not yet full blown Meme's themselves.

Perfect State
Children by their nature are not fully developed. They are in the process of integrating their Capsule selves into Zenith. This is their normal state of being and it is the most perfect state of being for Zenith. Children's thoughts and feelings are enacted openly and freely while their Grey Matter and Ruby absorb the world and its many amazing facets.

Abusive Of All
As the child grows older he is unwittingly abused at practically every step of the way. There is no deliberate intention to abuse no more than there is a deliberate intention to avoid abuse. These general abuses are not seen as abuse. Meme is abusive of all society, he doesn't just single out children for abuse, he abuses every body equally across the board including self.

The behaviour of Meme in society is unacceptable to Aura Bora. However, Meme feels he has a perfect right to express himself as he sees fit. The problem is his children are getting battered in the process through misappropriated values and attitudes.

This is why Aura Bora calls it child abuse. Society doesn't see it that way and perfect Meme certainly would have difficulty entertaining the idea. Nevertheless, that's the way it is in a Meme orientated society from the viewpoint of Capsule.

Running The Show
Child abuse and the many forms of other abuse begin with acceptance of reduced values and attitudes toward Zenith and toward society. As we saw earlier one of the knock on effects of misappropriating speed is reduced values and attitudes. Increased speed comes from abuse of time. Abuse of time comes from generator misalignment and generator misalignment comes from disconnection from Aura Bora. Disconnection from Aura Bora results in disconnection from Capsule. Disconnection from Capsule results in mindless behaviour. Mindless behaviour is the result of the three generators running the show without Aura Bora at the helm.

Manifesting War
With the three generators running the show children soon become Meme orientated. He experiences early symptoms that are passed off as an everyday part of life. Every symptom can manifest small conditions that in turn can lead to illness. Illness can lead to suffering that can lead to victim status and then to blame. Blame leads to anger and anger to fighting which likewise can lead to manifesting war. War leads to killing.

Big Trouble
Not only can this happen to every Meme, it happens to everybody he touches. It happens with his family, children, home, friends, relatives, workplace, environment, institutions, services, governments, countries

etc. Meme's problem is everybody's problem for he is running on generators and this affects everybody around him. When the large majority of the population are running around on generators the world and its people are in big trouble.

Total Extinction

Every intelligence every emotion, every reaction that Meme generates brings him to the logical conclusion of destruction. So intent is he on running his life without the lead of Aura Bora that he is generating himself to destruction. The logical conclusion to Meme activity is total extinction.

Focus Of Attention

To choose life rather than extinction needs to be the focus of attention, for if people continue to focus on Meme activities we will surely perish by our own hand. Meme is presently involved in strangling himself. Slowly but surely at first and then with ever quickening pace he is poisoning his own water supply, polluting his own air supply, stealing his own reserves, damaging his own world with toxins, rubbishing his ancestral home, killing his fellow inhabitants and blaming everybody else in the process.

Keep In Mind

The main thing to keep in Mind is to keep a Mind, for without Mind there can be no Capsule involvement in the world's development. Without Mind Meme is destined to travel through life making a complete travesty of the world.

Realizing Responsibility

Meme needs to take a look at his value system and go through his values with a fine-tooth comb and rake out the ones that cause him any kind of discord no matter how slight, for these are like leeches which if not dealt with can suck him bone dry.

By taking a look at his value system, he can begin to become aware of the values and attitudes he has let slip and can also begin taking positive steps toward realizing responsibility for connection to his Capsule. To begin with a small symptom would be advisable. For example, where he is experiencing anxiety he needs to first accept the anxiety, allow it to be without chasing it and ask Aura Bora to intervene (this is dealt with in more detail later on in the book).

THE WISDOM OF ORACLES
BY JOHN RYAN

CHAPTER 24

Awareness

I'm sorry for moving my lips
Permit me to breath very slow
I'd rather parade my two hips
If I did, I'm sure you would go.

I feel sore about this position
You don't allow very much room
Don't you think we could try the tradition
Of fair play from birth to the tomb? *pil*

Handing Them Back

The act of **unawareness** is prevalent in society. It is that unawareness that ensures Meme a life of illness.   **Yet initially it is only a small amount of awareness that is needed to rescue him from his demise**. At the beginning of his recovery from illness Meme will have to be constantly vigilant of his unawareness of minute symptoms. For once he notices his unawareness he will actually begin to become aware of what he is doing.

Having become aware of the symptoms Meme needs to know what to do next. What he needs to do next is to **allow Aura Bora to take care of the symptoms**. In other words, having become aware of the symptoms, he needs to let them go again by actively handing them back again to Aura Bora where they belong. **He must ensure Grey Matter doesn't gain control of the symptoms**. If Grey Matter is allowed into the control seat things can go quickly out of control.

An Eye Opener

The effect of Aura Bora running the show is an eye opener for the generators. To start, it's a very gradual process, the three generators are not in any way threatened or displaced and they can be utilized much more efficiently than before and in a way which is safe for both the generators and Meme.

The Smallest Progress

The beginning of allowing Aura Bora access to Meme is very much an experimental stage and can be taken at a pace that will suit all concerned. The generators will not at any point be rushed. It is not possible to make a mistake for it is not a test, and it is not possible for the generators to be discouraged or dissatisfied in any way with the process. The smallest progress will be a major success and will encourage the generators to try further experiments.

No Surprises

There is no danger to the generators or to Meme whatsoever. There are no backlashes and no surprises when they hand over control to Aura Bora.   From the beginning of the handover there is a sense of the generators becoming a natural part of life, of right order and of right placement.

Open Up

Meme as Zenith will become acutely aware of others and the amazingly ridiculous activities in which they get involved and will realize his own past involvement in similar activities. He will be able to differentiate between his own state of being and that of others. **His level of awareness will become more acute** and all the time he will be in total control of his life, which will become not only a pleasure, but also an amazing adventure. The whole world will open up in a way Meme never imagined possible.

What Was It All About?

If Meme does not allow Aura Bora access all the information that he has spent years gathering, all the work, all the worry, all the mistakes, all the triumphs, all the magic, all the memories will pass on with him and will be of little value to Capsule's evolution. As he looks back over his life he may ask a similar What? question asked by Adam and Eve, 'What was it all about?'

Meaningful

However, if Meme hands over responsibilities to Aura Bora his life will be much more valuable both to himself and eventually to Capsule. He can begin to live his life in a more meaningful way and the information accumulated during this period can then be a major contribution to the evolution of Capsule.

THE WISDOM OF ORACLES
BY JOHN RYAN

CHAPTER 25

TURNING AROUND

Channel

At this stage Meme realizes the need to connect with Aura Bora. This is the beginning of the turn around from a generated life. Zenith is Capsules representative in this created world. The three beings of Capsule depend on Zenith to channel his experiences of the world through to them. In that way Capsule benefits from the experience. However, when he goes it alone as Meme he makes no such connection and his journey through earth is of little value.

Evolve

The main reason Zenith is on earth in the first place is to assist Aura Bora, Osmosis and Oracle to evolve by partaking in the act of **creation**. Zenith does this by providing his invaluable experience whilst exploring on earth through his human creativity. Aura Bora's part of the deal is to bring Capsule knowledge and wisdom to the attention of Zenith and by doing so greatly assist his creative life on earth. It's a two-way situation. For this to happen he must connect with Aura Bora.

Basic Connection

All of the problems without exception that Meme experiences on earth are due to his lack of understanding of his basic connection to Aura Bora. By including his Capsule in his life he guarantees himself an easier passage through life on earth and also rightful expression of his creations (connection to Aura Bora is dealt with later in the book).

Freedom

It is in letting go of the responsibility that rightfully belongs to Aura Bora that Meme realizes freedom in his life for the first time maybe since he was a child. **With Aura Bora in the driving seat Zenith's generators can navigate the journey without taking on the driving as well**. Zenith can glide effortlessly through life, confident he has left behind all perceived illness, all perceived discord, discomfort, arguments, pain and suffering, all perceived hatred, guilt, evil, loss, abandonment, hunger, brutality, badness, fighting, war and death, in fact all perceived aspects of his life that make no sense.

Life Of Joy

Meme, having realized his place in the life of Aura Bora now lives a life of joy, of knowing, of wisdom, of real feeling and of active creation as Zenith. This is his real destiny, this is his birthright and this is his rightful connection to Aura Bora. Thus, he is living a creative mindful life of truth.

Temporary Resident

The act of living mindfully entails just one thing or one realization that of realizing Capsule. Capsule is the everlasting element and Zenith is the temporary resident not the other way around.

Zenith lives on earth for an average of seventy to eighty years. Some live for a shorter time and some for a longer spell depending on the different factors and the purpose for which Zenith was taken on in the first place. **This is precisely what happens Aura Bora takes on a body experience in Zenith for the express purpose of creating and advancing from an earth existence**.

THE WISDOM OF ORACLES
BY JOHN RYAN

CHAPTER 26

PASSING ON

Think once before ye go
For what you may wish to know
If leaving all that stays behind
Is what ye want to do. *pil*

Representative
Zenith is Aura Bora's representative on earth. Sometimes he lasts a very short time, however, in eternity time is not the important factor it is on earth. Zenith becomes part of Aura Bora from the time he becomes a fetus and begins to learn from his own life experience. Even when the fetus lasts a short time Aura Bora also learns from the experience.

A Short Life
A short life may have been Aura Bora's intention and this may be the only experience needed at this stage of Capsule's development. Sometimes a short life is not the original intention and for various other reasons Zenith fetus has a shortened life, in which case Aura Bora gains a fraction of the knowledge originally intended. This set of circumstances is not an upset to Aura Bora for Capsules cannot be upset it's not an aspect of their nature. Zenith, not having fully formed, as such doesn't experience loss.

Continue
Even with a cot death the baby will be always in Aura Bora and will have had little experience on earth. The essence of the baby Zenith returns to Aura Bora. Likewise, with a child's death the child

will have been in close contact with Aura Bora throughout its life on earth and will continue in the life of Aura Bora.

Built Up A Relationship
The older or adult Zenith passes into his Capsule world as an aspect of Aura Bora to continue the Capsule life that is always there. Although Zenith has lived this life on earth, his life lives on forever in Aura Bora. It is not a death as such but a moving on. The only reason we on earth experience moving on as death is because we have built up a relationship with the Meme aspect. This aspect of self is relating to the Meme of the person who has passed on and the emotion of passing on is experienced as death.

Passing on
However, death is not the case for Aura Bora is still very much alive. The problem is Meme has given total identity of the person to his human form only. Zenith is really Aura Bora's representative on earth. Passing on is a natural part of life. Its exactly the same as Aura Bora passing into fetus, fetus passing into baby, baby passing into child, child passing into adolescents, adolescent passing into adult, adult passing into old age, old age passing back onto Aura Bora. That's a normal cycle for most earth Zeniths.

The Reasons
Sometimes Aura Bora decides that its creation on earth doesn't need to be a full cycle and thus, Zenith passes on at an early stage. It really depends on the reasons why Aura Bora decides to create a body, what the creation on this earth needs to be. Once Capsule experiences what is necessary to evolve there is really

no other reason to be on earth. The experience is complete. Capsule already has creations on the other side some of which may also share a Zenith life on earth. However, there is no further benefit for this aspect of creation to stay on earth once Capsule has experienced what was needed from the stay.

Move On

The only problem is for Meme who may be attached to other Memes, which from an Capsule point of view makes no sense. It's a bit like an actor getting attached to a character he once played in a movie and continuing to live his life as the movie character instead of himself. The movie is finished and its time for him to move on. Capsule has a life, Zenith is not just an actor in a movie and likewise, he is not just Meme on earth. **He is in fact a created aspect of Capsule with a physical presence on earth**.

The Facade

There's no point in Aura Bora becoming attached to Meme for he is just a facade, a shell. The essence is in Zenith. Attachment to Meme is like eating the eggshell and throwing away the yoke or admiring the box and ignoring the chocolates. The essence of Aura Bora's invention is not in Meme.

Difficulty

Sometimes, when Meme passes on he can remain attached to earth. This rarely happens, as Zeniths know they belong to Capsule and earth world is just a temporary existence. However, Meme with earth bound issues can have difficulty passing over and may decide to stay or revisit earth until these issues are resolved.

Nothing Frightening

This is a most unfortunate situation for the wandering Meme. To people on earth it can seem like a frightening phenomenon but there is in fact nothing frightening about it and indeed nothing extraordinary either.

Nothing Evil

There is nothing evil about Memes not having fully passed over. Because earth bound Meme is so wrapped up in this world he perceives them to be something strange and fearful. There are no evil Aura Bora creations only the manifestation of a fearful Meme perception.

There are Memes that have passed over but not yet moved on wandering the earth, this is not unusual, its normal stuff. Because Meme has placed himself in a mindless world, fear is manifest out of ignorance. There is only Meme perceived fear, there is no actual fear.

Perceived Fear

The answer to this problem of feeling fear is for Meme to come in contact with his own Aura Bora. By doing so he will realize that there is nothing out there to fear.

Perceived fear is one of Meme's biggest problems for he experiences it at every turn. The avoidance of fearful situations punctuates his life. Meme at an unconscious level is on the constant lookout for sudden unwelcome attack.

THE WISDOM OF ORACLES
BY JOHN RYAN

CHAPTER 27

THE FEAR ORACLE

**I suffer a killer to tempt me
To sow little buds in my brain
And when these buds bloom
I hear the word 'doom'
In silence again and again.**

**So I go to my backroom and wait
For the day Life'll shew me the gate
For the moment Sir Death
Will lay on me his breath
For the finger he'll point much too
late.** *pil*

No Such Thing

The perception of fear comes in many forms for fear is manifested under many different headings. Meme fears his very existence and it is this fear that rules every step of his life. For example, his fridge is filled with food he doesn't need for fear he won't have enough. There is no such thing as fear in Capsule reality but in Meme world perceived fear rules and comes in multiple forms of oracles for these fears can be seen as having supernatural powers.

Doubt

The underwriter of perceived fear is perceived doubt and man's ability to perceive doubt in his self is tied up with his admiration for himself as Meme. It plagues him for in essence he knows that he is a falsehood hoping not to be exposed and that is one reason why Meme dresses to kill. He is hiding behind the facade behind the clothes, the uniform, the jewellery, the fashion, the impeccable home, the flash car, the enormous T.V., the P.C., the mound of old videos, piles of nick knacks, the attic crammed with I might need that's and the closet full of unused clothes.

The Props

Meme is the clown behind the makeup, the sad eyes behind the painted smile. When we peel away the facade that hides him all that can be seen is fear for without all the props he realizes that Meme is a fake. Deep down he knows the truth but deep down inside is where he's just not going to look.

Busy

There are ploys in which Meme engages to ensure he doesn't have to look at himself. Keeping busy is one. If he is kept busy then he doesn't have time to look at himself. Maybe next week when he's got a minute to himself Meme can look at that but right now he has too much to do.

Playing Catch-up

He is too busy because Meme makes sure the whole world is depending on him. The work is so demanding, the kids are a hassle always wanting something or other. With all the pressure there's never enough time for him to do all he has to do. So convinced is he that this is what living is all about, he continues through life always playing catch-up. Then, when he finally does get time to himself he spends it watching T.V., that great entertainment center of attention right smack bang in the middle of his home. The attention grabber that keeps him busy at the times that Meme is not busy.

Hiding

All this busy-busy, this facade, there's one name for it. It's called hiding. He is hiding behind the facade because he is scared. And why is he scared? He's scared that Meme will be exposed as a fake. And why is he scared of that? Because if he is exposed for the fake he will have to look at himself and he's scared there might be nothing there.

Deep down inside he knows Meme is a fake and he has no answer for that. This is a big problem for him. **If instead he looked deep down inside his Core he would find a completely different set of circumstances, for he would find truth in his Capsule** (Core is looked at later on in the book).

Terminal

Meme has misappropriated his life and he knows he is terminal that he will at some stage die. As long as he hides behind the mask and stays busy he won't have to look at that.

The News

Another of Meme's great inventions is distraction. He takes a great interest in the world around him. The news is a big thing in Meme's life. He thrives on the news especially what he calls bad news. Now he can act out his fears through others. When everybody else is engaged in fear chasing Meme fears don't seem so big. The bigger the disaster he sees on the news the more relieved is he that its not himself for he knows he could just as easily be on the news.

Bad News

There are plenty of other distractions though to ensure this day doesn't come. Meme takes a great deal of interest in local people. He's a people kind of guy. He likes to know everything that's going on, every bit of detail. He notices how other Meme's like to sometimes gossip and he doesn't like that. Not Meme, oh no, he would never sink that low as to be a gossip. He notices just how much 'bad' news there is even locally and that reinforces his belief in badness in the world.

The Weather

Why, even the weather is 'bad' sometimes, or its horrid or awful or wicked or shocking. It's never just windy or just cold or just wet or just showery or just snowy for Meme. Its got to be woeful, wet, windy weather, or a fierce, cold snap, a horrid, wet, wild wint'ry day and tomorrow we're promised shockin', heavy, sleety, snowy showers. Even if there's only one inch of snow he is determined, things out there are far worse off than for Meme inside.

Gone To Hell

The conviction that he couldn't be as badly off as anybody else consoles Meme. He sees that it's his surroundings that are bad. The way the country is being run is a disaster according to him. The educational system is abominable, the health service is a disgrace, the young people of today are a crowd of bowzies and the religion is gone to hell altogether. These are some of the great distractions that he invents to ensure that Meme keeps his eye off the ball.

Kept Busy

If Meme discovers the real truth he wouldn't know how he would react. So, he must be kept busy shopping for new clothes, making sure the house is kept clean all the time, working harder than anybody else, keeping pace with up to date events, avoiding the big bad world and all those terribly bad people who are making a dreadful mess of things, on that horrid, awful, shocking, wicked, wild, wet, drudgery of a day that the obnoxious financial minister put the already miserable welfare system under terrible pressure by rewarding those disgraceful reprobates an undeserved pay rise. Isn't Meme the perfect saint by comparison to all that's going on around him?

Battering

It's amazing how much we take this kind of conversation for granted. This is normal everyday interaction between Memes. No Meme exists that doesn't subscribe to the collective verbal battering of himself, his fellowman and the world around them. With these words come attitudes and from these attitudes an unhealthy value system is formed.

Unhealthy Values

Heading in only one direction, that or fear, is a value system and a way of life built up around words like obnoxious, terrible, dreadful, horrid, miserable and disgraceful. This is a value system built on loss, resentment, pride, judgement, arrogance, self-righteousness, manipulation, dissatisfaction, anger, poverty, hardship, speed, jealousy, worry and a whole range of unhealthy behaviours. This is in fact a glossary of unhealthy values that can only lead to dissatisfaction and fear.

Meme sees these values as a normal set of values. He sees nothing out of place with a set of values that include this list of behaviours. Indeed he is convinced that they are essential to his survival for this is the world in which he lives, the world he embraces and fully accepts without question with all its unhealthy values and attitudes. Not far from where I live there is a road sign that reads 'bad bends ahead'.

The Ultimate Mindless Act

It's only when Meme examines the list and stands back from it that he can see the situation he has nurtured for himself and see it for what it is. Everything has become turned so gradually he hasn't noticed that instead of living life filled with rewarding values he is choosing to live his life through destructive values. It is the acceptance of these values that is beyond comprehension from a Capsule point of view, for this surely is the ultimate mindless act.

The Best Of Intentions

To base existence on a set of values that are in no way complementary to a rewarding life may be logical and may be emotive and may be reactive but it is also mindless and without consideration of Capsule. It's a measure of how distorted life can become without the intervention of Aura Bora, and in a way it's not difficult to see how this can happen even with the best of intentions.

Keep The Head Down

Without mindful, Aura Bora guidance Meme can be turned in any direction and he won't even notice. On the occasions when he does notice he is helpless to do anything about it. For instance, there is a general acceptance of the rise in drug abuse and acceptance of poverty in the world. Better to just keep the head down and get on without complaint. Meme hopes it won't be so bad that he would have to get angry and argue, or even have to fight his corner, or indeed have to go to war.

In Danger Of Collapse

A value system built on dangerous attitudes, such as acceptance of political corruption, *has only one way to go irrespective of how well meaning is Meme. A value system is the foundation on which he builds his life. If this foundation is in any way corrupted or compromised or ill, he spends his whole life managing garbage.* It really is only a matter of time before it collapses. At the rate Meme is racing through life this shouldn't take too long.

Grasp The Nettle

Meme must realize his predicament and deal with the situation. However, unless he realizes just exactly what he is dealing with he will find it difficult to motivate himself.

He must 'grasp the nettle' and take a close look at his life. This is his call and no one else can do it for him. He must see the danger and appreciate the levity of the situation. *He must become aware of the possibilities of his own destructive behaviour and his own personal pattern of separating attitudes.*

Question His Values

Meme could set aside his sense of righteousness and his sense of good and bad, his logic of right and wrong, his notion of the fear oracle, the evil Meme, the boogey man, the big bad wolf etc. He could examine his acceptance of the notion of grandeur, his persistence toward acquisition, his willingness to downgrade his fellow man, his sense of importance in the world, his corruption of self. He could list his attitudes, question his values and examine their origins.

Rewarding Life

There is a more rewarding life of fulfillment, a life of health, a life of freedom, of painlessness, of joy, filled with wisdom, knowledge and creativity. It is the life of truth, a life that replaces this Meme life of fear and doubt. It is the birthright of everyone.

THE WISDOM OF ORACLES
BY JOHN RYAN

CHAPTER 28

TRUST

Confusion

Constant doubt causes worry and confusion in Meme who can be continually changing direction. Constant change puts a strain on the generators that can lead to illness in Meme. If he doesn't treat it by contacting Aura Bora it can develop and may even reach the point of breakdown in one or more of the generators. It's unlikely he's going to check in with Aura Bora while in Meme mode so a breakdown is imminent.

Mr. Doubt

So sure is Meme that he is going to be ill he takes out insurance for it, it's a guarantee. Insurance is not taken out just in case it might happen. Insurance is making sure it will happen. It's expected. This is the act of not trusting Zenith.

The very act of not trusting Zenith is Meme's downfall. It guarantees that he will be ill. The preoccupation Meme has with the insurance policy is astonishing. It's the 'just in case' syndrome. Meme is the epitome of Mr. Doubt. He has to have insurance just in case he burns down his home, just in case his T.V. gets stolen, just in case he falls and breaks his arm, just in case he crashes his car, just in case he can't work, just in case he gets sick. Meme places doubt into practically every situation in his life.

Not Trusting

Meme has gotten to the stage that he doesn't trust himself. Just imagine the implication of not being able to trust self. The only person on the planet that has custody of his welfare can't be trusted so Meme puts his welfare in the hands of a group of Memes. Not only that he pays the group of Memes handsomely for the privilege.

This is the ultimate insult to himself. This is the act of double binding for not alone is Meme not trusting of self but he trusts the ultimate mistrusting institutional Meme.

Cotton Wool

This Grey Matter logic is also backed up by Ruby fear and Young Nemo caution around taking action. Meme has bound himself up in cotton wool just in case he gets hurt while his generators batter the life out of him continually.

In Debt

Insurance is not the only way Meme mistrusts himself. He doesn't trust himself to look after his own money and has to ensure that his money is safely filtered through a Meme bank who charges an arm and a leg for taking care of his financial interests. He ensures that he has to borrow money to live a Meme life. This ensures he lives in debt to his generators and to Meme bank.

Unique Value System

Money is a common means of exchange where services are accountable and in Meme world the value of exchange is measured in financial terms only. His perception of what is of value needs to be questioned for he has a unique value system around his money.

Money, that's the ticket
Money, that's the cue
Honey, you can stick it
Just give me my due.
Pounds and pence a potion
Purer than pink gin
Lady, my one notion's
Not with you to sin.

Nickles, dimes and dollars
All give me a thrill
If the harpy hollers
Move in for the kill.

For money, that's the ticket
And, money, that's the cue
Honey, you can stick it
Just give me my due. *pil*

Lack Of Trust

Lack of trust in Zenith ensures Meme will always doubt his ability to take care of financial matters which forces him further into a contract with money. This lack of trust enslaves Zenith to Meme needs.

Important

The notion that Meme has about money is that money is an oracle and that nothing is more important, for indeed **nothing is more important to Meme than the acquisition of money**. Now Meme truly needs his generated brain to lead the way.

Safe Ground

The introduction of Aura Bora at this stage of the development can begin to bring Meme back to safe ground where the emphasis can be eventually changed toward Zenith values.

The Attitude

The outlook, the attitude and the value system that Meme has built up around himself is what is so dangerous to him, and not so much the financial situation in which he may find himself. When he changes his perception of the situation shifting from Meme to Zenith the circumstances around his money problems will shift toward a more positive direction.

Shifting

Shifting to Zenith with money matters means **taking the oracle element out of it** and placing money where it belongs, in the exchange for commodities area. Money is a commodity like any other. **When Meme stops treating money like an oracle his attitude around it shifts to a healthier set if values**. While he may still retain a Meme attitude around other matters he has made a significant start in shifting Meme values around money, thus, restoring a trust to his own ability in money matters.

Responsive Attitude

It is by examining the value system which we take for granted around each subject such as money, fear, good, bad, right, wrong, the weather, families, people, animals, the environment, Aura Bora, oracle, the government, the state of the country etc. that we begin to see the disproportionate values we place on everything. Which of these values would we hold onto if we were told the world would die in one week from today?

Even a shift from Meme to Zenith in a single subject means he has begun to turn toward a more responsive attitude to his surroundings. **This is the beginning of him trusting his own innate abilities.**

The Principal

It's the principal of the exercise that is most important. Once Meme accepts himself for what he is, he can change Meme principals to Zenith principals. He can develop a trust in his new attitude and remove the doubt manifested by Meme.

Acceptance

Acceptance is in itself a powerful ally for it is in acceptance of Meme that he realizes there is no one to blame and he can begin to change the circumstances around himself. By acceptance he stops arguing, blaming, resisting, complaining, worrying, feeling guilty, helpless or sad, gossiping, hoping, wishing, doubting etc. All these symptoms have only one result that of damaging Zenith's relationship with Aura Bora and guaranteeing a continued relationship under a mistrusting Meme.

Choice

Meme chooses to live his life as though living in a prison, a hospital or a mental institution. This is not because of a choice he made just once, he has made this choice time after time, minute after minute, hour after hour, day after day, week after week, month after month, year after year, decade after decade with hundreds of thousands of choices over his lifetime.

Through acceptance and allowing these symptoms without actively pursuing them Meme becomes active in his knowing of the symptoms. For him to shift to Zenith is a realization of free will and choice.

Very Small Symptoms

Every waking second of every day Zenith and Meme make choices from a mere inflection to a simple thought, a word, a look, a smell, a taste, a feel, a sensing, an awkwardness, a discomfort, a suggestion, etc. These very small symptoms are the beginnings of choice and can also be the beginnings of illness. **It is here he continually makes the choice** whether to go to prison or paradise, toward hospital or health center, toward mental institution or holiday camp. Here he decides in whom to place his trust Meme or Zenith.

THE WISDOM OF ORACLES
BY JOHN RYAN

CHAPTER 29

A CAPSULE ISSUE

Never be not what you are
When you go to encounter Life's call
Never watch Life from afar
Or gather Pride from a fall.

Never be not who you are
When you're into the quick and the free
Never shoot straight at a star
You're who you want to be. *pil*

Gradual Shift

The journey of choices begins when Zenith is a child and carries on through the rest of his life. Once after childhood he has begun to pass out of Zenith state he shifts back and forth from Zenith mode as a result of contact with the human world. This shift into Meme may take many years and is such a gradual shift he doesn't notice the changes in himself.

Over the course of the years Zenith makes hundreds of thousands of choices some bring him into Zenith and others into Meme and thus he fluctuates between modes.

Baby Generator

During the adolescent years there is a much more dramatic shift. With the introduction of puberty a new generator is born to provide Zenith with a reproductive system. Up to now the child has been operating on two generators. The introduction of Young Nemo means a new baby generator is born and like all new babies has no experience of the world. Young Nemo spends the first few years fluctuating between Zenith and Meme modes trying to find a level of acceptance.

At the same time the other two generators make tentative excursions into Meme mode trying to make sense of this new condition. Zenith flexes the muscles of the new generator to varying degrees of success and failure that brings him often in and out of Meme mode.

Physically Active

The physicality of Young Nemo ensures more of a ground, base, physically active and reactive approach to life for Zenith. How he has experienced life up to now will be the determining factors in how he greets this young generator.

Transition

Zenith operates through an Aura Bora value system for his early years. He gradually becomes more and more influenced by the world around him. He can make a smooth transition into adolescents if he still possesses a large amount of Aura Bora values. However, if these are continually called into question he may experience considerable confusion. Where he has a lot of uncertain or confused attitudes and values the introduction of adolescents can firmly establish Meme tendencies in him.

Cement His Values

A child may already have learned some values in the Meme mode. Adolescents will further reinforce these and as the years roll on more and more of his attitudes and values gradually end up with the Meme set of values with very few left in Zenith. He may further cement his values into Meme with the passing of the years.

Chipping Away

This eventually manifests a rock hard value system in Meme. Early grasping of the principals of change to Zenith is like chipping away at a rock with a hammer and chisel. How long it takes will depend on the effort he puts into the exercise. Careful study of the rock of values can uncover weaknesses that can make breaking it into sections easier.

Careful study doesn't mean Grey Matter intervention, this kind of study must be avoided at all costs because it brings him straight back into the What? question. **What? questions reinforce Meme mode and are unhelpful and indeed would produce a counter effect**.

An Aura Bora Situation

This is not a questioning process it is not a probing for information. *This is a feeling at Core process to find awareness. It has nothing to do with brain it has nothing to do with information and logic*. It has to do with knowledge.

A Feelings Issue

This has nothing to do with emotion either, so, *Meme needs to leave his heart out of it* also. Ruby may only upset the process by generating emotion around the issue and this would not be helpful for it is not an emotional issue. This is a feelings issue, there is no place to hang sadness or happiness here it's not about that. This is nothing to do with depression or levity it has to do with true feelings.

Upset The Process

Likewise, working through this process has nothing to do with action so Zenith needs to leave his reproductive system out of it. Young Nemo may only upset the process by generating physical interaction around the situation and this would not be helpful.

It is a pure creativity process there is no place for physicality here it is nothing to do with action and reaction it's not about that. This has to do with knowledge, feeling and creating from one's own purely innate perspective.

In The Present

Although it may be useful in certain situations such as in therapy, there is no need to examine past information for innate purposes because the answer is **not in stored Grey Matter information for the answer is in the present. There is no need to go over past emotional issues because the answer is not in stored Ruby emotion. There is no need to go over past actions and reactions because the answer is not there. The answer is in the present.**

From Meme Mode

Zenith in Meme mode would not benefit from generator intervention while they are also in the same mode. He has problems in the first instance as a result of being in this mode. A further reason for not deploying the generators is that this method of transferring from Meme mode **is non forceful and non invasive and is a truly mindful process**. There is no manipulation, no effort at driving home the message, no flattery, no persuasion and no subtle influences. **There is just allowing and acceptance**.

Seeking Of Truth

The process is for the seeking of truth in a world where misinterpretation is widespread. The genuine efforts of heartfelt, intelligent, hardworking people to come to terms with the perceived evil, with perceived badness, perceived wrongs, lies, hardships, sorrow, deception, loss and illness etc. is further hampered by widespread misinterpretation. The assumptions that are made in everyday language may be misleading, for example calling euphoria- love, happiness- joy, information-knowledge, and construction- creation etc.

Reach The Truth

Humanity has gone to great lengths to discover the path to truth. However, **the efforts of man to reach the truth are hampered by his starting point**. Truthful results, in the efforts to understand authenticity from the starting point of Meme, whilst immeasurably honorable, are nonetheless not possible. For example, the promise in court of a witness with the best intentions who is sworn in to tell the truth the whole truth and nothing but the truth is actually impossible where he is in Meme mode. Likewise a judge, lawyer or barrister in Meme mode is compromised in his efforts to reach the truth.

THE WISDOM OF ORACLES
BY JOHN RYAN

CHAPTER 30

THE CHANGE

Accept All Parts

Change begins with you, you must accept that which is you completely, warts and all. *Accept your generators as they are* as well as all parts of your body. You must *accept all parts of your Capsule as well not only Aura Bora but Osmosis and Oracle* also even though they may seem imperfect to you. You may not believe in their existence but *for the purpose of the exercise it is necessary to accept the possibility that they may exist*. Included is your acceptance of the pain and joy (but not necessarily forgiveness) in all of your experiences. From this starting point you can move forward. Both Aura Bora and the generators must accept themselves first in order to be able to then accept and work with one another.

Pertinent Questions

When you wish for understanding ask Aura Bora for whatever you need to bring that understanding forward. **If you don't know what you need then say just that and ask for knowledge of your needs**. The most important thing is to be **truthful and open**, you need not expected yourself to have answers **just questions. From questioning come the answers**. Get into the habit of asking pertinent questions (not What? questions) and expecting the rightful answers. This becomes a fun situation within a very short space of time.

Shifting Physically

Where there is a block, vibrate yourself with movement and sound. This could be in the form of walking and talking, moving and speaking, dancing and singing, jumping and shouting or whatever takes your fancy. The point is that **shifting physically and verbally causes movement and vibration** in the air.

Have Fun

If you need a place to experiment find a quiet place where you know you will not be interrupted. Any sound and movement will start you off. The important point at this stage is to keep your generators open to receiving direction from Aura Bora and do what comes to you naturally.

Remember, this should be an enjoyable experience it's not a test. So, **stay open to receive whatever messages come back from Aura Bora** and do just what you feel like doing. Have fun with it.

Lose Sensitivity

The process of working through Aura Bora is habit changing because it takes you out of your safe zone. This is very good for you because through habit you tend to lose sensitivity and your disfigured ego can take over from your original intention, for example, in hospitals some nurses and doctors, through habit of dealing with illness, often forget their patience are people and see only their condition. Ego needs to be brought into balance through Aura Bora.

Forgive Yourself

Loving yourself is tuning into Aura Bora that makes you realize your fears and denials in a safe way. You need to accept past behaviour rather than deny it **and then forgive yourself for not having accepted it before**. From now on you can **observe your actions** and your Aura Bora guided reactions and notice the difference rather than judging yourself for past reactions.

Live Longer

Instead of judging ask **questions of your Aura Bora that are pertinent to your situation. The deeper the question the deeper will be the answer**.

Do not force your body through its generators to do things it does not want to do and in this way you will not only improve your health but you will also live longer and happier. Your body needs to be allowed the freedom to come up with creative solutions to the situations life presents.

Rightful Order

Your life as a disconnected Meme up to this is not as was originally intended by Capsule. It is now time for you to take your rightful place in the world and to claim your birthright. To begin changing your life starts here and now in this moment. It is time for you to forget the past, to allow it to go from your memory and to use your body as it was intended, to realign the three generators by bringing them into play with the three beings of your Capsule. Without this rightful order there cannot be rightful living.

Tentative Beginnings

Your tentative beginnings toward realization can be just that. There is no need for large gestures of active enthusiasm**. Let the beginnings be small and deliberate so the effects of them can reach your inner realization**. Thus, they will become profound experiences and then they can be repeated with confidence. Small beginnings grow.

Important Step

There needs to be awareness of the differences between Zenith mode and Meme mode. This is an important step toward full awareness of Capsule self and can be combined with the first three steps mentioned earlier in the book.

First Three Steps

1   Realization of the need for change is the first step in letting go of Meme generated activity.
2   The act of recognition of another person is the second step.
3   Showing tiny deliberate acts of kindness toward another person is the third step toward awareness of Zenith self.

Difference

The Meme mode is self-gratification whereas Zenith mode by comparison is recognition of all people. A second difference is that both operate from different sources within the body. Whilst Meme only operates from the generators, Zenith operates initially through Corigonus. **All that is needed for the moment is for you to become aware of that subtle difference**. There is no need at the moment to do anything differently, just observe. Take note of your logic and intelligence toward any decisions. Take note of the fact that all Meme decision come by first accessing brain (later on in the book we will deal with access to Aura Bora through Core).

Become Aware

At the same time you could take note of your emotions, be aware overall in your body that you are in fact being emotive and from **what part of the body** is the emotion coming. It may be from any part of the body, not just the heart.

Similarly, you could take note of your body's **reactions** in relation to logic and emotions, again not to intellectualize your awareness but merely to become aware in the part of your body that the actions correspond to your logic and emotions. By these observations you will become more aware of the three generators in action. The more you observe these activities the more astute will be your awareness of yourself.

Responses

By doing this you will eventually become aware of the responses you have to each situation. You also begin to discover who is Meme in relation to Zenith. By observing yourself and examining Meme's reactions you realize that there are differences between Zenith and Meme and that Meme actions and reactions are a separate aspect from Zenith.

You may also begin to realize that you can have up to **three different reactions** at the same time to a particular situation. Instead of just one. You'll see that whilst your brain siftings go in one direction your heart's emotions go in another and your physical reaction in a third different direction.

Soak Slowly Through

The tendency for you as Meme will be to intellectualize about the situation and you need to avoid doing that. You need to become aware of your logic, your emotions and your reactions not in your brain but to **feel them in your body**. Just allow the awareness to soak through your body, keep Grey Matter out of it otherwise brain will run away with it and the exercise will be lost. Stay focused first on the external body overall and when that is achieved, allow your awareness to soak slowly through the skin.

Meme can take a backward step or indeed simply stop and wait and allow your body to take note. This exercise may take time at first but with practice it will become easier. Don't force yourself, just allow. As was mentioned before, it would be advisable to keep open communication and let Grey Matter in particular know your intention and how long this is likely to take so you will not be interrupted during the process.

Shifting

By becoming aware of the three generators reactions on the three different levels you are in effect allowing Zenith access into your body. This is in fact a Core activity (that will be discussed later). This is the object of the exercise and this is what needs slowly to be the aim. By encouraging this access you are inadvertently shifting gradually toward awareness in Zenith.

Fluctuate

All three generators are thus recognized and understood to be a separate part of the team with individual particular expertise. When this recognition of Zenith is realized then you can move on to the next stage of development. Even with this awareness you will have, unknown to yourself, already moved on in the next stage to Zenith. Becoming aware of the move is a different emphasis.

It's important for you to notice the process of awareness to Zenith and not to intellectualize on the shift but instead to feel it through the Core. At this stage you may fluctuate between Meme and Zenith. This can be expected at the early stages of awareness, indeed its very good progress.

One Team

The next stage, having become slightly aware even sometimes, is to become **actively encouraging of the lineup between the three generators**. When the generators are lined up they become active members of the one team. So, instead of activating individually and shooting off in three different directions, desperately generating to achieve their individual aims under the misguidance of Meme, they will in fact be united in a team effort under Zenith.

THE WISDOM OF ORACLES
BY JOHN RYAN

CHAPTER 31

CORIGONUS – CORE

A Lable's Very Able
A label's very able
A label's very neat
A label's not a fable
A label is a treat.

A label's quite unable
To fix on friend or foe
But a label's very able
Labels we all know. *pil*

Public Opinion

If we see the world and ourselves from the viewpoint provided by constant discord, how do we as a race progress? If we retain our current attitudes it is certain we can make very little progress, because with these attitudes and values embedded in our way of life there is no imaginative forward movement. When we look outside ourselves for the cure to our perceived problems we set ourselves up to be carried along by public opinion and if the majority of people are orientated toward doubt, life will naturally be allowed to fall into the same hole.

Occupy The Space

If for example we constantly take on board that which we are being told on T.V. news our lives will be filled with accounts of the worlds tragedies presented in sensational graphic form. The reported events **occupy the space in which awareness of our own lives needs to be. We are allowing ourselves to be constantly distracted from dealing with our lives by involving ourselves in** **that which is of no value** to Capsule and in turn damaging to our bodies.

If we continue to **bury ourselves in a busy lifestyle** and thus, **ignoring our Capsule needs** our bodies are paying the price through illness, misery, discontent, hidden anger, frustration and a multitude of self inflicted problems.

Responsibility

When your generators take on a responsibility for that which is innate, your body inadvertently disconnect from its innateness. There is no comeback when things don't work out because you have put your generators in control. There is no need for your human aspect to take *responsibility* for anything innate. Your innate self is there for that particular purpose. Unfortunately, your body keeps getting in the way and controlling the show. When your generators take on responsibility of your innate self they send away the innate aspect. The human you, is then *unavailable to do its own work* because it is *tied up* in what should be innate activity.

Misplacing

As human you have a specific function i.e. **to take care of the physical input** of your creations. However, if your human body is engaged in Aura Bora work you **are misplacing your energy and are leaving yourself unavailable for your own bodies work.**

You need to trust in your innate self, to stop doing the jobs you eagerly take on that are not your bodies to do. You are like the employee who thinks he should be the boss but neglects to look after his customers. The message you are sending out is that you **don't believe in yourself and what's more, that you don't trust your Aura Bora.**

Corigonus

Corigonus, otherwise known as Core is located just below the belly button. **By connecting with your Core self you can learn how to access the wealth of knowledge that is available directly to you from your innate self**. Its irrelevant whether or not you call it Capsule or by any other name.

The fact is you are inbuilt with the power to deal with any problem the world puts up in front of you. **There is no need to go outside of your own Capsule to gain access to knowledge**. What you need to do is learn how to **trust** yourself. By learning how to access your Core you will be taking the first steps toward trusting yourself and also taking the first steps toward living a joyful, healthy, knowledgeable, wise and creative life.

You were always meant to be in control of your own life, and **when you stop giving away control of your life** to other situations and gradually become aware of the many ways you may be doing this, **you will begin taking better care of your authentic needs** instead of your habitual exclusive practices.

A Fraction Of A Second

There is no need to beat yourself up about the past, **how you deal with here and now is what is important**. At any given time no matter what your situation Corigonus is always available to you. That's the advantage of Core **it can be contacted in a fraction of a second and consulted for any given situation large or small**. To start small would give you more opportunities to practice.

Straight

Messages through Core don't discriminate or judge or give unhealthy feedback or be in any way derogatory or abusive or critical. They just give it to you straight as it is, truthfully, knowledgeably and wisely. **Core cannot be manipulated or mismanaged it does not make assumptions. It does not play tricks or use complicated language**. Messages that come through Core communicate with you at your level of understanding and are clear, accurate and precise.

Through Core

The act of thinking does not come from the brain the act of thinking comes from the Core connection to Aura Bora. If you want to think you must engage Core for it is through Core you **come in contact with your Mind** and not through your brain as most people assume. Since the Mind doesn't reside in the brain **it makes no sense to go to brain to think**.

Imagination

Intellectualizing and being logical likewise is not thinking it is recalling already known information from the Grey Matter bank. It is information systemizing and requires no imagination. Thinking requires imagination and that does not reside in your brain. It resides in the Mind, in Capsule.

Act Of Creation

Aura Bora was created to utilize Capsule gifts, and humans were created to activate these gifts. When we are activating through these universal gifts we are in the act of creation. This is our purpose in life **to create through the mediums of knowledge, wisdom, love, joy and truth** and when we are not in the act of creating through these mediums we are in the act of constructing through generated activity. This in turn encourages Meme illness and our constructions will in themselves be destructive and also be filled with illness.

Nothing New

In order to be of maximum value to ourselves we must be able to use our thinking skills **properly** otherwise we are merely generating our intelligences. This does not encourage the development of any new information so nothing **new** can be learned by or created from this activity.

A Gamble

This is often why it is difficult for people in all walks of life to make any real advancement in their lives. While they may wish to live in different circumstances they simply cannot see a way of achieving their desires. A problem is that any scheme they come up with won't make any significant change and the fear of venturing into the unknown without a more realistic plan can be too much of a gamble for them to take. So, they may end up settling for what they already have and blame the world and its mother for the problems they've created for themselves. However, **it doesn't have to be this way with access through Core you can turn your life around**.

Engaging The Core

Lining up the three generators Grey Matter, Ruby and Young Nemo is achieved by access through Core. When you wish to move out of your current mode and realize Zenith mode you must turn yourself in the Aura Bora direction. In practical terms this means engaging with Core.

To engage Core, you need only to focus on Core and tighten your stomach muscles, which are in fact the muscles

around your Core. Hold this position for about ten seconds, at the same time ensure the rest of the body remains relaxed and has no tension. Just concentrate on the Core and let everything else go. Now release the hold and completely relax the Core muscles for a few seconds then re-engage the Core muscles only slightly once more.

Practice

The first time you do this it would be advisable to find a quiet space with no distractions for a few minutes so you can practice in peace. It may also help you to concentrate if you close your eyes and relax, whatever makes you comfortable. Later, you will be able to do it in any given situation.

Now the focus on Core comes from the three generators. Before you begin the connection process take a couple of deep breaths and focus on your three generators one at a time first the brain, next the heart and then the reproductive system. See them in a straight line down from your Grey Matter through your Ruby passing through your Core and to your Young Nemo. At your Core imagine a connection box and a second line going out to join up with Aura Bora in Capsule (see Zenith diagram at the beginning of the book).

Difficulty Imagining

If you are having difficulty imagining the generators perhaps you could substitute them with different colour tennis balls, blue for brain, red for heart and yellow for reproductive system and have them connected with a white telephone line going through each. At your Corigonus or Core, there could be a telephone junction box connected to the cable with a second cable coming out at right angles the other end of which is plugged into Aura Bora.

It may help you to tap the generator positions with your finger and draw an imaginary line also with your finger from one generator to the other down your body. You could place a hand at the Core position just below your belly button and this may help you to feel the connections. You may even consider making a quick drawing of the generators. However, don't get caught up with it if you're having any difficulty, it's not a test. Do the exercise even if you can't imagine it because the exercise still works without being able to imagine the generators.

Taking Control

It may take a few minutes at first to imagine the connections but with a small amount of practice it will be possible to make the connections in a fraction of a second. This act alone is empowering and it has the immediate effect of you taking control of the situation no matter what it is and becoming open to suggestions from your Aura Bora. You don't have to be in special circumstances to do the exercise, as every situation is appropriate to engage Core.

Patient

This is a critical stage in the changeover from Meme to Zenith. The three generators have been used to running the show up to now and won't at first know what is happening. You may need to be patient with the generators because they are not used to operating together and being coordinated with one another.

Take Charge

All three generators are by now used to operating in a discordant fashion and may be inclined to reactivate and try to take charge. This can be expected and you need to not get into a state about it when it does

happen. **Be gentle with yourself.** There are steps you can take to ensure your generators that all is well and they need not get ahead.

No Saboteur

Firstly you need to know that this is not an attempt by the generators to take over, they are simply responding as they have been used to doing. There is no part of you trying to take over for there is no part of you that is evil or destructive. There is no saboteur, no bad or good and there is no right or wrong. These are all shadows cast by Meme. These shadows don't exist in reality.

Responding

All of the generators are at your service and all are willing workers. However, your generators do not think and are unable to think and when there is no instruction from your Aura Bora they act and react on their own devices for your best interest. Because they have been used to responding to your every need they now see no reason for all this waiting.

Talking To The Generators

You may need to calm the generators if they interrupt the process. The way to calm the generators **is by talking to them as if you were talking to a child and explaining what is happening** and letting them know everything is all right that this process won't take long.

Once a reasonable explanation is forthcoming your generators are satisfied to wait as they are being asked. There is no need for you to get into a panic even though this may feel like a panic attack. This condition is simply an overenthusiastic generator wishing to serve. There is no danger to you and in fact all is well with your generators.

Very Precise

You may need to talk to the generators several times at first but as time goes on it will get much easier. One of the reasons the generators may interrupt is they may not have been told just how long this period will take. They are **very precise** on time. If you say it will take a minute, in exactly one minute and not a second before or after the generators will be anxious to get moving.

Precise And Truthful

Once the time for waiting has lapsed the generators will want to get back in action straight away for they are faithful. This is why you need to be **precise** with them and **truthful** with them for they do not know anything about dishonesty and **accept you at your word**. You need therefore to give an exact length of time that this situation could take, and if you are not sure exactly how long you must state this.

Communication

Communication is the key word here. It's advisable to have **open communication between you and separately with each of the generators. Remember to be gentle with yourself**.

Uninterrupted Contact

It's also advisable for you to have open communication with Aura Bora through your Core **all** the time. **Your three generators operate to the best of their abilities when you have an open and uninterrupted contact with Aura Bora all of the time**. It can take time to reach this level of awareness but the results are well worth the effort. When this contact is left open you **cannot** then be

in Meme mode. You inadvertently cut off communication with Aura Bora while you are in Meme mode.

Direct Enquiry

The three generators are now focused on your Core. They are not activating just waiting and focused. Imagine an energy coming from your generators through the line to your Core and connecting to the second line that leads to your Aura Bora. You can now make direct enquiry toward Aura Bora through your Core. The enquiry does not take the form of a question for this would activate your generators and they need to be still for the moment and waiting calmly. Activating Grey Matter in particular would bring you straight back to Meme mode.

The enquiry does not take the form of an emotion or heartfelt action or reaction for this would also bring you back to Meme mode. Nor does it take the form of a bodily action or reaction not even a slight gesture for likewise this would bring you back to Meme mode.

Underlying Intention

Your *underlying* intention is important. So, be clear about your needs and your intentions so that there is no confusion built into the process. It is the thought behind the thought that will take precedence. For instance, you may put your energy into a desire for a certain happening but at the same time on a deeper level be feeling that it somehow cannot happen without intervention. *The deeper feeling will be the direction in which circumstances pan out.*

Acceptance And Allowance

Your enquiry works best if it takes the form of **acceptance** *and* **allowance**. When you **accept** the situation for what it is without any input from the generators and **allow** whatever is happening to happen without generator intervention you are working not just on trust but *on a* **knowing basis** and the results are deeply satisfying. Be sure to remain alert for the reply from Aura Bora and be aware of the tendency within yourself to just cop out.

The generators may feel like they want to jump ahead and you may need to calm the generators **by talking to them and asking them to hold back** and let them know that it's out of their hands. You are waiting for your Aura Bora to take the lead. Aura Bora is fielding the situation at the moment and depending on the circumstances and how they were formed may give rise to a slight delay. It helps when there is a clear set of circumstances then Aura Bora can respond immediately.

Be Informed

It's important for you to inform your generators that it is not their duty to activate first with regard to situations, questions or doubts. They need only be **reactive to Aura Bora**. It would be an idea to set a time aside to talk with your generators and **let them know how you wish to continue with your life**. Grey Matter in particular will need to be informed of the change in direction you are planning to take in life. Once the generators are informed they will cooperate with you and support you for their only aim is to please.

Respect

When you point out to your brain its specific responsibility Grey Matter will in turn remind you if and when you breach the agreement, likewise the other two generators. With this open communication you show respect for your generators and they for you. You also acknowledge their rightful place in the scheme of things particularly in relation to Aura Bora.

Calm Control

This may seem like a cumbersome process and be slower at the beginning of the changeover. However, eventually the responses from Aura Bora will not alone be a great deal faster than generator response they will be precise and truthful no matter what your circumstances. You will be in calm control of all situations no matter what they may present for you will no longer be merely reacting to Meme's needs.

New World

At first it can seem strange talking to yourself, as this approach may not have been encouraged in you before. However, the more open your internal communication, the more you will realize the your many different and fascinating aspects and discover their capabilities while working with Aura Bora. This in turn will open up a whole new world of possibilities. You can begin to take back control of your life and to face the future with purposeful confidence.

Knowing

The experience of calm control in you is the knowledge that the three generators are lined up and facing in one direction, awaiting instruction from your Aura Bora. Now the generators are supporting one another under the direction of Aura Bora and you are operating in a smooth, coordinated, purposeful and focused manner under the direction of Aura Bora.

A Mere Incident

The return journey to safe waters may mean you could encounter many of the obstacles crossed on the journey thus far. However, now these obstacles will be crossed with the guidance of Aura Bora and you will experience them from a totally different and mature perspective. What may once have been a major problem will take on a different nature in your awareness and will fade into a mere incident, a happening not worth the mention.

Inevitable

You may lose Aura Bora several times at first on the journey. However, the missing Aura Bora will be noticed straight away **if you have informed your Grey Matter** to watch out for such an eventuality.

Where you persist in achieving contact with Aura Bora, these regular occurrences will become less regular as time goes by and eventually Aura Bora will end up as the guiding light in your life. It's inevitable when you **take the initiative and when you give the time to re-correcting your direction in life**.

New Set Of Values

With this re-correction you can reassess your attitude to life and over time insert a new set of values by which to live. These values will be the base from which you can achieve a completely coordinated integrated life.

New Value System

A new value system will be wise, knowledgeable and powerful that has as its main elements 1 Oracle, 2 Osmosis 3 Aura Bora and 4 your human element Zenith. It will be Capsule orientated, mindful and joyful and will be creative inventive, intuitive, inspirational and informative, will be timeless, painless, doubtless and free.

A Successful Transition

By maintaining contact with your Corigonus and being always aware that **Core engagement needs to be the first port of call**, you ensure a successful transition toward a life guided by your Aura Bora. **Awareness of your Core is automatic awareness of Aura Bora** and will ensure your three generators line up and await instruction and guidance from your Aura Bora.

Eventually, engaging with your Core becomes an automatic response when you stop to consider your options rather than going straight to Grey Matter with every enquiry. Allow the task to take as long as it takes. In other words, **you need to stay in the present moment**.

Distraction

Resistance to distraction may also take you away from Capsule contact. Allow the distraction to be itself rather than give it power. Your Aura Bora can then **direct you toward an action** rather than being **generated toward a distraction**.

Difficulties

Acceptance of difficulties in any situation in the form of **allowing there to be difficulty** without trying to change them, enables you to concentrate on solutions rather than be caught up in the difficulty. By accepting does not mean subjection. Subjection may automatically mean no acceptance and possibly closed to reasonable solutions.

By acceptance is meant acceptance *at your Core* and not just in your generators. Be careful you are not merely accepting through your generators. Any generator involvement concerning acceptance may merely point you in the direction of apathy where you could let go complete responsibility and this would be counter productive, thus enabling and empowering the difficulty.

The Arrangement

You need to be sure you **make an arrangement with your generators particularly Grey Matter to pass any questions or circumstances straight to your Core** and for the generators overall to be **non-accepting** of these situations **before** Core. Your brain must be specifically informed to not take over the lead from Aura Bora and in the event of a mishap **Grey Matter is responsible for ensuring that your Core is fully informed**. Use your own language to convey messages from generators to Core and visa versa.

Having guided the situation safely to your Core, the generators now must be alert to the response from Aura Bora through Core. This may be a little time consuming initially but eventually it will take only a fraction of a second and it won't be long before **there is a constant flow back and forth through your Core** between your generators and your Aura Bora. This is in fact the object of the exercise.

Pursuer

Resistance to and avoidance of a difficulty also empowers the difficulty and it becomes the focus, they do not send the difficulty away, the difficulty becomes your pursuer.

This in turn manifests fear. Active acceptance allows you to step back from the situation and *allows your Aura Bora to come up with a solution to the problem and then pass the knowledge to your generators*. Thus, can you get on with your life and leave the initial solution to problems in the capable hands of Aura Bora. One reason for fear in the past was the generators inability to deal effectively with a situation. Now you wont need to hold onto the fear because you have changed your approach and what may have seemed a problem before can be viewed from a new and mature perspective.

A Partnership

This doesn't mean you won't deal with the problem, but you'll deal with it in a different way to the usual Meme way. Having given it over to Aura Bora you need to **listen carefully for the answer that comes back to you** and follow through on it. By listening I mean listening with your body at Core. This is **a partnership** where all parties, generators as well as Core and Aura Bora, take responsibility for their own share. It means the human you, is not taking full responsibility without backup and likewise **not shirking the responsibility for dealing with the problem** but that you have a wise and sensible ally on which to call whenever needed. The generators, when they receive the truth of the situation, can at that point be called upon to respond and their response can be confidently effective and purposeful.

The object of the exercise is to deal with the questions, situations or difficulties effectively, truthfully, wisely and knowledgably. This can only be achieved through Core connection that allows open communication between Aura Bora and the generators.

Imperfection

One of the biggest tragedies you play on yourself is acceptance through Grey Matter of discord. The acceptance of **any imperfection** through Grey Matter is unacceptable to Aura Bora and only acceptable to Meme. You must instruct Grey Matter in no uncertain terms **to return immediately the slightest imperfection** to your Corigonus for Aura Bora's attention. Grey Matter needs to treat the imperfection like an unwelcome tennis ball and simply strike it over the net to your Core so Aura Bora can deal with the pass. The non-acceptance of discord in Grey Matter will open the way for rightful thought, rightful feeling and rightful creation in you.

Giving Power

When you avoid discord, resist it, retreat from it, see it as a danger, side step it, encourage it, you are **giving power** to it. However, when you merely **observe it** without getting involved mentally, emotionally or physically, as though it were an outside happening with no connection for yourself (but at the same time you are staying connected to yourself and awake for answers), you are allowing your Aura Bora to deal with the discord and you are open to receiving any messages from Aura Bora about the situation. You may identify it in passing as being alien to you but then pass on.

Once while on holiday in Stockholm I witnessed an incident. An irate driver was giving out to a cyclist whilst screaming into his face and gesticulating wildly and threatening. The cyclist stood listening but was not otherwise responding (he was allowing). What happened next both surprised and delighted me. A lady stood behind the cyclist, then a man then a couple stopped and a few more people also gathered. Nobody said anything, they just observed. Suddenly, the driver, who had been out of control with rage realized he was addressing not just the cyclist but a dozen people.

He stopped screaming and the cyclist was able to join in and give his point of view. Gradually, the crowd thinned out and the original couple exchanged their views in a civilized fashion. By simply being observed the driver got the message that his behaviour was unreasonable and unacceptable even to himself so he stopped being aggressive.

Stay Open

You may accept all aspects of a personality or a situation, even alien parts into your Core but then deal only with the aspects that are not alien.

You need to search for the truth not the Meme, to stay open and allow the mindfulness to reach you. The search for mindfulness is **not logical, or emotive, or reactive**. It is the **knowledge, feeling and creative** powers from your Aura Bora through your Core. You can bring any question to Core (except a What? question) and Aura Bora will answer it wisely and truthfully setting you on a true path.

In Grief

When we are in grief we feel the pain on three levels the brain, the heart and the reproductive system. It is the pain from these three levels that must be released.

Four miles from where I live there is King John's Castle in the heritage town of Trim. Built in the 11th Century, it provided the backdrop for Mel Gibson's film Braveheart. Outside the castle stands a large cannon gun. I use the image of this cannon to return any pain I'm experiencing to Aura Bora. Recently, I lost the love of a very wonderful woman and I used this method to release the thoughts, emotions and physical blockages that I experienced around the relationship.

All the regurgitating brain siftings and memories that were going around in my head I imagined being molded into the shape of a dense cannon ball. Likewise, I molded into a second cannon ball all the pent up heart felt emotions, fears, sense of loss, the emptiness etc. The third cannon ball was molded from the physical outbursts, the anger, frustration and crying etc. I wrote a message on each ball and set them down beside the cannon gun.

I placed the cannon gun at my Core facing it toward my Capsule and loaded it up with powder, fed in the first ball and lit the fuse. With an unmerciful 'BOOM' the cannon ball shot from my Core up into space and in through the open window of Capsule straight onto the lap of Aura Bora. The message I scribbled on the attached label read 'here's your ball of brain crap, I'm finished with it now'. I loaded the cannon three times in all and fired three shots and all was released from my body. I needed to do this several times over the next few days, particularly with my brain.

I remained open to Aura Bora for any feedback. Within a relatively short space of time the relationship had shifted to an invaluable friendship. This works for me, but you can use your imagination to get the best effect for you. Aura Bora just loves working with your imagination and creations.

Creator

The search for mindfulness is in itself creative and you must create to be purposeful. In fact this is your purpose in life to **be creator of life, of originality, of love, of joy, of beauty in all aspects of your life**, your family, home, friends, work, relationships etc. You are the creator of beauty on earth, the protector, the benefactor and also the beneficiary.

For you to realize your true potential you must never again look In the direction of Meme and must never again be tempted into accepting a Meme orientated life. Once you embrace your new life fully, you will never knowingly experience or accept discord, illness, discomfort, pain, sorrow, sadness, arguing, frustration, resistance, fighting, war, hunger, disease, or any of the multiple symptoms associated with Meme.

A New Truth

A life of beauty, joy, caring and peaceful understanding, a life of thinking, loving and creating, a life of imagination, intuition, wisdom and of powerful presence awaits. A new awareness is born in you. You are as a new creation, a new truth.

The Next Chapter

The next chapter on Truth looks at one of the most established value systems, The Ten Commandments. Whether we are religious or not this set of values has given rise to an overall attitude that permeates society and is taken for granted as the guidelines for human behaviour even though their interpretation appears to be generated and while it is not the intention of this book to challenge accepted interpretations, it is important to note that no set of rules for any institution or way of life needs to be taken on board without question.

It is imperative that questioning be encouraged so that we can be accountable for our own decisions and responsible for our own advancement on a personal level. To allow institutions, authorities, religions and governments etc to make decisions for us without questioning being a natural and encouraged part of the process is to hand over the responsibility for yourself to somebody else.

We need to realize the importance of **the art of forming questions** for **it is in the questioning that we arrive at the answers**. The deeper the question the more profound will be the answer. A surface or What? question will yield a shallow answer.

The ability to ask a pertinent question is a most important tool in the advancement of the human race.

THE WISDOM OF ORACLES
BY JOHN RYAN

CHAPTER 32

TRUTH

What difference do the changes make
What's brought about that's new
What odds the fresh steps that we take
To give each one their due?

What's there that wasn't there before
What isn't now that is
What evens up the ancient score
What gives the drink its fizz?

What sweet sounds out of silence
break
What harmony is sung
What music does the singer make
By any other tongue?

What difference do the changes make
What's brought about that's new
What odds the fresh steps that we take
To give each one their due? *pil*

The Ten Truths

As was mentioned earlier in the book The Ten Commandments currently in use is an interpretation written several hundred years after the original Truths or Commitments that were handed down by Moses. The Commandments appear to be a generated interpretation of The Truths and as such provide a particular view to what could be interpreted as a substantially broader subject.

The Ten Truths provide us with knowledge, wisdom and truth pertaining to man and to the makeup of the universe. This information has been with us for approximately 2,500 years. However, we have chosen up to now to interpret them from a generated What? perspective, in other words from a Meme viewpoint.

The following interpretation is just that, an interpretation and is intended as a means of offering a broadened perspective and of raising questions about and awareness of the infinite possibilities available to us. It also points to the importance of punctuation and how it can alter completely the meaning intended.

The Ten Truths are clearly written with Zenith in mind and are meant as a guide for him.

The First Truth

I – Am - The Lord, Thy, God - Thou shalt not have strange gods before – me.
This Means, I – Cosmic – Osmosis, Aura Bora, Oracle – Zenith shalt not have strange oracles before – Meme.

This is The First Truth it is not a command. The First Truth could be interpreted as having five separate statements. Combined into one sentence they leave us with a particular interpretation. However, when they are divided into five statements they provide us with a much deeper meaning. Lets take a closer look at each of these statements in The First Truth.

The first statement of The First

Truth is – **I.**

The most profound statement in the universe is written with the smallest letter in the alphabet. I - encapsulates all that Is. If nothing else I shows us that I is brilliantly uncomplicated. I - couldn't be simpler and paradoxically couldn't be more complex.

I – makes no statement of power but is omnipotence. I - makes no statement of presence but is omnipresence. I - makes no statement of knowing but is omniscience. I - is all there is the One, the

Only, the Supreme.

The second statement of The Frst Truth is – Am. Cosmic - is the second statement in The First Truth.

Am / Cosmic

Am encapsulates all that is created by I. To proclaim Am is to bring I into Being, into Cosmic. I - becomes creator in Cosmic. Cosmic - is the condition of I.

The third statement of The First Truth is – The Lord, Thy, God. Osmosis, Aura Bora, Oracle (Capsule) - is the third statement in The First Truth.

Oracle

Oracle **is** the wisdom, truth and knowledge in Capsule (Mind).

The Osmosis

The Osmosis is the manifestation and accumulator of the wisdom, truth and knowledge in Capsule (Mind). The – implies Osmosis has a clear and precise purpose (to supply knowledge, truth and wisdom to Aura Bora).

Aura Bora

Aura Bora, is the activator or instigator of wisdom, truth and knowledge in Capsule (Mind). The Osmosis, Aura Bora and Oracle are the three innate beings that combined make up the Capsule of Zenith. Each Zenith explorer is attached to a Capsule (Mind). There may be several Zeniths attached to a Capsule (For more information on Oracle, Osmosis, Aura Bora and Zenith refer to chapters 1, 5, 7, 10 and to the diagram at the beginning of the book).

The fourth statement of The First Truth is – Thou shalt not have strange gods before. Zenith shalt not have strange oracles before - is the fourth statement in The First Truth

Obligation

This is an interesting statement for although it may appear to be an instruction it is in fact not an instruction, nor is it a suggestion. In fact there is nothing forceful or commanding about the statement. As with all The Truths, the statement merely makes clear the inevitability or an obligation.

Zenith

Zenith is not part of Capsule and also, clearly has the obligation not to have strange oracles before him. Aura Bora knows the need to inform Zenith of his obligations and knows the possible pitfalls if and when they become disconnected from one another.

Shalt Not Have

Zenith is obliged to not hold, to not possess, to not have even the slightest experience of, or be in the slightest affected by, or obliged to – strange oracles before him.

This little 'have' word encapsulates a great deal. For one thing it shows how precise are these Truths. There is not one word in The Ten Truths wasted. ***Every word is filled with meaning and every word deserves close scrutiny to gain the true essence and value of their meaning***.

Strange Oracles

Strange oracles don't actually have to have supernatural powers they need only to **appear** to have supernatural power or be an odd or unusual object of worship.

In other words any tiny feeling or logic, any tiny action or small symptoms, any perceived right like the right to share an ignorant opinion, the right to mislead others with sifted emotive action, **in fact any symptom given notice that only appears to have supernatural powers is a strange oracle**.

Manifest perceived illness for instance doesn't actually have power on its own. Perceived rights and opinions appear to have supernatural power and carry authority when spoken on T.V., radio, printed in newspapers or magazines, written up on advertisements as do sports stars, pop stars, movie stars and the whole conglomeration of possible other strange oracles.

Before

Before – means in the presence of Zenith and in preference to, The Osmosis, Aura Bora and Oracle (Capsule).

The fifth statement of The First Truth is – Me. Meme – is the fifth statement in The First Truth.

Meme

Meme is placed alone, as I is also alone. However, there is one significant difference between Meme and I. Meme is at the opposite end of The Truth to I.

Meme is a manifestation of earth bound Zenith and this is why all The Truths are intended for Zenith. When he faces in the direction of Meme he turns his back on I, Cosmic, The Osmosis, Aura Bora and Oracle in favour of Meme.

A Mere Indication

The First Truth obliges Zenith to swing toward Aura Bora. **With just a mere indication in a Meme direction, Zenith slips through the net**. All the sickness,

all the poverty, the danger, fear, arguing, opinion, disfigurement, drug abuse, prostitution, robbing, fighting, murder, war etc. are all caused through choice where Zenith chooses Meme over Cosmic.

Truth One

The First Truth means, **I** – The Almighty exists.
Am – Is Cosmic in the form of the universe.
The Osmosis, Aura Bora, Oracle – Are innate beings, invisible bodies of the universe in triune form, in other words, is Capsule (Mind).
Zenith A creation of Aura Bora living on earth **shalt not have strange oracles before** - is obliged not to get involved in the worship of earthly matters.
Meme – Is the catalyst, to be avoided, is Zenith transformed.

The Next Nine Truths

The next Nine Truths are also directed at Zenith. They are sequential, a follow on from The First Truth. In fact The First Truth is profound and were Zenith to follow it to the letter there would be no need for the next Nine Truths. But Aura Bora knows that Zenith can be sometimes easily misled.

The Second Truth

Thou shalt not take the name of The Lord, Thy, God in vain.

This Means

Zenith shalt not take the name of The Osmosis, Aura Bora, Oracle in vain. The Second Truth points at Zenith's ability to take the name of the whole Capsule.

In Vain

To be vain is to be excessively proud, bound

to fail or futile. In vain, however, means something completely different. In vain means unsuccessfully, so while it is possible for Zenith to take possession of Capsule, he can only do it unsuccessfully. From where can Capsule be removed and to where? - From its position with Zenith and into Meme.

Truth Two

The Second Truth means Zenith is obliged to not remove, possess, accept or assume Capsule's reputation to be that of Meme or to exist in the state of Meme and that any attempt to turn Meme into an oracle will be unsuccessful.

A Natural Progression

The Third Truth is a natural progression of The Second Truth and indicates how Zenith can avoid becoming a Meme.

The Third Truth

Remember – To keep holy – The Sabbath Day.
There are three messages in The Third Truth; 1- Remember, 2- Remember to keep holy and 3-Remember to keep the Sabbath Day.
The first message of The Third Truth is – Zenith, remember.

Remember

To remember is to retain in ones Grey Matter something that may need to be recalled later. Remember is also two words, Re, meaning again and member, meaning the individual makeup of a body or society. The only membership is that of the Capsule triune, The Osmosis, Aura Bora and Oracle.
The second message of The Third Truth is – Zenith, remember to keep holy.

Remember To Keep Holy

Zenith is obliged to instill in his brain the responsibility for his connection to the triune or Capsule. This is indeed a huge implication for Grey Matter heretofore never realized. Now it is up to Grey Matter to take the initiative in a Capsule matter. What The Truth is saying is **when Zenith fields a question to his brain, Grey Matter is required to remember to 'not' take the question on board**.

Grey Matter is not culpable if brain hasn't been properly informed of The Truth, for once Grey Matter is informed Grey Matter will not forget. *Grey Matter has never been informed and up to now has automatically fielded the questions even though the second part of The Third Truth clearly states that Grey Matter is obliged to not take any questions*. They are clearly Aura Bora's concern.

The third message of The Third Truth is – Zenith, remember to keep the Sabbath Day

The Sabbath Day

The words Sabbath and Day are both separate messages. The word Sabbath relates to the activities of love, admiration and the rest time that is also important. The word 'Day' relates to the time that these activities take place and that is during the time of normal activity, *which in effect means all of the time*.

This one word completely reverses our current assumption that there is one day per week set aside and makes it clear that *every moment of every day* is the time for reuniting. In other words Zenith is obliged to never disconnect from Aura Bora.

Truth Three

The Third Truth means Zenith you're obliged to inform your brain to always stay connected and open to Aura Bora. You are further obliged to not give Grey Matter any direct questions and *should a question inadvertently be fielded directly toward brain that Grey Matter is to reject it*. At *all* moments of the day Zenith, remember to *be mindful* and keep your connection to Aura Bora.

The Fourth Truth

Honour Thy Father and Thy Mother.

This Means

Honour Aura Bora's Father and Aura Bora's Mother. The Fourth Truth is directed at Zenith and specifically points to Aura Bora's relations.

Honour

Honour is respect, personal integrity, pleasure or privilege.

Aura Bora's Father

Aura Bora's Father is not the father of Zenith, or Meme. Aura Bora's Father is Oracle.

Aura Bora's Mother

Likewise, Aura Bora's Mother is not the mother of Zenith or Meme. Aura Bora's Mother is The Osmosis.

Truth Four

The Fourth Truth reinforces and is a natural follow on from The Third Truth where Zenith is obliged to stay connected to Aura Bora. He now can honour the knowledge, wisdom and truth of Father, Oracle manifested in Mother, The Osmosis.

The Fifth Truth

Thou shalt not kill.

This Means

Zenith shalt not kill. Zenith is obliged to ensure that having honoured Oracle and The Osmosis that he doesn't now somehow kill that knowledge, wisdom or truth.

Kill

To kill is to cause the death of, to put an end to. Death is the permanent end to all function of life. It is not possible for Zenith to kill whilst connected to Aura Bora, only whilst connected to Meme. The act of killing something is to dishonour it.

The one sure way for Meme to kill is to dishonour knowledge, wisdom and truth and thus kill the reputation of Oracle, The Osmosis and Aura Bora on earth and in the process eventually bring about the death of everything and everyone in his path.

We need look no further than the direction in which humanity is progressing to appreciate the wisdom of these words.

Death By Ignorance

Acceptance of information is the death of knowledge. Acceptance of logic is the death of wisdom. Acceptance of honesty is the death of truth. 'Beware of the fruits of knowledge'. By ignoring his true destiny Meme brings to the universe the unique talent of being able to kill all around him and encourages death by ignorance.

The Sixth Truth

Thou shalt not commit adultery.

This Means

Zenith shalt not commit adultery.

Midnight Blue
I'm a liberated lady
From the year of Eighty-two
A sorta greeneyed Sadie
In tights of midnight Blue.
I'm very much the mistress
Of all I say and do
And men I seek to distress
With what is trite and true.
I don't subscribe to Marriage
Or Patriarchal Law
I'm a queen without a carriage
A crab without a claw.
I'm a liberated lady
From the year of Eighty-two
A sorta greeneyed Sadie
In tights of Midnight Blue. *pil*

Partnership

Not alone can Zenith bring death but he can do it in partnership. The subject of honour raised in The Fourth Truth and in The Fifth is advanced in this Sixth Truth.

Commit Adultery

To Commit Adultery is to pledge to a cause or course of action that is the sexual unfaithfulness of a husband or wife.

Husband Or Wife

Zenith is derived from Aura Bora and the only husband and wife are the Father and Mother of Aura Bora.

Solemn Promise

Committing adultery is not just the act of unfaithfulness it's also the act of pledging a cause or course of action which causes sexual unfaithfulness of Oracle or The Osmosis. To pledge, Zenith must make a solemn promise or arrangement.

Marry

One way Zenith can make a solemn promise is to get married. For Zenith to marry whilst in Aura Bora mode presents no problems. However, to marry in Meme mode can mean taking an unsuitable partner thus committing adultery on the truth, knowledge and wisdom of Oracle by manifesting a false alignment.

Truth Ignored

Where Zenith in Meme mode marries another the obligation in The Sixth Truth is ignored and Zenith by consummating the false marriage commits adultery. He is obliged to consider his partner from a Capsule perspective and not just from a Meme perspective.

Since Capsule can send out many explorers the possibility may be that partners can, but not necessarily, come from the same or sister Capsule. When we consider the number of marriages built on Meme values that end in divorce it serves us well not to misinterpret this truth from a Meme perspective.

The Seventh Truth

Thou shalt not steal.

This Means

Zenith shalt not steal.

Zenith in Aura Bora mode does not need to steal anything for Aura Bora already has everything. However, Zenith in Meme takes on a different emphasis and is incomplete. What does Meme need that Aura Bora has?

For Meme to be complete or acknowledged he must steal Aura Bora's reputation. Meme achieves this by denouncing Aura Bora's existence and the existence of Aura Bora's companions Oracle and The Osmosis so Meme can become the complete capsule.

Capsule's Reputation

Now Meme is not only the important being but has become the only being in Meme awareness by stealing the one thing worth stealing, Capsule's name. The Seventh Truth is further emphasis and progression of The Second Truth where Zenith is obliged to not assume Capsule's reputation to Meme.

Strange Oracles

Zenith shalt not steal the reputation of Aura Bora, Oracle or The Osmosis for in doing so Meme can but put in place strange oracles such as information, honesty and emotion in place of the knowledge, truth and wisdom of Capsule.

The Eight Truth

Thou shalt not bear false witness against Thy Neighbbour.

This Means

Zenith shalt not bear false witness against Aura Bora's Neighbour.

Aura Bora's Neighbour

Aura Bora's neighbour is Oracle.

Cease Support

In The Seventh Truth Zenith is obliged to not steal Capsule's reputation. In essence, The Eight Truth is saying, where Meme has stolen Oracle's reputation, the essence of Capsule, Zenith is now not to support the deception once it has been witnessed and realized.

Compassionate

The Truth offers a way out even if the worst happen. This is truly compassionate. The Ten Truths recognize the possible breach of right order and simply remind Zenith of his obligation by intimating to his current situation.

Solutions

The Truths do not seek retribution. Even when The Truths have been breached there is a solution sought to deal with the problems manifested. This is the essence of truth. There is no blame for there is no one to blame. There are only solutions and no one is wrong or bad only misguided.

Cease Support

Zenith shalt not bear false witness against Aura Bora Neighbour means Zenith, having realized Meme's untrue state, is obliged to cease support of that which is not knowledge, truth and wisdom. This intimates back to The Third Truth in which Zenith is encouraged to employ Grey Matter to remember to keep holy.

The Ninth Truth

Thou shalt not covet Thy Neighbour's Wife.

This Means

Zenith shalt not covet Aura Bora's Neighbour's Wife.

Covet

To covet is, to long to possess (what belongs to someone else).

Aura Bora's Neighbour's Wife

Aura Bora's Neighbour is Oracle and Oracle's wife is The Osmosis. This Truth is specific in that it points to the single most dangerous occupation in modern society that of misappropriating the manifistation of Mind, in other words, manifesting a false mind.

A Further Development

The Ninth Truth means Zenith is obliged not to long to possess Mind. This is a further development for in The Seventh Truth,

Zenith is obliged not to steal the reputation of Capsule, The Eight Truth obliges him to not support the deception and in The Ninth Truth he's not to manifest a Mind that doesn't include wisdom, truth and knowledge. The Ninth Truth is in fact man's first warning in the Garden of Eden, 'beware of the fruits of knowledge'.

The Tenth Truth
Thou shalt not covet Thy Neighbour's goods.

This Means
Zenith shalt not covet Aura Bora's Neighbour's goods.

Aura Bora's Neighbour's Goods
Goods come in the form of property and merchandise. But we're talking about Oracle's goods here so we're not talking about worldly goods. Oracle is a spirit, a being with supernatural power and this is what Zenith in Meme wants, to be the object of worship, to be idolized. This is a follow on from The Ninth Truth. Having alluded to the desire to possess Mind, Zenith is cut off by The Ninth Truth, so he may seek solace in the only thing left, worship.

The Problem
In The Tenth Truth Zenith is obliged not to desire worship or adoration, it is in the act of *desiring* worship or wishing to be treated singly and as an idol the problem lies.

Self Worship
The idea of worshipping strange oracles was originally introduced in The First Truth. The Truths in turn, allude to the variety of strange oracles and the varied directions Zenith can take in pursuit of them. In The Final Truth Zenith is pinned down to the realization that *any* worship of strange oracles is in fact self-worship.

Without Command
The Ten Truths bring Zenith through every combination of possible infringement without command or demand, without intimidation or subtle manipulation, without instruction or rules, without force or suggestion. The Ten Truths merely *intimate the obligation* of Zenith to be receptive to Aura Bora rather than to Meme.

In No Way Bound
This is indeed wise, truthful and knowing for Capsule would not possibly influence Zenith's free will. He has a perfect right to ignore Aura Bora in favour of Meme. He is in no way bound to The Ten Truths. However, The Ten Truths indicate the pitfalls of such a decision, even offering means of realigning with Aura Bora in The Third Truth – Remember, to keep holy – is how Zenith through his brain can reconnect with Aura Bora. It's interesting that although brain or Grey Matter is the culpable party *Grey Matter is also the pathfinder on the route to recovery*.

Doubt Be Banished
We need to look closely at the structures we have placed in our societies **from a different perspective, that of Aura Bora.** Zenith will finally awaken to his true calling and rediscover his original intention and his unique place in union with his Capsule. Thus, will doubt be banished forever and a new sense of confidence will inhabit humanity, the confidence of Capsule creation derived from truth, wisdom and knowledge.

For what will come
We all must pray
There is no cause
To stay and stay. *pil*

Conclusion

In our efforts to engage with the world we take for granted that we are responsible for its welfare on one hand, whilst on the other we take every opportunity to place the world at risk. The earth can and will take care of itself even if it means eliminating the offending human race in the process. No matter what we do to it earth will survive for it is clearly more intelligent than we are, but we may not survive.

We place an inordinate importance on the human aspect of our being. However, the important element of humanity, our innateness, is almost completely ignored. We have within ourselves the ability to tap into the power of the universe and to use that power for the good of all. We have through our misinterpretations not been able to tap into that power up to now, perhaps because we are only capable of using this power destructively.

However, once the human race acknowledges its connection to the cosmos, the power of the universe will open up and humanity can advance on a totally different level of awareness. What we consider to be miraculous will become everyday events.

We will be able to cure ailments completely, to travel at a thought, to communicate without using spoken language, to motivate energy at all levels of possibility and much more. We will discover new ways of curing our planet and taking care of all our needs without destruction and realize a new level of creation.

When we as a race orientate ourselves in the direction of creation rather than destruction, it will be possible to engage infinity, timelessness, truth, wisdom, intuition, insight, imagination, invention, inspiration, consciousness, mindfulness and all the innateness of the universe.

As we develop a new way of engaging the universe the emphasis toward our professions and activities will shift naturally. Those who are involved in education, for example, will develop a different way of approaching education to include a Capsule approach. Likewise religion, medicine, science, politics, banking, the law etc. will each in turn move gradually toward a new Cosmic approach.

Our old systems will be found unnecessary as we embrace a new way of life. There won't need to be public outcry to change, for people will simply cease to support the outdated models and it will be necessary for them to change or become extinct for they do not in their current state provide the answers needed for the new world.

It is time to embrace the most exciting time in the world's evolution. A new and extraordinary world awaits us. All we need to do is to change our attitudes.

So far so good or so bad
To have made your acquaintance,
I'm glad
And whether I am an Ella or Sam
With your blessings, I'll never be sad! *pil*

E n d.

THE WISDOM OF ORACLES
BY JOHN RYAN

Acknowledgements

My deepest appreciation to my brother Seamus (James Daniel Ryan) who passed over but left behind an invaluable collection of his works which were truly ahead of my time. I'm proud and deeply honoured to be able to include some of your poetry. My only regret is I was unaware of your uniqueness and insights while you were still alive. Through this book, in which I felt your guidance at every turn, I'm only beginning to realize your wisdom and the level of acceptance and allowing in your gentle knowing nature. Seamus, your starlight shines timelessly though you have since moved on.

Sincere thanks to Kate O'Neill who took great pains to read the handwritten manuscripts and subsequent copies, for your guidance, patience, understanding and clear, professional, earthed appraisal with a no-nonsense approach.

Sincere thanks also to Marie Byrne who worked on the second hand-written draft as well as subsequent drafts. You enabled me to learn from your invaluable awareness, your sharp observations, incisive perspective and ability to follow each question to the end.

My utmost appreciation to Frank Ryan, you took on the unenviable task of knocking into shape the third draft going through the manuscript with a fine-tooth comb (a talent I fully appreciate) questioning many of the early loose, indefinite passages and assumptions, you added stability and a grounded realism to the message in the book and made it more accessible, my thanks.

Thank you Nick O'Neill, a fellow explorer, for your open and questioning mind that makes the conversation ever satisfying. My thanks to Pat Cullen and Alan Maher you gave a direct appraisal coupled with sound suggestions and much food for thought.

Thank you Maria Salazar, your truthful and straight opinions made it clear to me the need for a second book on this subject orientated toward a different approach also for your encouragement and help with technical matters and your invaluable friendship.

Thanks also to Deirdre Ryan, Tony McGrath, Eamonn Ryan, Laura Flynn, Maria Flynn and Angela O'Sullivan for your input and helpful suggestions that enabled my understanding from the reader's point of view - your support is greatly valued.

I appreciate the input of Liam Douglas who has a track record for the sheer number of books on similar subjects he has read and absorbed. Your opinion is appreciated, as is your discovery of new information in the book. Thank you for sharing your wisdom, knowledge and understanding in context.

Thank you to Lillian Roberts Finley for your encouragement and views as an experienced writer.

A very special thanks to Meath County Council's Library Services particularly the staff at Navan Library you are extremely helpful, good natured and good humoured which makes it a pleasure for me to research in your library.

Thanks also to Meath County Council's Arts Office for presenting me with an invaluable bursary to The Tyrone Guthrey Centre, very much appreciated.

Thanks to Belinda Quirke and her staff at Solstice Arts Centre, Navan for all your help.

I feel very privileged with and blessed by my wonderful family and friends who are ever supportive and encouraging and even more so while I was writing this book.